ASTRONOMY

A LABORATORY TEXTBOOK
WITH INTERNET EXERCISES

Third Edition

John W. Wilson

Georgia State University

CONTEMPORARY PUBLISHING COMPANY OF RALEIGH, INC.

CPC

6001-101 Chapel Hill Road • Raleigh, NC 27607 • (919) 851-8221

Publisher: Chuck Grantham
Editorial Assistant: Erika Kessler
Typesetting: Contemporary Publishing Company of Raleigh, Inc.
Copyediting: Sheryl Fowler
Director of Marketing: Sherri Powell
Printer: Edwards Brothers, Inc.

ACKNOWLEDGMENTS

Writing a manual of this nature requires the assistance of many people. I would like to give special thanks to Dr. David W. Wingert for contributing his lab on "Eclipse Predicting," which he wrote, and is included in this manual with his permission. In addition he has been extremely helpful in critically reading and commenting on the text of this entire manual. I also want to thank Mollie C. Raby for typing this manual in TEX formats.

Most of the photographic observing projects are based on some practical astrophotography techniques that I learned as an amateur. I would like to thank Robert L. Adams, President of the Southeast Missouri Astronomy Club, for the many hours spent helping me develop these skills.

Laboratory exercises 8 and 15, **"Relative Ages of Martian Landscapes"** and **"Galaxy Classification,"** are modifications of laboratory exercises written by Dr. Donat G. Wentzel at the University of Maryland and are published with his permission.

The star charts for observing project 20 were made using the program code **"StarChart"** Version 3.2, rewritten in March 1990 by Craig Counterman from the original **"StarChart Software Suite"** written in 1987 by Alan Paeth.

During my years at Southeast Missouri State University I was a teaching assistant under the direction of Dr. Leo P. Connolly, now at California State University–San Bernardino. It was during this time that he developed some of the materials included in exercises 4, 9, and 14, **"Planetary Orbits," "Atomic Structure and Spectroscopy,"** and **"The Period-Luminosity Relation."** I would like to thank Dr. Connolly for all the time spent showing me his teaching philosophy and for the use of some of his lab materials.

ISBN: 0-89892-202-X

PREFACE

The laboratory exercises in this book have been developed over a period of eighteen years. During this time they have been used by thousands of introductory astronomy students at Georgia State University. In the fall of 1998, our university system switched from quarters to semesters. Thus, our two-quarter lab science sequence expanded to become a two-semester sequence. Our Astronomy 1010 students complete labs 1 through 9 from this book. In addition, they do several of the labs from the CLEA Project at Gettysburg College. Similarly, our Astronomy 1020 students do labs 10 through 17 from this book and several CLEA labs. During both semesters, all astronomy lab students are expected to complete one observing session outside of the regularly scheduled lab periods. At these sessions, the students have the opportunity to do one of the observing projects, labs 18 through 24. The last exercise in this section, lab 26, is used at GSU as an optional lab for students who need to make up for a missed lab period. It can be completed entirely on the student's own time. However, this is an important issue for astronomy and could be used as part of a course requirement. Even though GSU uses this manual for a two-semester course, it clearly has enough lab exercises for a one-semester astronomy lab course.

John Wilson
Spring 2000

TABLE OF CONTENTS

BASIC DRAWING AND MEASURING

OBJECTIVES

After completing this exercise, the student should be able to:

1. make measurements using cm and mm.
2. use a protractor to measure angles to the nearest degree.
3. use a compass to draw circles.

STUDENT MATERIALS

pencil
compass (to draw circles)
protractor
ruler (mm)
calculator

LAB MATERIALS

none required

STUDENT REQUIREMENTS

This lab is to be done individually without lab partners. After completion of the excercise, turn in **Figs. 1 – 4** and **Tables I & II** in page order sequence.

INTRODUCTION

In Astronomy labs you will be asked to measure lengths in centimeters and millimeters, use a protractor to measure and construct angles, and draw circles with a simple compass. You will also be expected to do simple arithmetic such as finding the average of a data set or working with powers-of-ten. This exercise is designed to help you remember these skills. Please be sure you can perform all the objectives of this exercise by the next laboratory period.

PROCEDURE

Length and Distance

One of the tools you will use for measuring length is a simple ruler which has a metric scale along one edge. When using a ruler it is a good idea to place your eye directly above the ruler and look straight down in order to reduce parallax errors. To further reduce errors a measurement should be made at least three times and the average used as the best value. An average is calculated by adding up the measurements and dividing the sum by the total number of measurements.

Your ruler should have a metric scale which is divided into centimeters (cm) and millimeters (mm). The centimeter is divided into ten equal parts which are called millimeters; these are the smallest divisions on your ruler. You should see that 1.0 cm = 10 mm. With your ruler you can accurately measure length to the nearest tenth of a centimeter. However, with the aid of a magnifying lens you can estimate length to the nearest tenth of a millimeter.

Angles

The main instrument you will use to measure angles is a protractor. Since each protractor is somewhat different in design, it is not practical to describe how to use each one. If you are unfamiliar with how your protractor is to be used, please ask your instructor for some assistance. Measure the angles A, B, C, D, indicated by the arrows in **Fig. 1**. Your measurements should be to the nearest degree. Record your answers in the spaces provided along the right margin. In the blank area on **Fig. 2**, construct angles to within one degree of 26°, 129°, 250°, and 311°. Be sure to use an arrow and the letters A, B, C, D to indicate the angle as was done in **Fig. 1**.

A Scale Drawing of the Solar System

Drawing planetary orbits is a very important part of this course. Most planetary orbits can be approximated using an off-center circle. In order to practice drawing circles you will make two scale drawings of the solar system. One drawing will be for the inner planets and the other one will be for the outer planets.

A compass is used to draw circles. The compass point and the pencil tip should be separated a distance equal to the radius of the circle you wish to construct. This is best done by placing the compass point and pencil tip along the edge of a ruler and opening the compass to the desired amount using the ruler's scale. Do not use the scale on the compass itself because these scales are not accurate.

The distance between the Earth and Sun is called an astronomical unit (AU). In **Tables I** and **II**, a list of the planets and their distances from the Sun in AUs is given. Note that two different scales have to be used because the outer planets are significantly farther from the Sun than the inner planets. For continuity Jupiter is repeated in both scales. Multiply each planet's distance in AUs by the scale factor given for each table and record your results in the last column of **Tables I** and **II**. These distances are in cm and will be used to make your scale drawings.

In the center of **Fig. 3** is a dot which will represent the Sun. With a compass draw circles centered on the Sun which have radii equal to the scale distances of Mercury through Jupiter as listed in the third column of **Table I**. Label each circle with the name of the planet whose orbit it represents. You have completed a scale drawing of the inner planets and one outer planet, Jupiter. Notice that a rather large gap exists between Mars and Jupiter. It is known to be filled with thousands of small rocks called asteroids. On your model, label this gap as the *Asteroid Belt*.

In the center of **Fig. 4** is a dot that represents the Sun. With a compass draw circles centered on the Sun which have radii equal to the scale distances of Jupiter through Neptune, as listed in column 3 of **Table II**. Label each circle with the name of the planet whose orbit it represents. Notice how much smaller Jupiter's orbit is on this drawing than on the previous drawing of the inner planets. This is because we had to change scales to fit the outer solar system onto a single page. Pluto's orbit is so eccentric that its center is basically near the orbit of Saturn and not near the Sun. Therefore place the point of your compass on Saturn's orbit (use the side nearest the bottom of your page) and draw Pluto's orbit with a radius equal to the scale distance in **Table II**. Notice that Pluto's orbit actually comes inside Neptune's orbit.

MEASUREMENTS AND POWERS–OF–TEN

2

OBJECTIVES

After completing this exercise, the student should be able to:

1. make calculations using scientific notation.
2. round off numbers to the correct number of significant digits.
3. estimate errors associated with a data set.
4. graph data and represent it with a visually estimated best-fit line or curve.

STUDENT MATERIALS

The student is expected to bring the following items:

> pencil
> mm scale (ruler)
> calculator

LAB MATERIALS

The lab instructor should provide the following items:

> one 2-meter stick for the whole lab class
> one magnifier lens and a wooden block
> (or appropriate substitute) for each student

STUDENT REQUIREMENTS

This lab is to be done individually without lab partners. Each student is expected to do his own work. After completing this excercise, turn in **Tables I, II,** and **III,** the **Problem Set,** and **Figs. 2** and **3**.

INTRODUCTION

During the analyses of data, astronomers must frequently deal with extremely large and small numbers and perform mathematical calculations with these numbers. This lab will help you learn how to make these types of calculations. You will also learn how to analyze data and how to estimate errors associated with a data set.

PROCEDURE

I. Powers–of–Ten

The average distance from the Earth to the Sun is 149,600,000 km. Because of all its digits, this number can become difficult to handle in a calculation. A better way to express this distance is to write it as a power-of-ten in scientific notation. This means you write the number so that it is between 1 and 10 with a power-of-ten multiplier representing the remaining digits. So, this distance can be written as follows:

$$149,600,000 \text{ km} = 1.496 \times 100,000,000 \text{ km}$$
$$= 1.496 \times 10^8 \text{ km}.$$

Similarly, very small numbers can be written as negative powers-of-ten. For example, the wavelength of yellow light is about 0.000055 cm. Expressing this in scientific notation means you move the decimal to be placed between the 5's and multiply by a negative power-of-ten equal to how many places to the right you moved the decimal point. So, the wavelength of yellow light can be written as

$$0.000055 \text{ cm} = 5.5 \times 10^{-5} \text{ cm}.$$

In column 1 of **Table I** are some large and small numbers. Write these numbers in scientific notation and place your answer in column 2. Do not try to fill in column 3 at this time.

II. Significant Figures

Measurements of physical quantities cannot be made with infinite precision. For example, the mass of the Earth has been determined to be
$$5.9742 \times 10^{24} \text{ kg}.$$

This number has five significant figures. The 5, 9, 7, and 4 are most certainly accurate, but the last 2 is uncertain. It might really be 1, or 2, or 3. Therefore, it makes no sense to write this mass as 5.974274×10^{24} kg because the 2 is already uncertain and the digits 7 and 4 are completely meaningless.

To determine the number of significant figures in a measurement you start counting at the first nonzero digit on the left and count to the first uncertain digit on the right. The number 264.62 has 5 significant figures while the number 0.007256 has only four significant figures. The three leading zeros are not significant. Confusion can be reduced if these numbers are written in scientific notation. The first number, 2.6462×10^2, has five significant figures and the number 7.256×10^{-3} has four significant figures. If in doubt, write the number in scientific notation and then count the significant figures. How many significant figures are in the number 2.6750×10^5? The answer is five, because the last digit of 0 is the first uncertain digit and should be counted.

In the lab, you will need to make calculations using numbers which have different amounts of significant figures. In this case, the mathematical result **cannot** be any more precise than the least precise value used in the calculation. Suppose a block of wood is measured to be 20.9 cm long. How long is 1/3rd of the block (i.e., 1/3 = 0.3333)? When you multiply by 0.3333 or divide by 3 the answer is 6.9666 cm. This result should be rounded off to have the same number of significant figures as the least accurate number used in the calculation. The number 20.9 cm has three significant figures and 1/3rd has an infinite number of significant figures, so your answer should be rounded to 6.97 cm.

In column 3 of **Table I**, state the number of significant figures of each value listed in column 2.

III. Calculations Using Powers-of-Ten

In the lab, you will need to multiply and divide numbers written in scientific notation. This may

seem difficult but it is actually simple. Suppose you want to multiply 2000 by 300; you would write $2000 \times 300 = 600000$. In scientific notation it would look like

$$(2.0 \times 10^3) \times (3.0 \times 10^2) = (2.0 \times 3.0) \times (10^3 \times 10^2)$$
$$= 6.0 \times 10^{(3+2)} = 6.0 \times 10^5$$

which is 600000. In other words, you multiplied the 2.0 and the 3.0 together and the new power-of-ten is obtained by adding the two exponents. This is similar to simply counting the zeros on 2000 and 300. Similarly, division is like canceling the zeros in the numerator and denominator. For example

$$\frac{600000}{300} = \frac{6000}{3} = 2000, \text{ in scientific notation it becomes}$$

$$\frac{6.0 \times 10^5}{3.0 \times 10^2} = \frac{6.0}{3.0} \times \frac{10^5}{10^2} = 2.0 \times 10^{(5-2)} = 2.0 \times 10^3, \text{ which is 2000.}$$

Solve the problems given in the Problem Set at the end of this lab. Be sure to show your work and to round off your answers to the proper number of significant figures. Express all your answers in scientific notation.

IV. Data Collection

Colecting data always has errors associated with it which are related to the collection process and are not considered mistakes. In other words, each piece of data does not have infinite precision and is limited to how well the measuring instrument can be read. To explore this further, we will take a simple set of data.

Measure the height of your lab instructor, or of a student volunteer, several times. Record your results to the nearest tenth of a centimeter (cm) in **Table II**. You should notice that the measurements are not all exactly the same. This variation is the data error and represents a statistical variation, not a real change in the person's height. The best height for the individual is the average of all the measurements. Calculate the average height of the person by adding all the values together and dividing the total sum by the number of measurements taken. Since the person is a constant height and because you used several measurements which were precise to a few tenths of a centimeter, your average is certainly good to a tenth of a centimeter and may be good out to a hundredth of a centimeter, depending upon how many individual measurements were taken. At the bottom of **Table II** record the person's average height, making sure to round off your answer appropriately. In the space at the bottom of **Table II** list three possible sources which may have contributed to the data error.

Now you will make some measurements of a small block of wood or some other object specified by your lab instructor. Make three separate measurements of the wooden block's length to the nearest tenth of a centimeter (example: 15.2 cm). Record your values in column 1 of **Table III**. These numbers may or may not be exactly the same value.

It is possible to read your ruler to the nearest hundredth of a centimeter. In order to do this you will need to use a magnifier lens to estimate between the tenths of a cm lines on your ruler. If the measurement falls half way between two lines, then write a 5 in the hundredths spot (example: 15.15 cm). If the measurement is just a tiny bit past a line, then you would estimate the value to be 1 or 2 hundredths of a cm (example: 15.12 cm). Similarly, if the value appears to be almost to the next line, then you would estimate 8 or 9 hundredths of a cm (for example:

15.18 cm). (**NOTE:** The numbers given in the above examples may not be the values you actually measure; they are only examples of how to write your estimate.) You should notice that the accuracy of these estimates is only good to + or – 0.01 cm. It is not possible to read your ruler to any higher accuracy. So, the errors in your data will be mainly caused by your inability to read the ruler accurately to a hundredth of a centimeter. Try to estimate the length of your wooden block to a hundredth of a centimeter and record your results in column 2 of **Table III**. The best value for the wooden block's length is the average of the numbers in column 2. Calculate this average.

V. Graphing Data

You have probably done graphing with an x/y coordinate system in a math class. When you did this, you calculated positions of points on the graph and drew straight lines, parabolas, etc. by connecting the plotted points. In order to visualize patterns or trends, a scientist plots data in much the same way you did in your math class. Usually this is done by plotting the dependent variable along the y-axis and the independent variable along the x-axis. Two examples of such graphs are shown in **Fig. 1** (Velocity vs. Distance and Brightness vs. Time). As you have just seen in part IV of this lab, data have inherent errors produced during the collection process. So when data are plotted, it represents a trend or pattern. Therefore, data points should not be connected by lines or curves as you did for your math class.

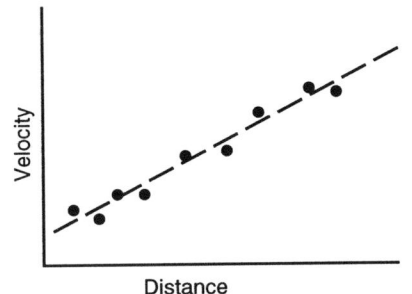
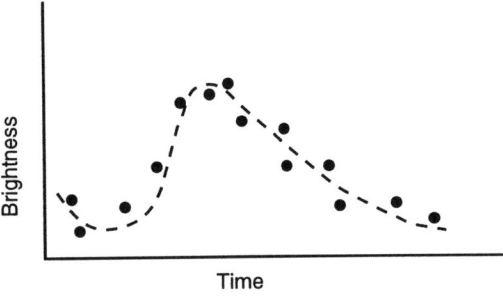

Fig. 1: Examples of a best-fit-line and a best-fit-curve which are commonly used in astronomy.
Notice that both the line and the curve follows the data but they do not connect consecutive data points.

Instead, a best-fit line or curve is drawn in such a way that it divides the data equally as shown in **Fig. 1** for two data sets. A best-fit line or curve may or may not pass through actual data points but it should always be close to the data it represents.

You will now make graphs of two different data sets and construct an eyeball best-fit-line or best-fit-curve for each of the data sets. The data in **Table IV** are believed to represent a straight line. Plot this data on the graph in **Fig. 2** and use a straight edge or ruler to draw in the best-fit-line. **Table V** has data which can be fit by a smooth curve. Plot this data on the graph in **Fig. 3** and represent it with a freehand best-fit-curve.

After a graph has been constructed it can be used to estimate values which lay between data points. On your graph in **Fig. 2**, go along the x-axis to the value X = 2.0. At this x value, lightly draw a straight line up until you intersect the best-fit-line you drew. Now, lightly draw a line over to the y-axis and read off the value of Y which corresponds to an X of 2.0. Write the value obtained for Y near the location intersected on the y-axis. Similarly, determine the velocity of the binary at the position of 220 degrees. Again, write your result near the intersection of the velocity-axis.

PROBLEM SET

Example: $(2.76 \times 10^5) \times (5.2 \times 10^{-2}) = 14.352 \times 10^{5+(-2)} = 14.352 \times 10^3 = 1.4 \times 10^4$

1. a. $2.0 \times (2.8 \times 10^5) =$

   b. $5.6 \times (6.725 \times 10^{-6}) =$

   c. $(3.77 \times 10^5) \times (4.8 \times 10^3) =$

   d. $(5.29 \times 10^3) \times (6.8 \times 10^{-7}) =$

Example: $\dfrac{2.54 \times 10^7}{1.3 \times 10^{-2}} = 1.95 \times 10^{7-(-2)} = 1.9 \times 10^9$

2. a. $\dfrac{9.65 \times 10^3}{2.0} =$

   b. $\dfrac{5.6 \times 10^5}{1.6 \times 10^5} =$

   c. $\dfrac{3.2 \times 10^9}{2.4 \times 10^5} =$

   d. $\dfrac{2.99792 \times 10^8}{5.520 \times 10^{-7}} =$

Table I

	Scientific Notation	Significant Figures
206265		
6378		
365.256366		
3.1416		
0.006214		

Table II

Trial Number	Height in cm
1	
2	
3	
4	
5	

Average height = _____

List three possible sources of data error.

1.

2.

3.

Table III

Trial	cm ± 0.1	cm ± 0.01
1		
2		
3		

Average length = _____

Table IV

The data below represents a linear relation.

X	Y
1.24	4.23
1.25	4.24
1.28	4.23
1.34	4.27
1.43	4.25
1.56	4.28
1.75	4.33
2.03	4.35
2.46	4.41
3.21	4.55

Table V

The data below represents the velocity curve of a binary star.

Degrees	Velocity (km/sec)
6	−110
27	−133
81	−150
87	−149
111	−114
121	−110
140	−72
166	−41
217	−12
227	+10
240	+21
253	+6
297	−26
324	−64
342	−89
348	−99

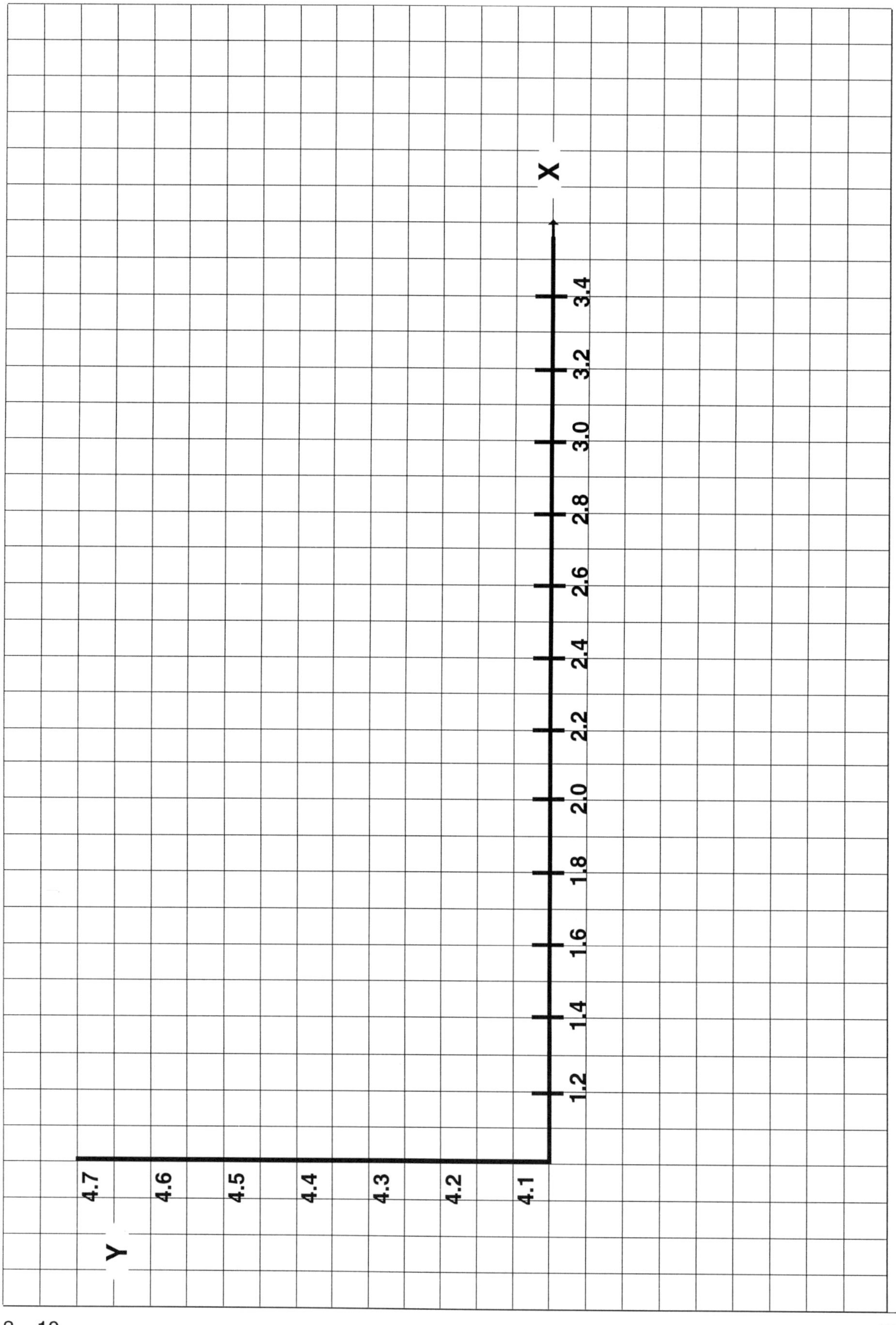

Fig. 2: Graph of a best-fit straight line.

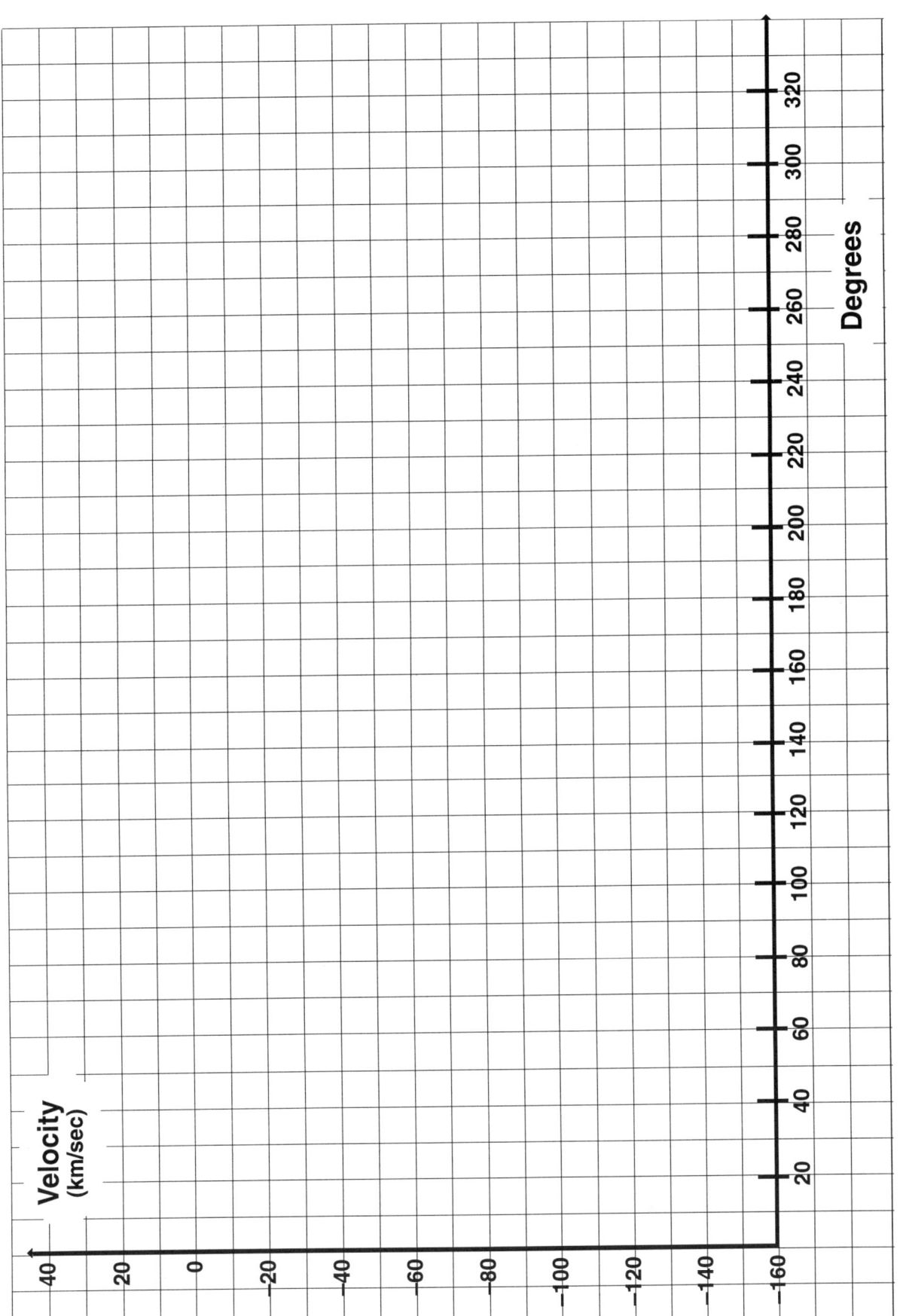

Fig. 2: Best-fit radial velocity curve for a binary star

THE CELESTIAL SPHERE AND PLANISPHERES

3

OBJECTIVES

After completing this exercise the student should be able to:

1. locate stars and planets on a celestial globe using R.A. and Dec. coordinates.
2. identify the locations of the celestial poles, equator, and ecliptic.
3. use a celestial globe to find the Sun's position along the ecliptic for any day of the year.
4. use a planisphere to identify stars and constellations in tonight's sky.
5. use a planisphere to estimate the rising and setting times for bright stars and planets.

STUDENT MATERIALS

pencil
planispheres (optional)
current issue of *Astronomy* and/or *Sky and Telescope* (optional)

LAB MATERIALS

celestial globes
current planet coordinates
planispheres
current issue of *Astronomy* and/or *Sky and Telescope* (optional)

INTRODUCTION

You are probably taking this course because you are interested in learning about the night sky or because it was the only class which fit into your schedule. Assuming the former, then the best way to learn about the sky is to go outside and observe it for yourself. If you do go and observe the night sky, it will appear to be a giant sphere with the stars painted onto it. The celestial sphere is an imaginary sphere of infinite radius on which we imagine all the stars to be attached. As this sphere appears to rotate from east to west, it carries all the stars and constellations with it. One of the first things you can see is the daily

rotation of the Earth. The celestial sphere appears to rotate from the east to the west. This is simply a reflection of the Earth's west-to-east rotation. Careful observation reveals that the celestial sphere makes one complete rotation in 23 hours and 56 minutes. Since our day is based on exactly 24 hours, then a star seen rising in the east tonight will rise 4 minutes earlier tomorrow night. It is this 4 minute daily shift which causes us to see different stars and constellations in summer than in winter. This westerly shift of the sky is caused by the Earth's orbital motion around the Sun. Notice that in one week the star will rise 30 minutes earlier and in a month it will rise 2 hours earlier. As this continues, you can deduce that eventually the star will be rising in the middle of the day and could not be observed at all. After one full year, you could again observe the same star rising at exactly the same clock time.

This annual shift of the sky is very easy to observe. Go out at some particular time, say 10:00P.M. and locate some bright star which is directly over a tree or antenna in the distance. In one week, go stand in this same location at 10:00P.M. and you will see this same star to be slightly west of the tree or antenna. You are actually observing the Earth's revolution around the Sun. Some time this week, try this observation for yourself; I think you will find it to be fun and educational.

By observing the night sky over several evenings, you will probably notice that your eyes begin to see patterns among the stars in the sky. These figures are not real but your brain loves to arrange things in logical terms, so it causes you to see boxes, lines, etc., among the stars. It is exactly this type of thinking that caused ancient people to place figures of heroes, fish, and other objects into the night sky. We know these figures as the constellations. Modern astronomers still recognize areas of the sky as being within the boundary of a particular constellation, but the figures of birds and monsters are generally not used.

However, it is still fun to try and visualize the original figures of the constellations. Currently there are 88 officially recognized constellations in the entire sky, including both northern and southern hemispheres. You will see many of these constellations on the celestial globes used in today's lab work. These globes are great for helping you visualize the celestial sphere in 3-D but they are not very good for helping you to learn to identify constellations in the actual night sky. A star wheel or planisphere is a much better tool for constellation finding. A planisphere is a flat disk which can be set to show you the sky at any time of day on any date of the year. It is a nifty little device.

During this lab exercise, you will use both a celestial globe and a planisphere to learn about the night sky. I hope you will use the techniques in this lab to go out and observe the motions of the sky and to become friendly with the brighter stars and constellations. After you learn the stars and constellations, they sort of become your "friends" and you look forward to seeing them each year. In addition, you will be able to impress your friends and neighbors by pointing out bright stars and constellations to them.

PROCEDURE

I. The Celestial Sphere

DO NOT MAKE ANY MARKS ON OUR CELESTIAL GLOBES. THANK YOU VERY MUCH FOR KEEPING OUR EQUIPMENT NEAT AND CLEAN.

The celestial globes are small, 3-D representations of the entire sky. The first thing you will notice on the globe are the drawings of the constellations and the bright stars. Each globe maker writes the names differently. Your lab instructor may need to point out which names belong to constellations and which ones are for stars. Some other things you should find on your globe are the celestial equator, the north and south celestial poles,

and the ecliptic. On many globes, the celestial equator is where the manufacturer has glued the two halves together. The north and south celestial poles are located at the two rotation points because the real sky appears to rotate around these same two locations. Unfortunately, the real sky does not have these nice mechanical supports and so the celestial poles are more difficult to find when you go outside. In addition, you can only observe the north celestial pole from locations north of the Earth's equator. The ecliptic is the apparent path of the Sun among the background of stars and it runs around the globe making a 23.5 degree angle with the celestial equator. Be sure that you can locate the celestial equator, celestial north and south poles, and the ecliptic on your celestial globe. If you are having trouble, feel free to ask your lab instructor for assistance.

In order to locate objects on the celestial sphere, astronomers have developed a two-dimensional coordinate system which is attached to the sky and rotates along with it. This system is similar to the longitude and latitude positions on the Earth's surface. The east-west coordinate is called Right Ascension (R.A.) and is measured in units of time, such as hour (h), minutes (m), and seconds (s). Declination (Dec.) is the north (+) and south (−) coordinate, and is measured in angular units of degrees (°), arc minutes (´), and arc seconds (´´). The origin of this system (R.A. = 00h 00m 00s, Dec. = 00° 00´ 00´´) is located at the Spring Equinox, where the ecliptic intersects the celestial equator in the spring. Locate this equinox on your celestial globe by finding where the ecliptic crosses the equator in a south-to-north direction near March 21st. Looking along the globe's equator, find the R.A. hour lines which run north and south and are usually labeled with the hour coordinate from 00h to 23h. You can estimate between the hour lines to the nearest 10 minutes of time. It is not possible to read the R.A. to any higher precision. To the north (+) and south (−) of the equator, the Dec. coordinate circles can be seen. These are usually drawn on the globes at intervals of 5, 10, or 15 degrees, depending upon the globe makers preference. You should be able to estimate the Dec. coordinate to within 1 or 2 degrees. The equator has a Dec. of 0° and the north and south

ECLIPSE PREDICTING

OBJECTIVES

After completing this exercise the student will be able to:

1. convert Universal Time to the observer's local time zone, such as EST, EDT, CST, etc.

2. compare times of new or full moon to the time of nodal passage to predict the dates and times of all eclipses during the given calendar year.

3. determine which eclipse will possibly be visible from his or her observing location.

STUDENT MATERIALS

pencil
mm scale
protractor
compass
calculator

LAB MATERIALS

eclipse data for current year (optional)
contact angles for an eclipse during current year (optional)

STUDENT REQUIREMENTS

This lab is to be done individually, without lab partners. After completion, turn in answer sheet and **Fig. 1** in page sequence order.

PREDICTION RULES FOR 1996

1. An eclipse can occur only when the moon is new or full. The **time** of **mid-eclipse** is the **time of new** or **full moon**.

2. An eclipse will occur only if the moon is also **close** to a **node** (a point where the moon's path crosses the Sun's path). For example, at the ascending node the moon crosses from the south to the north side of the ecliptic (Sun's path).

3. Solar eclipses (only at **new** moon):

   a. **Central** solar eclipses: the moon passes directly in front of the Sun, as viewed from a narrow band on the Earth's surface.

      The eclipse will be central if a node is passed within 20 hours of the time of the new moon.

      These central eclipses can be:

      i. **Total**: the moon is large enough to cover the entire Sun.

      ii. **Annular**: the moon is within 8 days of apogee, making its image too small to cover the Sun even at mid-eclipse.

   b. **Partial** solar eclipses: as viewed from a fairly large area on Earth, the moon only partially covers the Sun's disk.

      The eclipse will be only partial if the time between new moon and a nodal passage is greater than 20 but less than 28 hours.

4. Lunar eclipses (only at **full** moon):

   a. **Umbral eclipses**: the darkest part of the Earth's shadow is the umbra. No direct sunlight reaches the moon in this region.

      A lunar eclipse will be umbral if a node is passed within 20 hours of the time of the full moon.

      The exact geometry of each umbral eclipse determines whether it will be total (the entire moon enters the umbra) or only partial.

   b. **Penumbral eclipses**: the penumbra is the region around the umbra, where some sunlight still reaches the moon. The shading of the moon in the penumbra is subtle and may go unnoticed, unless you are aware that an eclipse is in progress.

A lunar eclipse will be only penumbral if the time between full moon and nodal passage is more than 20 hours but less than 28 hours.

5. The eclipse limits of 20 and 28 hours used above are approximate and may be slightly different from year to year.

6. Remember that solar eclipses are seen only from a small area. Generally, if the moon is north of the ecliptic, that area will be somewhere in the northern hemisphere. (The moon is north of the ecliptic during the time from ascending to descending node.) The exact location of the eclipse path on Earth requires a complex calculation.

7. Lunar eclipses are visible to anyone who can see the full moon, which is the entire nighttime hemisphere of the Earth.

8. All of the times in the **Data Table** are given in Universal Time (UT). This is standard time at the Greenwich Meridian.

   Eastern Standard Time is UT minus 5 hours (EST = UT – 5).

   Eastern Daylight Time is UT minus 4 hours (EDT = UT – 4). We now observe daylight time from the first Sunday in April until the last Sunday in October.

PROCEDURE

I. SOLAR ECLIPSES

There were two solar eclipses in 1999. Answer the following questions for each solar eclipse on the separate **answer sheet**.

1. Comparing the times of new moon and nodal passages, what is the UT date and time of the eclipse?

2. What is the Eastern Time and date of mid-eclipse? (April 7 – October 27)

3. Using the ecliptic limits given in the general instructions, will the eclipse be central or partial?

4. At the time of the eclipse, is the moon slightly north or south of the ecliptic?

5. If the eclipse is central, do you expect it to be total or annular?

6. Considering your answers to questions 2 and 4 above, is there any chance that the eclipse will be visible from your location?

II. LUNAR ECLIPSES

There were two lunar eclipses in 1999. Answer these questions for each lunar eclipse on the **answer sheet**.

7. What is the UT date and time of the eclipse?

8. What is the Eastern Time and date of mid-eclipse?

9. Using the ecliptic limits, will the eclipse be umbral or penumbral?

10. Considering your answer to question 8, was the eclipse visible from your location?

III. DETAILS OF A LUNAR ECLIPSE

The steps outlined below will enable you to construct a diagram of the second lunar eclipse. Your diagram should be done on **Fig. 1**.

1. Draw a north-south vertical line (north will be **up**) in the middle of the page.

2. Draw a 2.6-cm-radius circle centered on this line. This represents the umbra of the Earth's shadow.

3. The moon first enters the umbra at a point 47° clockwise around the umbra from the north. Extend a line outward from the center in this direction, well beyond the umbra's edge.

4. Centered on this line, draw a 1.0-cm-radius circle which lies outside the umbra, just touching its edge. This circle represents the moon at its **first contact** with the umbra.

5. **Last contact** comes at a point 30° counterclockwise around the umbra from the north. Draw a line from the center in this direction and repeat step 4 for last contact.

6. Draw a line through the centers of the first-and-last contact lunar images. This line represents the moon's path through the umbra.

7. Find the midpoint of the line drawn in step 6, halfway between first and last contact. Draw a 1.0-cm-radius lunar image at this location. This circle represents the moon at mid-eclipse.

8. The scale of your drawing is about 1 cm = 0.25°. The moon moves at about 0.5° per hour through the shadow (2 cm/hr on the diagram). You already know the time of mid-eclipse. Using the distances on your drawing, find the precise times of first and last umbral contact.

9. Using the same center as the umbra, draw a larger circle of 4.6 cm radius. The space between the umbra and this circle is the penumbra. The shading of the moon in the penumbra becomes noticeable only near the umbra itself.

1999 ECLIPSE DATA

Dates and Times are UT Date Hr:Mn

Hint: Remember that events near the end of one month may occur close in time to something else at the beginning of the next month.

NEW MOON	FULL MOON	ASCENDING NODE	DESCENDING NODE	PERIGEE	APOGEE
Jan 17 15:46	Jan 02 02:49 Jan 31 16:06	Jan 05 02:26	Jan 19 13:34	Jan 27	Jan 11
Feb 16 06:39	Feb none	Feb 01 13:06 Feb 28 19:38	Feb 15 21:52	Feb 21	Feb 09
Mar 17 18:48	Mar 02 06:58 Mar 31 22:49	Mar 28 00:37	Mar 15 07:09	Mar 20	Mar 08
Apr 16 04:22	Apr 30 14:55	Apr 24 01:54	Apr 11 13:56	Apr 17	Apr 05
May 15 12:05	May 30 06:40	May 21 03:18	May 08 16:55	May 16	May 02 May 29
Jun 13 19:03	Jun 28 21:37	Jun 17 07:56	Jun 04 17:56 Jul 29 02:38	Jun 13	Jun 26
Jul 13 02:24	Jul 28 11:25	Jul 14 16:14	Jul 01 20:48	Jul 11	Jul 23
Aug 11 11:08	Aug 26 23:48	Aug 11 01:53	Aug 25 10:22	Aug 08 Sep 29	Aug 20
Sep 09 22:02	Sep 25 10:51	Sep 07 09:36 Oct 31 13:48	Sep 21 17:41	Sep 03	Sep 17
Oct 09 11:34	Oct 24 21:02	Oct 04 13:12	Oct 18 22:26	Oct 27	Oct 15
Nov 08 03:53	Nov 23 07:04	Nov 27 15:52	Nov 15 00:13	Nov 24	Nov 11
Dec 07 22:32	Dec 22 17:31	Dec 24 22:56	Dec 12 01:46	Dec 22	Dec 08

Answer Sheet

Solar Eclipses	**1**	**2**
1. UT Date and Time:	_____	_____
2. Local Date and Time: (Specify **A.M. or P.M.** and EST, EDT, etc.)	_____	_____
3. Central or Partial?	_____	_____
4. North or South?	_____	_____
5. Total or Annular?	_____	_____
6. Possibly visible from your location?	_____	_____

Lunar Eclipses	**1**	**2**
7. UT Date and Time:	_____	_____
8. Local Date and Time: (Specify **A.M. or P.M.** and EDT or EST)	_____	_____
9. Umbral or Penumbral?	_____	_____
10. Possibly visible from your location?	_____	_____

NAME: ______________________

LAB SECTION: ______________________

Contact Times:

First Contact = ______________________

Last Contact = ______________________

Fig. 1: Drawing of a lunar eclipse.

PLANETARY ORBITS

OBJECTIVES

After completing this exercise, the student will be able to:

1. draw a simple ellipse using two thumbtacks and a loop of string.

2. calculate the eccentricity of an ellipse.

3. use a series of lunar photographs to make a scale drawing of the moon's orbit.

4. be able to confirm the elliptical nature of the moon's orbit by determining the major axis, minor axis, and eccentricity of the orbit.

STUDENT MATERIALS

pencil
mm ruler
compass
protractor
calculator
Sky and Telescope reprint, "The Moon's Orbit," from back of lab book

LAB MATERIALS

two thumbtacks per student
one loop of string per student
a piece of cardboard (~8 ½×11") per student

STUDENT REQUIREMENTS

This lab is to be done individually without lab partners. After completing the lab, turn in **Table I**, **Fig. 1**, and **Fig. 2** in page order sequence.

PROCEDURE

A. Kepler's Laws and the Elliptical Orbit

You will draw an elliptical orbit on the page provided (**Fig. 1**). To do this you will need a piece of cardboard, two thumbtacks, and a loop of string.

1. Remove **Fig. 1** and place it on the piece of cardboard.

2. Insert a thumbtack through the two focus points labeled **F1** and **F2**.

3. Make a loop of string which is large enough to go around both tacks at the same time. The loop should stretch about 8 to 10 cm, but its actual size is not important.

4. Place the loop of string around the tacks and stretch it taut with a sharp pencil point as demonstrated by your instructor. While holding the pencil vertically and keeping the string taut draw an ellipse by moving the pencil around the two tacks. The orbit you have drawn is similar to that of some comets and asteroids.

5. Draw a line longwise through the ellipse which connects **F1** and **F2**. This line is called the major axis. Label the major axis on your drawing.

6. The minor axis is perpendicular to the major axis and divides it in half. The midpoint of your major axis is halfway betwen **F1** and **F2**. Locate this point and label it **c**. Now draw and label the minor axis on your ellipse drawing.

7. Kepler's 1st law states that the Sun is at one focus of an elliptical orbit. Pick one of the foci and label it **Sun**. The other focus has no physical significance.

8. Perihelion is the closest approach to the Sun. Aphelion is the farthest point from the Sun. Perihelion and aphelion are on the orbit at each end of the major axis. Find and label these two points on your orbit.

9. The distance from the center **c** to either perihelion or aphelion is named the semi-major axis. Label this distance as **a** on your orbit. The

distance from the center to one of the foci is named **x** in this exercise. Label this distance on your orbit.

10. On your orbit, measure, in AUs (1 cm = 1 AU) the perihelion distance, the aphelion distance, and the major axis, the semi-major axis, and the distance, **x**. Record your results to a tenth of an AU in the spaces provided below your drawing.

11. How much an ellipse deviates from a circle is called its eccentricity, **e**. Calculate your orbit's eccentricity using the relation **e = x/a**, and record your answer in the space provided. Note that eccentricity is a ratio and has no units.

12. Kepler's 3rd law states that the orbital period, **P**, is related to the orbit's semi-major axis, **a**, by the relation $P^2 = a^3$, where **P** will be in years if **a** is in AUs. Use the 3rd law to calculate the period of your orbit. Record your answer to the nearest tenth of a year in the space provided.

B. The Moon's Orbit

As applied to the moon's orbit, Kepler's 1st law would state that the moon's orbit is an ellipse with the Earth at one focus. If the moon's orbit is an ellipse its distance from the Earth should change during one complete orbit. This means the moon should appear larger at perigee (closest approach to Earth) than it does at apogee (farthest from Earth). The *Sky and Telescope* reprint provided in the lab packet at the back of this book shows a series of lunar photographs. These were obtained as the moon passed several different positions in its orbit. It is possible to use these photographs to determine a few orbital properties of the moon.

1. Measure the diameter, **d**, of each lunar image shown. Be careful not to simply measure the illuminated portion. Make all measurements more or less vertically. Estimate each value to a **tenth** of a **millimeter** using a magnifier. Record your measurements in the column provided in Ta-

ble I. (**Note:** these values should range between 40 mm and 60 mm.)

2. From each diameter measurement the relative distance to the moon can be determined. This distance will be scaled down to fit on a piece of graph paper. Calculate the scale distance, **D**, (in mm) to the moon using the relation **D = 4000/d**, where **d** is the diameter recorded in column 4 of **Table I** and 4000 is a scale factor. Record your values of **D**, to its nearest tenth of a millimeter, in the last column of **Table I**.

3. Calculate the average scale distance, D_{ave}, to the moon and record your answer in the space provided at the bottom of **Table I**.

4. Plot the moon's orbital position on the polar coordinate graph paper given as **Fig. 2**. You will have to plot longitude vs. scale distance, **D**. On the graph paper longitude starts at the bottom, labeled **0°**, and increases counterclockwise. This will correspond to the true direction of the moon's orbital motion as viewed from above the Earth's north pole.

To plot the first data point, place the edge of your millimeter ruler along the line labeled **270°** (longitude). Be sure that 0 mm is at the origin of the graph paper, which corresponds to the Earth's position on this diagram. Now measure out along the 270° line and place a pencil dot at your value of **D** for a longitude of 270°. Continue in this manner for the remaining data in **Table I**.

5. If you examine the plotted data on **Fig. 2** it can be seen that they are **not** centered around the Earth. In order to draw the moon's orbit you must first establish the orbit's center. Open your compass equal to the D_{ave} calculated in step 3. Remember to use the edge of a ruler to properly set the compass. Locate the center by placing the compass point on three or four of the plotted data points and draw a small arc near the center of the graph. Ideally these should all cross at one place, the center. In reality, they will show you only approximately where the center should be.

6. Place the compass point within the small area enclosed by your arcs drawn in part 5. Check to see how well the compass pencil passes through the data points. This will not be perfect. Adjust the compass point's location until a best-fit circle can be drawn. Once you have located the center, draw in the moon's orbit with your compass. You are thus representing the elliptical orbit of the moon with an offset circle instead of an ellipse.

7. The compass hole is the center of the moon's orbit. One focus is located at Earth, which is at the origin of the graph paper. Use these two points to draw and label the major and minor axes of the moon's orbit. Hint: How are the center and foci related to the major and minor axes in **Fig. 1**?

8. Label perigee (closest) and apogee (farthest) on the moon's orbit. These may, or may not, be at data point locations.

9. Measure the values of **x** and **a** in millimeters. Calculate the eccentricity of the orbit using **e = x/a**. Record your results in the spaces provided on the graph paper.

TABLE I

MOON'S ORBIT

IMAGE	DATE (Nov.)	LONGITUDE (°)	d (mm)	D (mm)
1	7.44	270°		
2	8.46	283°		
3	10.46	309°		
4	12.46	336°		
5	14.46	5°		
6	15.81	27°		
7	17.84	57°		
8	19.94	87°		
9	22.92	127°		
10	24.79	151°		
11	26.90	176°		
12	29.92	212°		

$D_{avg} =$ _____

• F2

• F1

Perihelion = _____   x = _____   P = _____

Aphelion = _____   a = _____

Major Axis = _____   e = _____

Fig. 1: Drawing of an elliptical orbit.

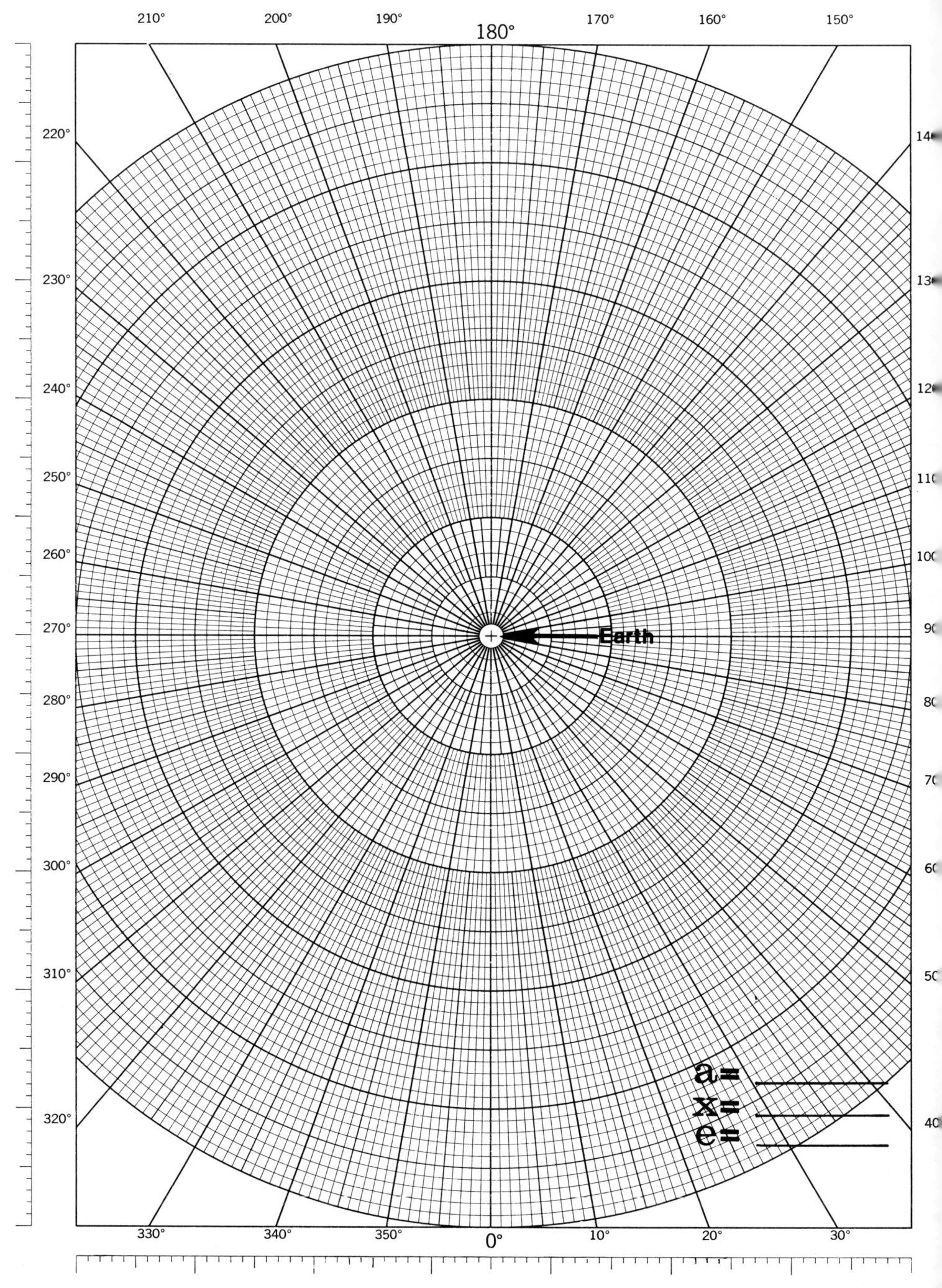

THE MASS OF JUPITER

OBJECTIVES

After completing this simulation, the student will be able to:

1. observe the motions of Jupiter's moons.
2. use Kepler's 3rd Law to determine the mass of Jupiter, based on the student's observations of the Galilean Moons.

STUDENT MATERIALS

pencil
mm ruler
calculator with logs

LAB MATERIALS

"Dance of the Planets" software by ARC, Inc. MS-DOS or Macintosh computer with at least 640K of RAM, 360K drive, VGA monitor

STUDENT REQUIREMENTS

Data may be collected by individuals or by pairs of students. All data reductions and analysis, graphs, and answers to questions should be completed individually, **not** by pairs or groups. Turn in **Table I**, **Figs. 2a**, **2b**, **2c**, **2d**, and your answers to the questions and calculations.

INTRODUCTION

During 1609 and 1610 the Italian astronomer Galileo Galilei was the first person to use a simple telescope to observe the moons of Jupiter. He noted that the Jovian moons appeared to behave like a miniature solar system, with Jupiter replacing the Sun and the moons playing the role of planets. In part this helped to support the Copernican Heliocentric Model of the solar system, because these moons did not orbit the Earth. The center of their system was

Jupiter. So not everything orbited the Earth or had the Earth at its center. About this same time a German mathematician and astronomer, Johannes Kepler, was developing his three laws of planetary motion. The four Galilean satellites of Jupiter appeared to obey these laws.

About 50 years later, In 1666, Issac Newton developed his Law of Gravity and revised Kepler's three Laws of Planetary Motion. Kepler's 3rd Law was rewritten to include the masses of the two orbiting bodies. Mathematically, this law can be written as

$$P^2 (M_1 + M_2) = a^3 \qquad \text{(Eq. 1)}$$

where: $P =$ orbital period in years

$a =$ semi-major axis or the radius of the orbit in AUs

M_1 and $M_2 =$ masses of the two orbiting bodies in solar masses

Rearranging terms, **Eq. 1** can be solved for the masses M_1 and M_2,

$$(M_1 + M_2) = a^3/P^2 \qquad \text{(Eq. 2)}$$

Notice that **Eq. 2** gives the total mass of the two orbiting objects, not the individual masses of each body. In the case of a large planet and a tiny moon, such as that of Jupiter and one of its moons, it can be assumed that the satellite has almost no mass relative to the very massive planet. Thus, $M_2 = 0$, **Eq. 2** becomes

$$M_1 = a^3/P^2 \qquad \text{(Eq. 3)}$$

and M_1 is effectively the mass of the planet.

During this lab exercise you will use **"Dance of the Planets"** software to simulate observations of Jupiter and its four Galilean satellites as viewed with a small Earth-based telescope. Data will be collected on the orbit of one Jovian moon and the mass of Jupiter will be calculated using **Eq. 3**, above. The orbiting moons are really fun to watch, so enjoy yourself while doing this simulation.

OBSERVING PROCEDURE

Your lab instructor will assign each group of students a Galilean Moon to observe using the software "**Dance of the Planets**." Io is rather close to Jupiter and only takes a couple of days to orbit the planet. At the other extreme is Callisto, which is relatively far from Jupiter and takes about three weeks for one revolution. Thus the time interval needed to observe each moon through a complete orbit is different for each satellite. Io must be observed every few hours for two or three days and Callisto should be observed once per day for several weeks. The frequency with which you should make observations for your assigned moon is given below:

Io: Observe every 2 hours for 2.5 days.

Europa: Observe every 4 hours for 5 days.

Ganymede: Observe every 8 hours for 9 days.

Callisto: Observe once per day for 18 days.

1. To start the software, use the following steps:

    a. Turn on the computer and monitor.

    b. At the prompt type **cd dance,** and press **[enter]**.

    c. Type **dance** and press **[enter]**.

    d. When the white screen appears, press any key to continue.

    e. When the title screen appears, press any key to continue.

    f. To make selections and communicate with the program, use the highlighted letters or numbers for the keyboard stroke.

2. Use the following key commands to set up observations of Jupiter as viewed through a 64× telescope on the Earth.

    a. Select the menu, [**M**].

    b. Select Earth view, [**E**].

    c. Select Menu [**M**], Planets [**P**], and Jupiter [**5**].

    d. Select Zoom [**Z**], use cursor keys (arrows) to choose a magnification of 64×, and press [**enter**].

    Jupiter and its moons should now be seen on the screen as you might see them in a small telescope at 64×.

3. Select pace [**P**], use cursor keys (arrows) to choose a pace of 20, and press [**enter**]. Now you should see an image of Jupiter and its four Galilean Moons orbiting around it.

    In step 4, below, you will start collecting data for your satellite's orbit. **Fig. 1** shows an example of data collected for Io during August of 1995. Use this example to interpret the directions given in the following steps.

4. Press [**L**], and the simulation pauses and labels the moons by name. While the simulation is pausing make the following measurements.

    a. Use a mm scale to measure the diameter of Jupiter. Record this value in the space provided at the top of **Table I**.

    b. Use the clock in the lower left corner of the screen to determine the date and time of your observation. The bold-faced numeral is the month, the lighter numeral is the day, the last two numbers are the hour of the day. The clock face (above the month and day) tells you the number of minutes past the hour shown.

    Example:

    mmddhr

Record in **Table I** the date and time of your observation to the nearest 30 minutes.

c. Use a mm scale to measure from the center of Jupiter to your assigned moon. If you are measuring to the left of Jupiter, this value is considered to be negative (–). Measurements to the right are considered positive (+).

d. Continue collecting data at the suggested intervals given for your moon at the beginning of this section. To resume the simulation press the space bar or **enter**. When you want to pause the simulation to collect data, press [**L**].

5. After you have finished taking data, stop the simulation by selecting menu [**M**], exit [**X**], and yes [**Y**].

DATA REDUCTIONS AND ANALYSIS

1. Convert your mm measurements in **Table 1** into Jovian Diameter (J.D.) units. Divide each mm value in column 3 by Jupiter's mm diameter written at the top of **Table I**. Record your J.D. distances in column 4 of **Table I**.

2. Make a graph of J.D. vs. Time for your assigned moon on **Fig. 2a**, **2b**, **2c**, or **2d**, whichever corresponds to your satellite. The time scales are in hours. The beginning of a new day is represented by a large tick mark. Label these large tick marks with the dates of your observations as shown on the example graph of **Fig. 1**.

3. After plotting all the data, draw a best-fit curve through the data. This curve should be smooth and free of any kinks or sudden jogs. See **Fig. 1** for an example of how your curve should look.

4. Use the curve you have just drawn in **Fig. 2** to determine the orbital period, P, for your satellite. In order to use Kepler's 3rd Law, you will need the period in units of years. However, it will probably be easier to determine the period in hours or days and convert these into years. Record your value for P in the spaces provided on **Fig. 2**. See **Fig. 1** as an example of how to determine P.

5. The amplitude of the curve in **Fig. 2** represents the orbit's diameter, or major axis. To use Kepler's 3rd law, you need the value of the orbit's semi-major axis, a. Because the orbit is elliptical and because we view the orbit from varying locations, you need to measure the full amplitude of the curve (top to bottom) as shown in **Fig. 1**. this is the orbit's diameter or 2a, so divide by 2 to get the orbit's semi-major axis, a. Record this value in the space provided in **Fig. 2**. In order to use Kepler's 3rd Law, you must convert this value into AUs by multiplying it by 9.545×10^{-4} AU/JD. Record your answer in the space provided in **Fig. 2**.

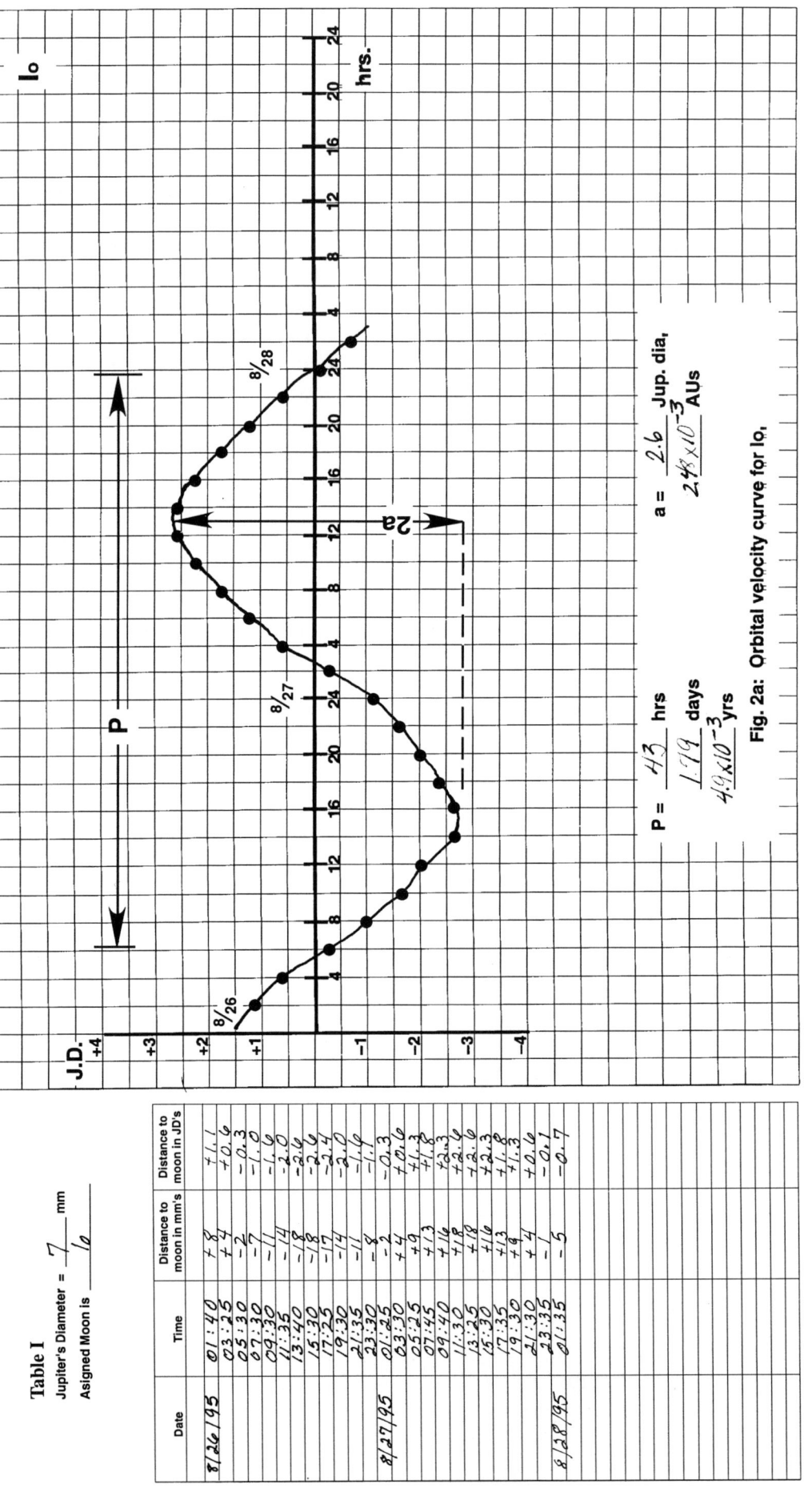

Fig. 1: An example of the results obtained for Io.

Table I

Jupiter's Diameter = __7__ mm

Assigned Moon is __Io__

Date	Time	Distance to moon in mm's	Distance to moon in JD's
8/26/95	01:40	+8	+1.1
	03:25	+4	+0.6
	05:30	-2	-0.3
	07:30	-7	-1.0
	09:30	-11	-1.6
	11:35	-14	-2.0
	13:40	-18	-2.6
	15:30	-17	-2.4
	17:25	-17	-2.4
	19:30	-14	-2.0
	21:35	-11	-1.6
	23:30	-8	-1.1
8/27/95	01:25	-2	-0.3
	03:30	+4	+0.6
	05:25	+9	+1.3
	07:45	+13	+1.8
	09:40	+16	+2.3
	11:30	+18	+2.6
	13:25	+18	+2.6
	15:30	+16	+2.3
	17:35	+13	+1.8
	19:30	+9	+1.3
	21:30	+4	+0.6
	23:35	-1	-0.1
8/28/95	01:35	-5	-0.7

$$P = \frac{43}{1.79} \text{ hrs} \atop \frac{1.79}{4.9\times10^{-3}} \text{ days} \atop \text{yrs}$$

$$a = \frac{2.6}{2.43\times10^{-3}} \text{ Jup. dia,} \atop \text{AUs}$$

Fig. 2a: Orbital velocity curve for Io,

Table I

Jupiter's Diameter = _____ mm

Assigned Moon is _____

Date	Time	Distance to moon in mm.	Distance to moon in JD

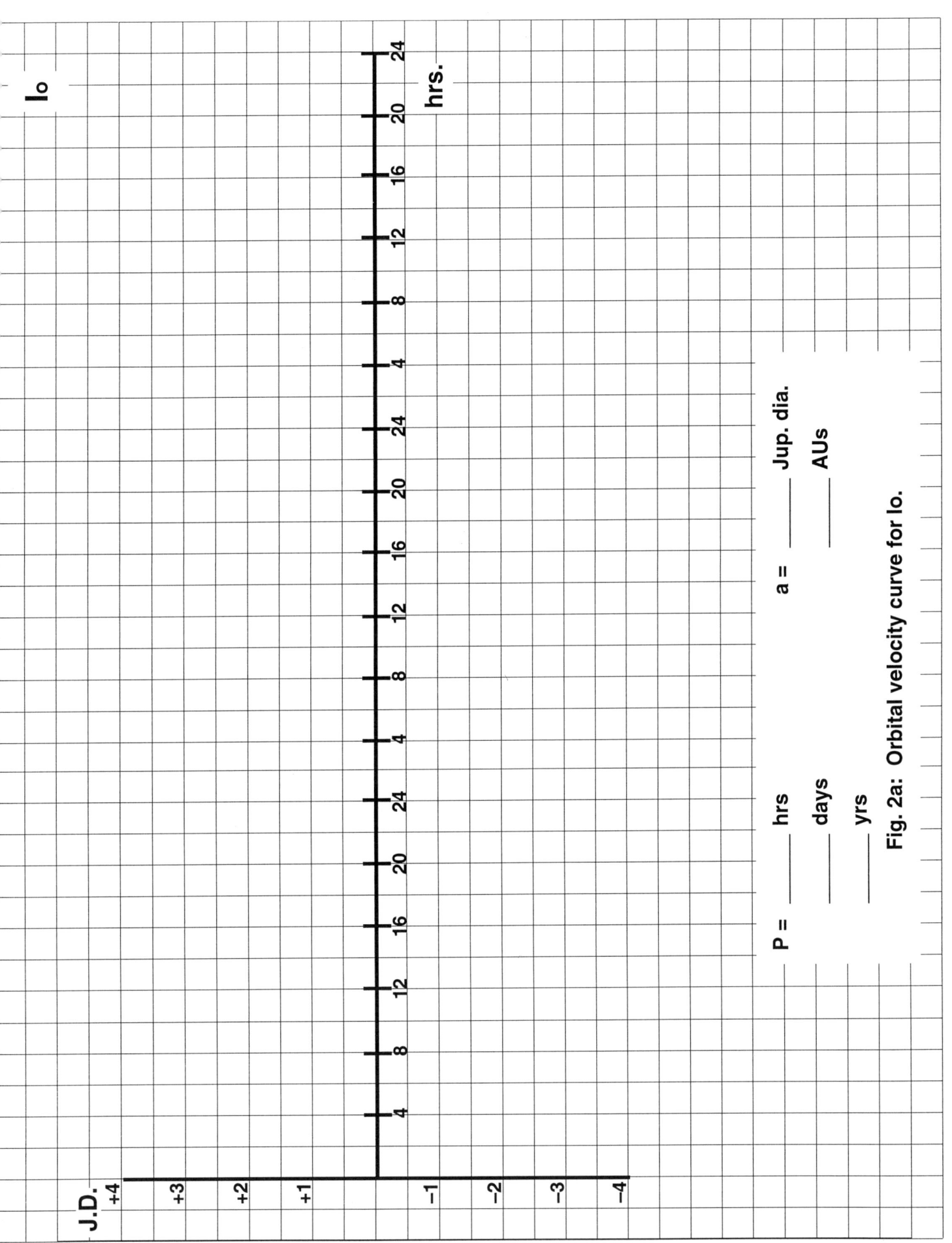

Io

J.D.

+4

+3

+2

+1

−1

−2

−3

−4

4   8   12   16   20   24   4   8   12   16   20   24   4   8   12   16   20   24   hrs.

P = _____ hrs   a = _____ Jup. dia.

_____ days   _____ AUs

_____ yrs

Fig. 2a: Orbital velocity curve for Io.

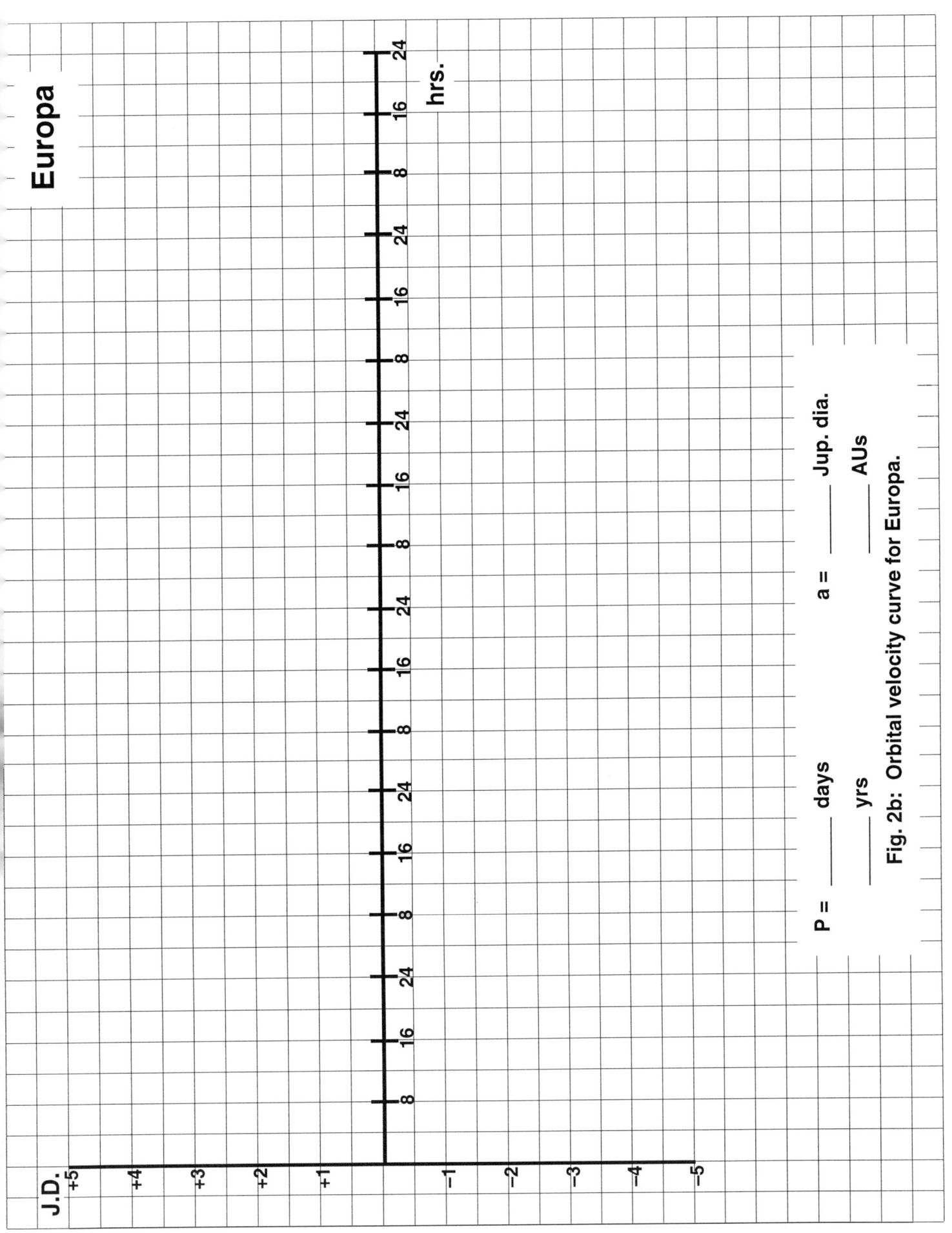

Europa

J.D.

+5
+4
+3
+2
+1

−1
−2
−3
−4
−5

8 16 24 8 16 24 8 16 24 8 16 24 8 16 24 8 16 24 8 16 24 8 16 24
hrs.

P = _____ days   a = _____ Jup. dia.

_____ yrs   _____ AUs

Fig. 2b: Orbital velocity curve for Europa.

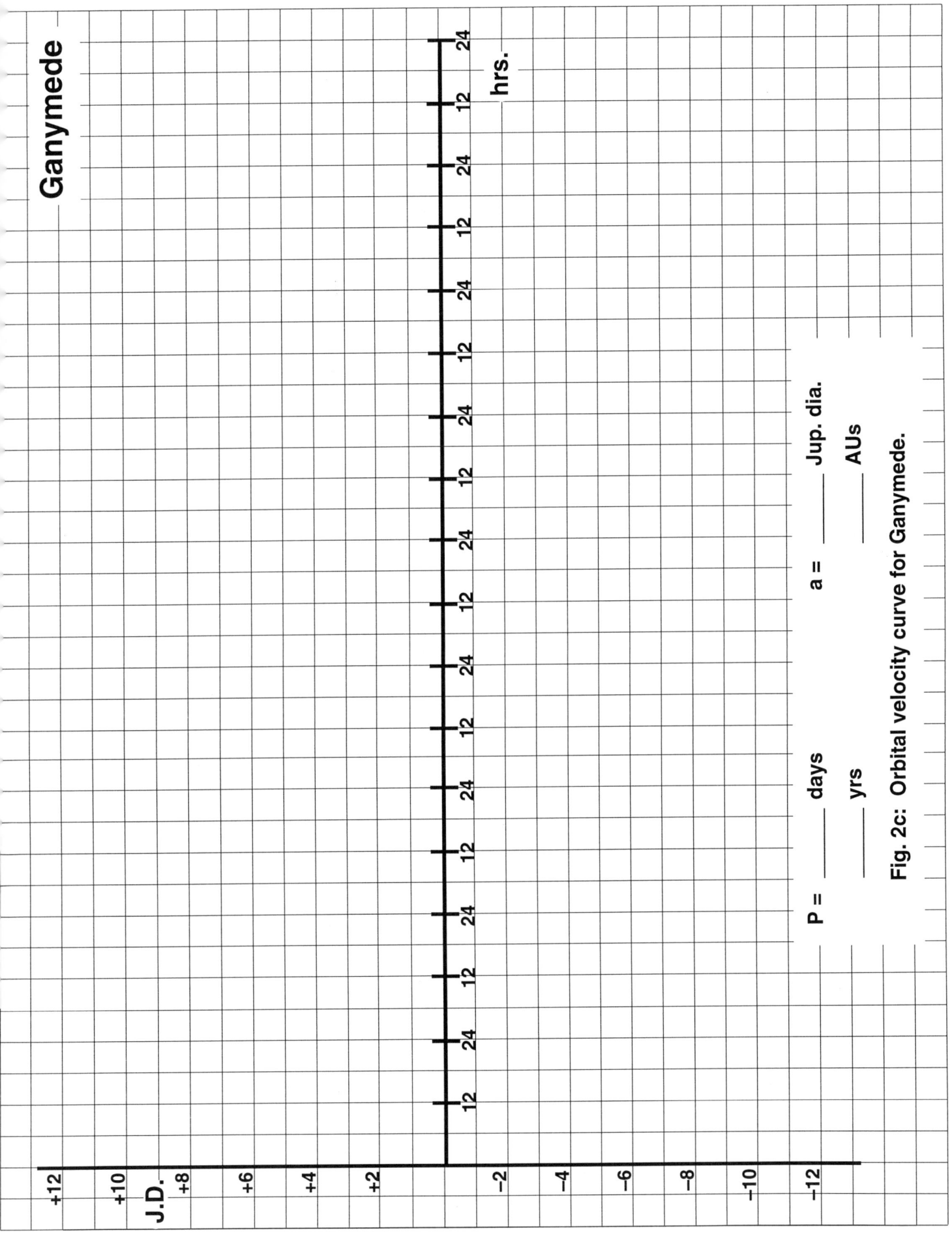

Ganymede

J.D.

+12
+10
+8
+6
+4
+2
-2
-4
-6
-8
-10
-12

12 24 12 24 12 24 12 24 12 24 12 24 12 24 12 24 12 24 12 24 12

hrs.

P = _____ days   a = _____ Jup. dia.

_____ yrs   _____ AUs

Fig. 2c: Orbital velocity curve for Ganymede.

Callisto

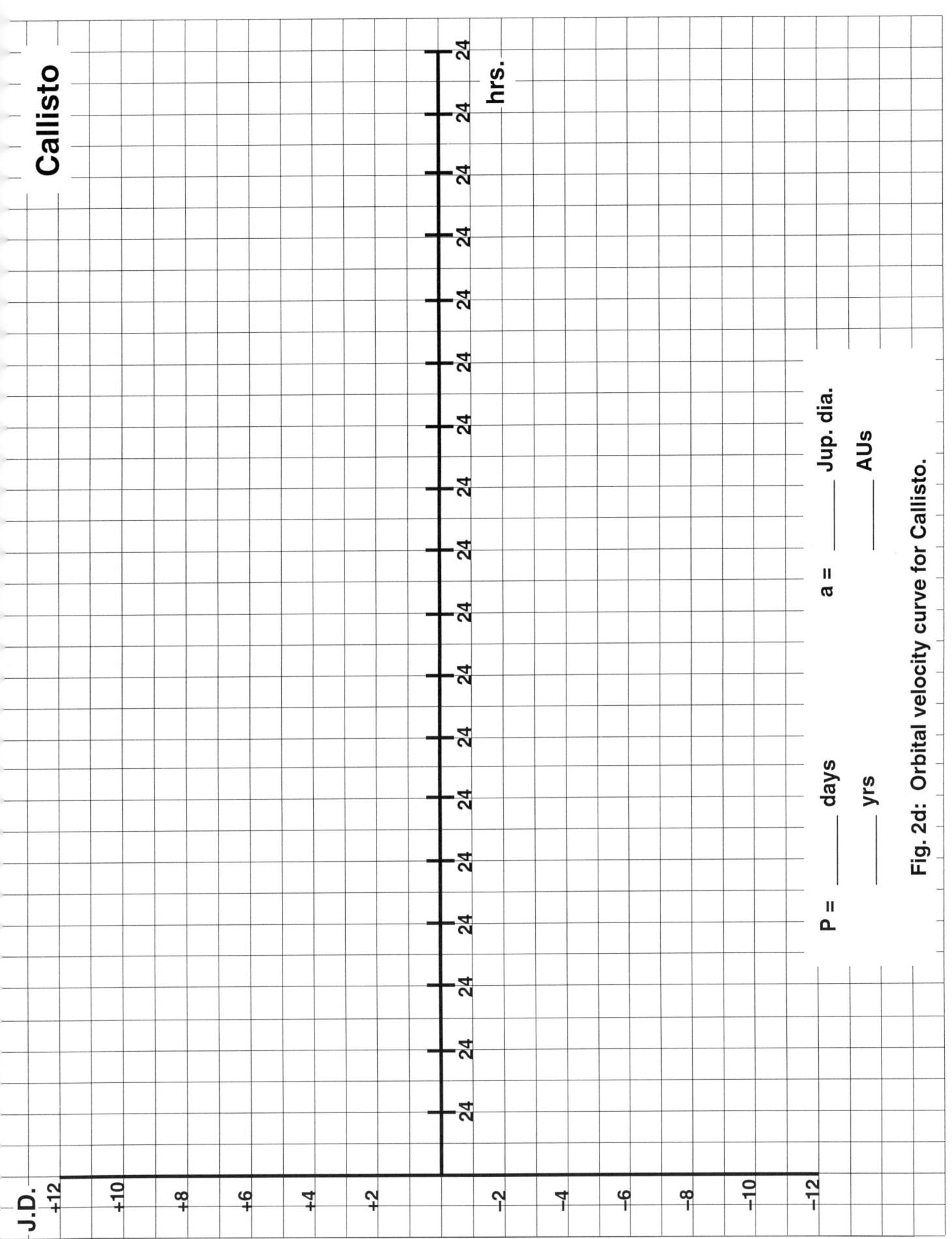

hrs.

P = _____ days   a = _____ Jup. dia.

_____ yrs   _____ AUs

Fig. 2d: Orbital velocity curve for Callisto.

J.D.

Questions and Calculations

1. Use **Eq. 3** in the Introduction section of this lab to calculate the mass of Jupiter in terms of the Sun's mass ($M_\odot$). SHOW YOUR WORK.

    $M_J =$ _____ $M_\odot$

2. The Earth has a mass of $3.0 \times 10^{-6}\, M_\odot$. Convert the mass of Jupiter in question 1, above, into Earth masses (M_+) by dividing the mass of Jupiter by the mass of the Earth, given above. SHOW YOUR WORK.

    $M_J =$ _____ M_+

3. The accepted mass of Jupiter is about $318\, M_+$. Calculate the percent error in your Jovian mass calculated in question 2. The percent error is calculated using

    $$\% \text{ error} = \frac{\text{accepted value} - \text{your value}}{\text{accepted value}} \times 100\%$$

    SHOW YOUR WORK.

    $\%$ error = _____ $\%$

4. The smallest known stars have a mass of about 10% of the Sun's mass ($0.1\, M_\odot$). Based on your Jovian mass calculated in question 1, how many times more massive does Jupiter need to be in order to become a small star?

Example 1: A sample calculation of Jupiter's mass based on data in Figure 1.

$$P^2 (M_1 + M_2) = a^3$$

$$M_1 + M_2 \quad = \frac{a^3}{P^2} = \frac{(2.482 \times 10^{-3})^3}{(4.900 \times 10^{-3})^2}$$

$$= \frac{15.29 \times 10^{-9}}{24.01 \times 10^{-6}}$$

$$= 0.6368 \times 10^{-9-(-6)}$$

$$= 0.6368 \times 10^{-3} \, M_\odot$$

$$= 6.4 \times 10^{-4} \, M_\odot$$

REFRACTION AND REFLECTION OF LIGHT

OBJECTIVES

After completing this exercise the student will be able to:

1. measure the index of refraction for Plexiglas.

2. calculate the speed of light in Plexiglas.

3. graphically determine the focal length of a spherical mirror by using the law of reflection.

STUDENT MATERIALS

compass
mm ruler
protractor
calculator
pencil

LAB MATERIALS

4 straight pins per student
1 Plexiglas square per student
1 plane mirror per student
2 mirror stands
1 piece of cardboard (~8$\frac{1}{2}$×11") per student

STUDENT REQUIREMENTS

This lab is to be done individually without lab partners. After completion, turn in **Figs. 3**, **5**, and **6** in page sequence order.

INTRODUCTION

Most astronomical instruments use lenses and/or mirrors to gather and focus light. These devices use the *Laws of Refraction* and the *Law of Reflection* to produce an image of astronomical objects. In this lab you will study these basic laws of optics so you can better understand how optical equipment functions. As light waves pass from one material into another material at some angle, other than 90°, they are bent or refracted. This bending follows the four *Laws of Refraction* stated below:

1. When a ray of light passes at an angle from a medium of lesser density to one of greater density, it is refracted toward the normal.

2. When a ray of light passes at an angle from a more dense to less dense medium, it is refracted away from the normal.

3. A ray of light which enters a new medium at right angles (90°) to the surface is not refracted and has no change in direction.

4. No matter what the angle of incidence, the index of refraction for any two media is constant.

The normal referred to is a line which is perpendicular to the surface at the entry point of the light rays.

When light reflects from a shiny surface it follows the *Law of Reflection*. Simply stated, the angle of reflection is equal to the angle of incidence.

PROCEDURE

Part A. Refraction of Light

Use **Fig. 1** as an example of the procedure below.

1. Place your Plexiglas on **Fig. 3** about center and *carefully* outline it with a pencil.

2. Remove the Plexiglas plate. With a protractor, construct a normal 1 cm from the top right edge of the Plexiglas. A normal is a line which is perpendicular to the optical surface. Label the place where the normal meets the top edge of the Plexiglas as **A**.

3. On the right side of the normal, draw a line from **A** at any angle out from the Plexiglas. This will represent a ray of light going into the glass.

4. Place **Fig. 3** on a piece of cardboard. Replace the Plexiglas and align it with the outline drawing. Stick one pin on the incident ray near the Plexiglas and another pin near the end of the ray. Be sure these pins are as vertical as possible. Label these pin positions **1** and **2**.

5. Look into the Plexiglas from the lower edge and line up the images of the two pins you see. (Only the bases of the pins are visible through the glass.) Place two more pins between your eye and the Plexiglas so that they line up with the images of the two pins you see through the glass. Label these two pin positions **3** and **4**.

6. Remove the Plexiglas and pins from the page. Draw a line through pin positions **3** and **4** and extend it until it intersects the outline of the Plexiglas. Label this point **B**.

7. Draw a line through the square connecting **A** to **B**. This is the refracted ray. It shows you the path the ray took through the Plexiglas. The line joining pins **3** and **4** shows you how the light traveled after it came out of the glass. This existing ray should be parallel to the incident ray joining pins **1** and **2**.

8. Construct a normal at point **B**.

   Calculating the index of refraction. Use **Fig. 2** as an example of the following procedures.

9. Draw a circle of 6.5 to 7.0 cm radius on your drawing in **Fig. 3** with point **A** as the center. Record the radius used on **Fig. 3**.

10. Where the circle cuts the incident ray, label point **R**. Point **S** is where the circle cuts the refracted ray. Label point **S**.

11. Using a protractor draw a line from **R** perpendicular to the normal. Label this intersection **M**. Also draw a line from **S** perpendicular to the **same** normal. Label this intersection **N**.

12. Measure the length of lines **MR** and **SN** in millimeters. Record your answers on **Fig. 3**.

$$\text{Index of refraction} = \frac{MR}{SN}$$

Calculate the index of refraction of Plexiglas, and record your answer on **Fig. 3**.

13. The index of refraction **n** is the ratio of the speed of light in air to the speed of light in some substance such as Plexiglas. Mathematically this can be written as

$$n = \frac{\text{SPEED OF LIGHT IN AIR}}{\text{SPEED OF LIGHT IN PLEXIGLAS}}$$

Calculate the speed of light in Plexiglas using your experimental value for **n** and assuming the speed of light in air is 3.0×10^8 m/sec. Show your work at the bottom of **Fig. 3**. Express your answer using powers-of-ten notation.

Part B. The Law of Reflection

Use **Fig. 4** as an example for the following procedure.

1. Use your protractor to construct a perpendicular dashed line near the center of the line **AB** in **Fig. 5**. Label the point of intersection **C**, and label the end of the line as **D**.

2. Starting at **C** draw a line at any angle to the left of the normal **CD** and in front of the mirror. This line will represent the incident ray. Label the end of this line as **E**.

3. Place **Fig. 5** on a piece of cardboard. Hold the plane mirror facing you and place its back edge along line **AB**. Be sure to use the back edge because the reflecting surface is on the back side of this mirror.

4. Stick two pins vertically into the incident ray. Label these two pin locations **1** and **2**.

5. Looking into the mirror from the right side of line **CD**, sight the images of pins **1** and **2** in the mirror. Turn the board until the images of pins

1 and 2 are aligned and appear as a single image. The image of one pin will appear to be in front of the other pin's image.

6. With the images of pins **1** and **2** aligned, stick pins **3** and **4** into the page so that they are lined up with the images of pins **1** and **2** which are seen in the mirror.

7. Label the locations of pins **3** and **4** as you did for pins **1** and **2**.

8. Remove the mirror and all four pins from the page.

    Draw a line connecting the locations of pins **3** and **4** and point **C**. Label the end of this line **E´**. Line **CE´** represents the reflection of line **EC**.

9. The angle of incidence, **i**, is the angle between the incident ray **EC** and the normal **CD**. Use a protractor to measure this angle and record its value on the figure.

10. The angle of reflection, **r**, is the angle between the reflected ray **CE´** and the normal **CD**. Measure this angle and record its value on the figure. These two angles should be the same to within 3°.

    Reflection from a spherical surface.

    Fig. 6 shows a concave spherical mirror which has seven incident light rays striking its surface. You will now use the *Law of Reflection* to draw the reflected rays and determine the approximate focal length of this mirror.

11. The mirror's center of curvature is labeled **C** and is on the optical axis. Any line drawn from **C** to the mirror's surface is perpendicular to the surface. At the point where ray **1** strikes the mirror draw a straight dashed line to point **C**. This dashed line represents the normal for ray **1**.

12. Measure the angle of incidence for ray **1** and construct the reflected ray as a solid line. Be sure it is long enough to cross the optical axis along ray **4**.

13. Repeat the above procedure for the other incident rays **2** through **7**.

14. All the reflected rays tend to cross the optical axis at or near the focal point. The focal length of a mirror is the distance along the optical axis from its surface to the average focal point. The rays reflected from the mirror's edge do not focus at the same place as rays reflected from near the center. Your drawing probably shows some spherical aberration. Measure the mirror's focal length and record your answer in the figure. Spherical mirrors suffer from spherical aberration.

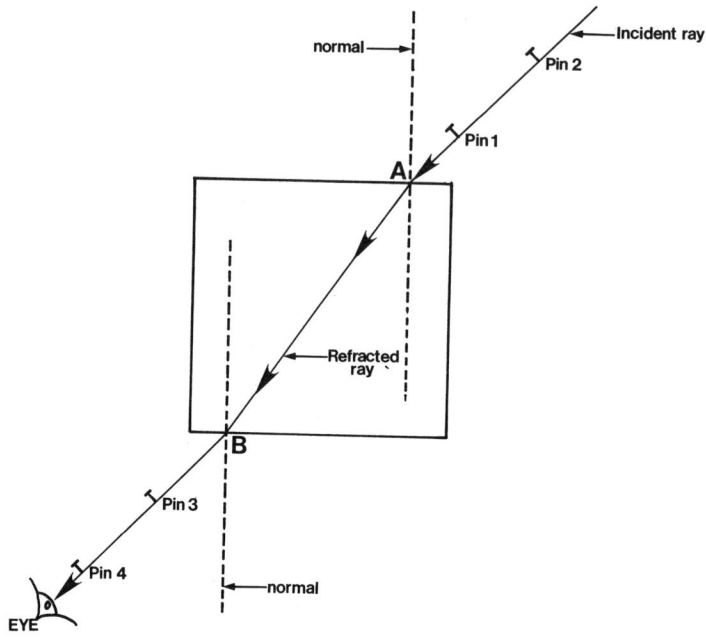

Fig. 1: An example of locating the refracted ray in Part A.

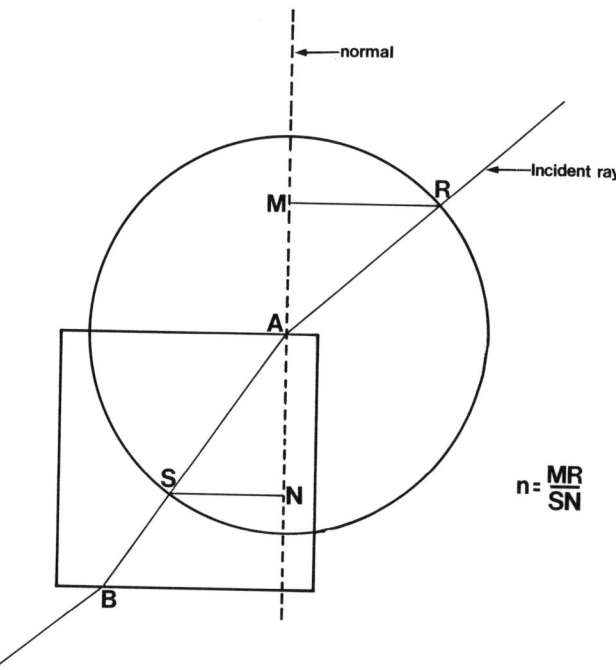

$$n = \frac{MR}{SN}$$

Fig. 2: An example of how to measure the index of refraction in Part A.

NAME: ____________________

SECTION: ____________________

Radius of circle = ____________________

Index of refraction for Plexiglas = ____________________

Speed of light in Plexiglas = ____________________

Fig. 3: Refraction of light through a Plexiglas plate.

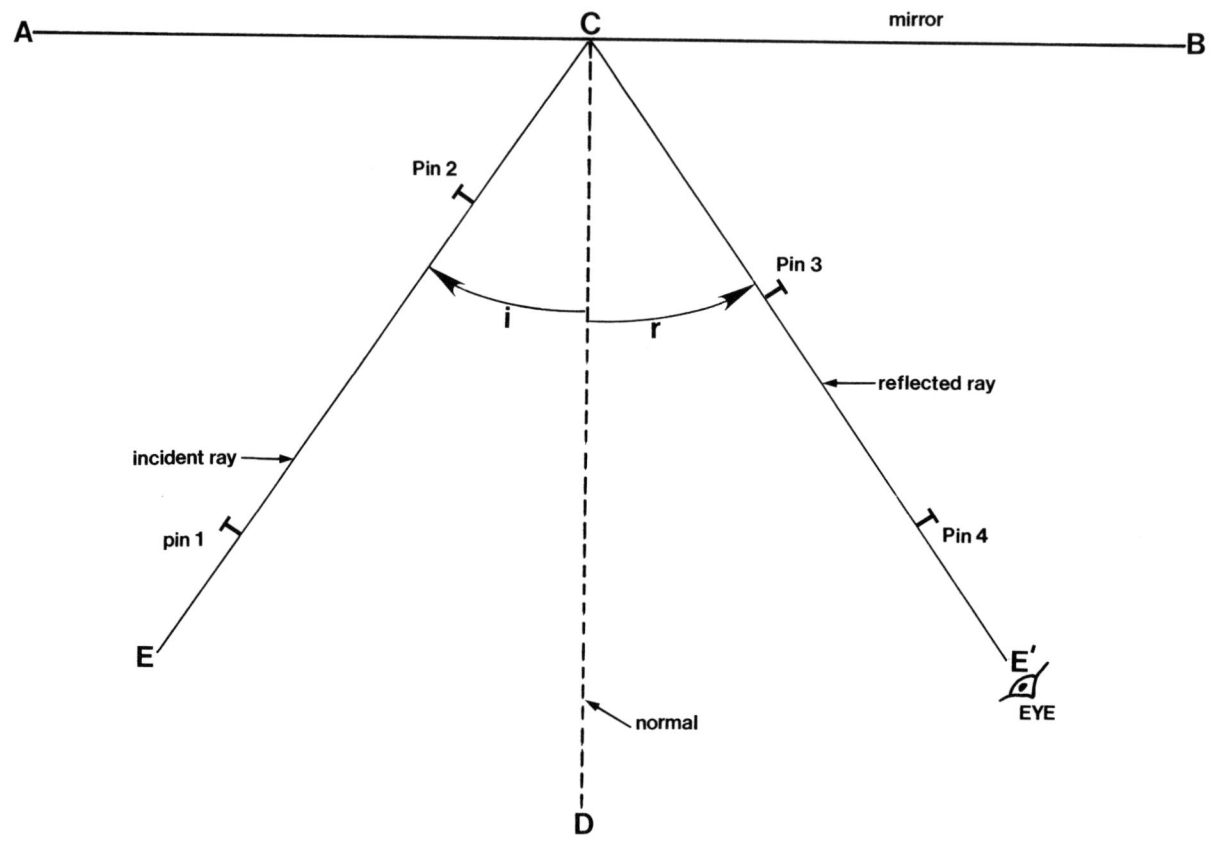

Fig. 4: An example of reflection of light from a plane mirror for Part B.

NAME: ____________________

SECTION: ____________________

A ____ B

i = ________

r = ________

Fig. 5: Reflection of light from a plane mirror.

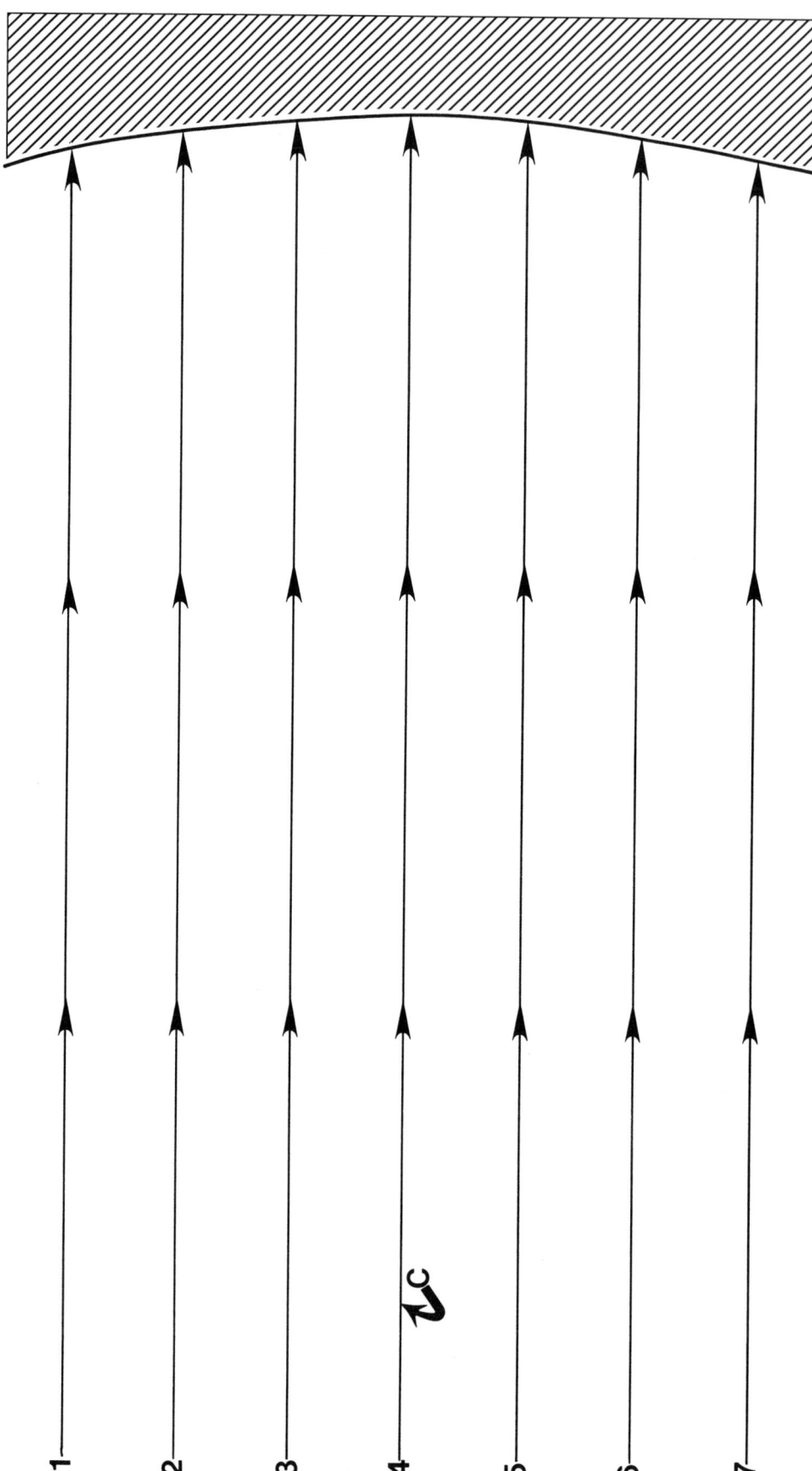

Fig. 6: Reflection of light from a spherical mirror.

SIMPLE LENSES AND TELESCOPES

OBJECTIVES

After completing this exercise the student will be able to:

1. use an optical bench to find the focal length of a lens.

2. find the focal length of a lens when an object is placed at infinity.

3. calculate a telescope's resolving power, focal ratio, and magnification.

STUDENT MATERIALS

pencil
calculator

LAB MATERIALS

Each setup requires:

2 different lenses with different focal lengths
1 illuminated light source and/or object
1 screen and screen holder
1 lens holder
examples of several different types of telescopes should be set up around the lab room (one example of each type)

STUDENT REQUIREMENTS

This lab is to be done with a lab partner during the data collection period. You are to make calculations individually and to answer questions using your own words. After completing the lab, turn in answer sheets for **Parts A** and **B**.

INTRODUCTION

In the last lab you learned about the Laws of Refraction and Reflection. These basic laws of optics guide the construction of optical instruments that use lenses and mirrors. Lenses are used in many forms, from eyeglasses to microscopes to binoculars to telescopes. As parallel light passes through a convex lens, the light bends so that all the rays intersect at one point in space, called the focus (**Fig. 1**). The distance from the center of the lens to the focus is the

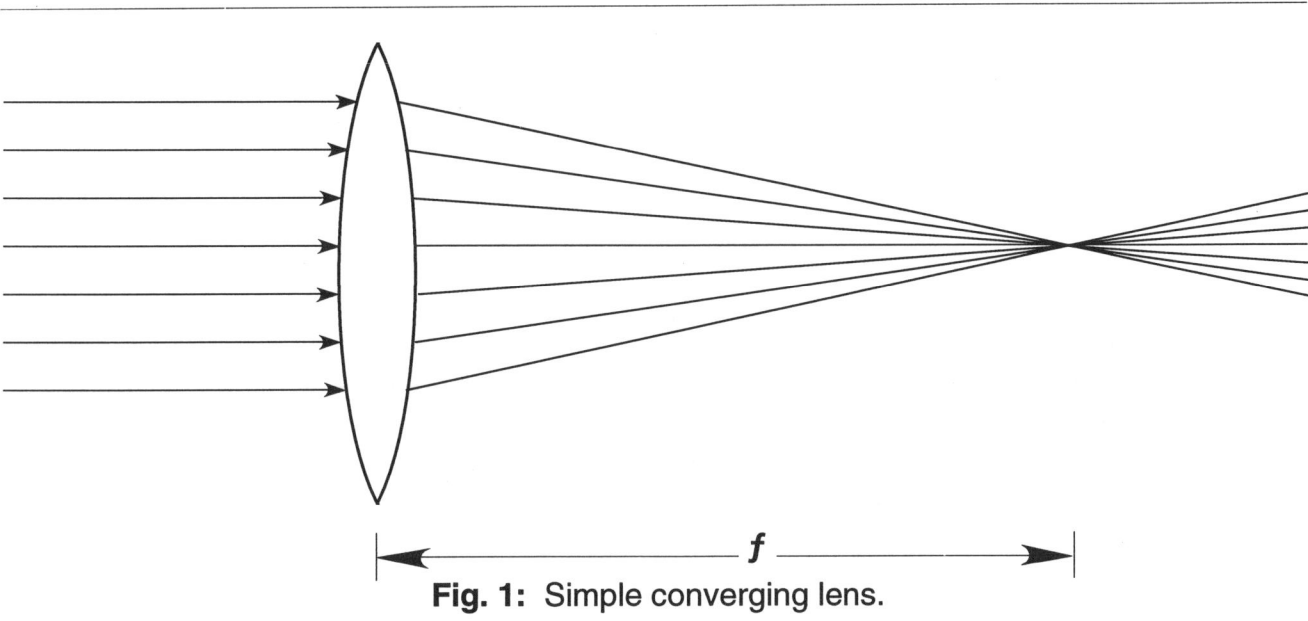

Fig. 1: Simple converging lens.

focal length. The focal length of a lens is constant and is determined by the lens's shape and material (glass, plastic, etc.).

Parallel light means that the light source is a point an infinite distance away from us. We can assume this is the case for stars. We cannot assume this for sources of light which are close to us (such as light bulbs). A finite-sized light source (like a light bulb) a finite distance away (like 30 centimeters) will emit light in all directions, not just parallel to the axis of the lens. In this case, **Fig. 1** does not show the correct situation. To find the focal length we must use the simple lens equation:

$$f = \frac{(S \times I)}{(I + S)}$$

where

f = focal length of the lens

I = image distance = distance from the lens to the image

S = object distance = distance from the source to the lens.

This equation says that:

focal length = image distance times object distance all divided by the sum of the image distance and object distance.

PROCEDURE

A. Measuring the Focal Length of Lenses

1. Set up your optical bench as shown in **Fig. 2**. The arrow is your source. The screen will hold your image. Note that the ruler in the bench is movable. Place the 0 cm mark so that the arrowed source is at 0 cm.

2. Be careful to touch only the edge of any lens. Carefully place the lens with orange paint on its edge, in the lens holder. Move the screen until you see a sharp image of the arrow. Record the object distance, **S**, and the image distance, **I**, on your lab report.

3. Move the lens on the optical bench to a new location and refocus. Again record **S** and **I**. Repeat this procedure a third time. You have now mea-sured the numbers you need to determine the focal length of this lens.

4. Calculate the focal length using the simple lens equation for each position of the lens. Record your answers to a tenth of a centimeter. Calculate the average focal length and record the result.

5. Use the lens with blue paint on its edge. Repeat steps 2, 3, and 4.

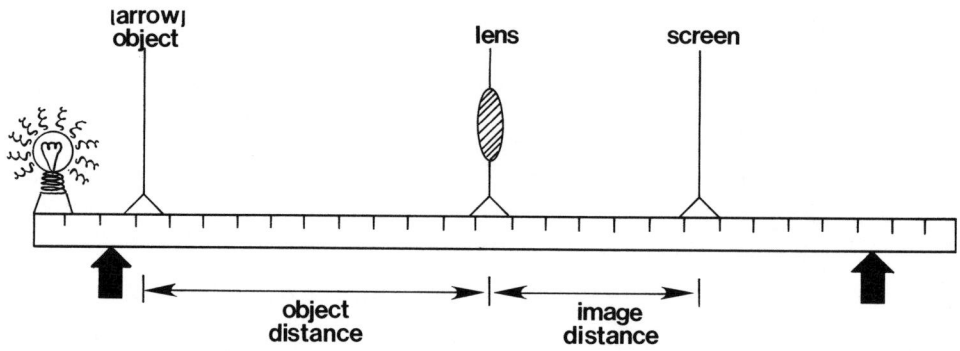

Fig. 2: Use this optical bench setup for the first part of this exercise.

6. Now carefully place both lenses together in the lens holder. Repeat steps 2, 3, and 4.

7. Carefully slide the light bulb (it is **HOT**) and arrowed object off the optical bench.

8. Place the orange lens in the lens holder. Aim the optical bench so that it points toward a window or down a long hallway. Adjust the screen until you see a sharp image of the scene. This image may be difficult to see. Record the image distance on your report form. (**Note:** There is no object distance because it is infinity.)

9. Move the lens to two more positions and measure the image distances.

10. Calculate the average value of **I**. How does this image distance compare to the average focal length for this lens, as obtained from the optical bench part? They should be about the same value.

11. Repeat steps 8 and 10 for the blue lens.

B. Telescopes

One or more telescopes have been set up around the room to be used for this part.

1. On each telescope is a card with the telescope's optical design, aperture, focal length, and eyepiece focal length. Record this information about each telescope on your answer sheet.

    While you are at each telescope, look at some scene outside the room. Notice the image's brightness, orientation and general quality.

    The steps below will reveal some important specifications about each telescope.

    Return to your seat for steps 2 through 5.

2. The focal ratio of a lens or telescope is an indicator of its photographic speed or image brightness. It can be calculated by dividing the telescope's focal length, f_o, by its aperture, D. Mathematically, this is written as

$$\text{focal ratio} = \frac{f_o}{D}$$

Since this is a ratio it is important that f_o and d be expressed in the same units. The larger the focal ratio is, the fainter the telescope's image will be. Thus a large ratio means a slower photographic speed.

Calculate the focal ratio for each telescope set up in the lab room and record your answer in the space provided.

3. A telescope's angular resolution is its ability to see tiny angles. Usually, the resolution is expressed as an angle in seconds of arc or arcsec. For most optical telescopes the angular resolution can be calculated using

$$\text{angular resolution} = \frac{11.6}{D}$$

where D is the telescope's aperture in centimeters. The smaller the angular resolution, the smaller the details the telescope can see.

Calculate the angular resolution of each telescope set up in the lab room and record your answers in the spaces provided.

4. One reason astronomers build large-aperture telescopes is to gather more light. You can catch more rainwater with a large bucket than with a small one. A telescope's light-gathering ability is directly proportional to the primary lens or mirror's surface area. Because most telescope optics have a circular lens or mirror the surface area is simply the area of a circle, which can be written as

$$\text{telescope's surface area} = \pi \left(\frac{D}{2}\right)^2$$

where $\pi = 3.14$ and D = telescope's aperture.

Calculate the surface area of each telescope set up in the lab room. Record your answers in the spaces provided.

5. Magnification is simply the ratio of the telescope's focal length, f_o, to the eyepiece's focal

length, f_e. This can be written as

$$\text{magnification} = \frac{f_o}{f_e}$$

where f_o and f_e must be expressed in the same units. Notice that magnification is a ratio and therefore has no units. However, the symbol × is sometimes used to indicate how many *times* the object is enlarged. An example would be 150× for a magnification of 150 times.

Calculate the magnification of each telescope set up in the lab room. Record your answers in the spaces provided.

Please straighten up your lab area before you leave.

ANSWER SHEET

NAME: _____

SECTION: _____

PART A: Measuring the Focal Length of Lenses

Steps 1 to 6

Orange Lens

Trial No.	S in cm	I in cm	f in cm
1			
2			
3			

f_{ave} _____

Blue Lens

Trial No.	S in cm	I in cm	f in cm
1			
2			
3			

f_{ave} _____

Orange and Blue

Trial No.	S in cm	I in cm	f in cm
1			
2			
3			

f_{ave} _____

Steps 7 to 11

Trial No.	I (orange)	I (blue)
1		
2		
3		

average I (orange) = _____

average I (blue) = _____

ANSWER SHEET

NAME: _____

SECTION: _____

PART B: Telescopes

1. Optical Design = _____

   aperture = _____

   focal length = _____

   eyepiece focal length = _____

   Calculate: focal ratio = _____

                          resolution = _____

                          surface area = _____

                          magnification = _____

2. Optical Design = _____

   aperture = _____

   focal length = _____

   eyepiece focal length = _____

   Calculate: focal ratio = _____

                          resolution = _____

                          surface area = _____

                          magnification = _____

3. Optical Design = _____

   aperture = _____

   focal length = _____

   eyepiece focal length = _____

   Calculate: focal ratio = _____

                          resolution = _____

                          surface area = _____

                          magnification = _____

LUNAR FEATURES

OBJECTIVES

After completing this exercise the student should be able to:

1. use a lunar photograph to find examples of features such as maria, mountains, and basic crater types.
2. use a lunar map to identify, by name, features visible on a lunar photograph.
3. estimate the diameters of craters and maria visible on a lunar photograph.
4. determine the height of a lunar mountain when the moon is photographed near one of its quarter phases.

STUDENT MATERIALS

a pencil
mm ruler
calculator

LAB MATERIALS

Each lab setup needs:

meter stick
large poster or photograph of a quarter moon (with corners weighted down, if necessary)

STUDENT REQUIREMENTS

This lab is to be done with a lab partner. All calculations are to be completed individually. Turn in only the answer sheet.

INTRODUCTION

The moon has a large number of features on its surface. Some of these features, such as the maria, appear as dark patches to the naked eye. A few of the largest craters can be viewed with binoculars. Many more surface features, such as mountains and smaller craters, can be viewed with a telescope. The height of the features can be calculated by analyzing their shadow length. In this exercise you will learn how to identify some lunar features and how to estimate their diameter and height.

PROCEDURE

A. Lunar Map

A lunar map from Sky Publishing has been provided in the packet at the back of this book. So that you can find craters and other features you will want to use the selenographic coordinate grid which is drawn on your map. Lunar longitude is the distance in degrees east (+) or west (–) of the meridian passing through the center of the moon as observed from Earth. Lunar latitude is the distance in degrees north (+) or south (–) of the moon's equator. Notice that east is to the left and south is to the top of your map, so it conforms to the moon's orientation as viewed through an astronomical telescope.

On the back of your lunar map each crater is listed by number (1 to 300) along with a selenographic longitude and latitude of the coordinate grid intersection that is *nearest* each crater. Thus, to find the crater Abenezra (**1**) on your map, locate longitude +10° and latitude –20°. What is the name of the crater located at –20° and +10°? Write your answer on the report form.

B. Identification of Lunar Features

1. At each lab table is a photograph of the moon, taken at either first quarter or third quarter. On your data sheet indicate which lunar phase your photograph represents.

2. Compare the lunar photograph to your map and orient the photograph to match the map. Locate five maria on the photograph and list their names

on your report form. These will be different for first-quarter moon and third-quarter moon. (**Note:** third-quarter moon photos have a large mare named Oceanus Procellarum. This is one mare, not two.)

3. Locate any mountain ranges visible on the photograph. Use your map to find out the names of these mountains and list three of them on your report form.

4. Inspect the craters on the photograph. Some craters have flat or smooth bottoms that have been filled with lava. Other craters have a central mountain peak that was probably caused by the meteor impact which formed the crater. Still other craters have prominent ray systems emanating from them which may stretch for hundreds of kilometers over the lunar surface. These rays may be thought of as the material splashed from the crater during meteor impact. On your report form name at least three examples of these types of craters seen on the photograph.

C. Size of Lunar Features

1. To determine the size of any lunar feature you must first determine the scale of the photograph. Use a meter stick to measure the diameter of the lunar image to the nearest millimeter. The moon's actual diameter is known to be 3476 km. Determine the scale of your photograph, in km/mm, by dividing the moon's actual diameter by the measured diameter of your photograph. Record the scale on your report form.

2. On the chalkboard, your instructor will make a short list of lunar features visible on your photograph. Measure each feature's diameter in millimeters. To determine the feature's true diameter, multiply the measured diameter by the scale of your photograph. On your report form, record the name of each feature and its calculated diameter in km.

D. Height of a Lunar Mountain

The height of certain lunar features such as mountains can be calculated by analyzing the length of their shadows. In **Fig. 1** you are viewing the moon from above one of its poles.

In this diagram **MB** represents the height of the mountain, **CB** is the moon's radius, **SM** is the length of the shadow as seen from Earth, and **TB** is the distance of the mountain from the terminator. By inspection it can be seen that the triangle **CTB** and **SBM** are similar right triangles (*i.e.*, they have equal

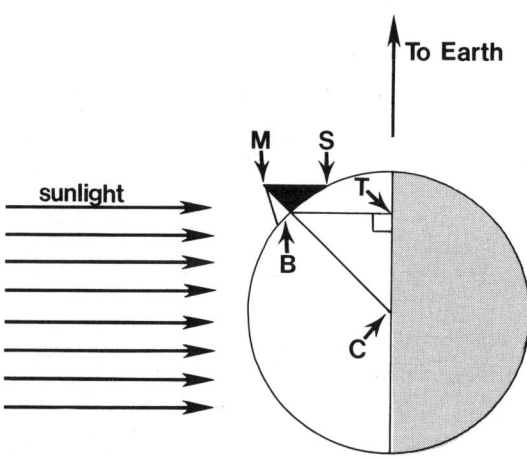

Fig. 1: Geometry used to determine the height of a lunar mountain.

angles). Therefore, the ratios of the sides must be equal. So it can be written that

$$\frac{MB}{SM} = \frac{TB}{CB} \qquad (1)$$

Rearranging terms, this can be solved for the height of the mountain, **MB**, and written as

$$MB = \frac{(SM)\,(TB)}{CB} \qquad (2)$$

The moon's radius, **CB** in km, is already known. Both **TB** and **SM**, the distance of the mountain from the terminator and the shadow's length, can be measured on your photograph. Thus, you have all the needed information to calculate a mountain's height, **MB**, using equation 2.

Your instructor will give you the name of a mountain whose height you are to estimate.

1. Locate this mountain peak on your photograph and record its name on your report form.

2. Measure the length of its shadow in millimeters. Multiply by the scale factor and record the answer in kilometers.

3. Measure the distance from the mountain's center to the terminator. Multiply by the scale factor and record the result in kilometers.

4. Calculate the moon's radius in km and record this on your report form.

5. Use equation 2 to calculate the height of the mountain in kilometers and record your answer on the report form. Does your answer seem reasonable to you? If not, ask for some help and try again.

Turn in your lab report form. Be sure to clean up your table and leave it in better condition than you found it.

LUNAR FEATURES

NAME: _____

SECTION: _____

A. Lunar Map

Crater at −20° and +10° is _____

B. Lunar Features

1. Phase of photograph: _____

2. Maria visible

   a. _____   d. _____

   b. _____   e. _____

   c. _____

3. Mountain ranges

   a. _____   b. _____   c. _____

4. Craters

flat bottoms	central peaks	rays
a. _____	a. _____	a. _____
b. _____	b. _____	b. _____
c. _____	c. _____	c. _____

C. Size of Lunar Features

1. Scale of photo = _____

2.

Feature Name	Diameter in mm	Diameter in km
a. _____	a. _____	a. _____
b. _____	b. _____	b. _____
c. _____	c. _____	c. _____

D. Height of Lunar Mountains

1. Name of mountain _____

2. Length of shadow, SM = _____

3. Distance to terminator, TB = _____

4. Moon's radius, CB = _____

5. Height of mountain, MB = _____

RELATIVE AGES OF MARTIAN LANDSCAPES

10

OBJECTIVES

After completing this exercise the student should be able to:

1. identify major features on Mars.
2. determine relative ages of surface features by superposition.
3. determine relative ages of features by using crater density.

STUDENT MATERIALS

pencil

LAB MATERIALS

Each lab setup needs:

a large Mars map obtained from spacecraft mapping missions (with corners weighted, if necessary)
a Martian globe or two

STUDENT REQUIREMENTS

Students may work with a lab partner. All questions are to be answered individually, using your own words. Turn in the answers to all questions.

INTRODUCTION

From spacecraft photography and mapping of planets it is possible to determine the relative ages of surface features on some planets such as Mars. In other words they help determine whether a canyon or volcano was formed before or after some cratering events for that planet. Unfortunately this method of relative dating cannot determine the actual age of the feature. Thus these techniques cannot tell an astronomer if a canyon is one million or one billion years old. The actual dating of craters, volcanoes, etc., can only be done through radioactive age dating. In practice, this has only been done for Earth and moon rocks brought back by the Apollo astronauts.

Superposition is a method of determining the relative ages of features. If one feature is on top of or partially obliterates another feature it must have formed after the feature it was superimposed upon it.

Crater density is another important method used to estimate the age of one landscape relative to another landscape. This method is based on a theory of solar system creation in which the number and size of meteoroid and asteroid material decreases in both number and size with time. This implies that landscapes which have large numbers of big and small craters were formed early in the solar system's formation period while the amount of meteoroid and asteroid material available to form impact craters was high. As time passed, the quantity of this material decreased. Landscapes which formed later in the solar system's development have smaller and fewer craters per square kilometer than those which formed earlier. Thus by counting the number of craters within two areas of equal size the relative ages between these areas can be determined. The one with the largest and most craters can be considered to be the older landscape.

In the lab you will use superposition and crater density to estimate the relative age of several Martian landscapes.

PROCEDURE

1. Inspect the Preliminary Mars Chart and locate two basins in the southern hemisphere. The western basin, Argyre Planitia, is near longitude 40° and latitude –50°. The eastern basin, Hellas Planitia, is near longitude 290° and latitude –40°. These two basins were probably formed by giant impacts of meteoroids. The smooth surfaces are lava flows. Do you think these lava flows occurred before or after most of the bombardment and cratering activity? _____

2. Use a magnifying lens to inspect the rim of the two basins. Look to see if the rims have more craters than the lava field inside the rim. Also look for ghost craters which have been filled with lava. Based upon the appearance of the rims, which of the following historical accounts is most likely? Circle your choice, **a** or **b**.

    a. These giant impacts occurred early, when most of the other impacts occurred, and excavated the large basins with their surrounding rims. The lava filled the basins much later after most of the cratering activity was over.

    b. The giant impacts just happened to occur very late after most of the other craters had formed and the lava filled the basins immediately after their formation.

    State what evidence you used in making this decision.

3. Look carefully at the crater density along the rim of each basin. Is the Hellas or Argyre basin older?

    _____

    Why?

    You also have two enlarged, detailed maps. One shows a volcanic region and is marked "V." The other one shows a large canyon area and is labeled with a "C." If you compare maps **V** and **C** with the Preliminary Mars Chart you can see that the eastern edge of map **V** will fit next to the western edge of map **C** along the 90° longitude line.

4. Locate the areas shown on maps **V** and **C** on the Preliminary Mars Chart. Remember that high crater density implies an older surface. Compare the volcanic and canyon areas to the large highlands area (cratered terrain) east of the canyon. Are the volcanic and canyon areas older or younger than the highlands? _____

5. Inspect the area south of the canyon, between longitudes 45° and 100°. (Use both maps **V** and **C** placed side by side.) Notice that this area is not uniformly cratered or wrinkled. A boundary seems to occur at what longitude?_____   Is the younger surface to the east or west of this boundary? _____

6. On map **V**, look at the smooth plain named Tharsis Montes. Does the crater density suggest that Tharsis Montes is older or younger than the region south of the Valles Marineris? _____

7. On map **C**, inspect carefully the edge of the canyon between longitudes 70° and 75° and between latitudes –3° and –8°. Does this area suggest that the canyon is older or younger than the plains to the north? _____

8. Look at the crater density inside the Valles Marineris on map **C** and choose one of the following historical accounts of the canyon's formation.

    a. The canyon formed before the surrounding plains, and the lava flows which made the plains did not reach the canyon.

    b. The canyon was cut into the rock by a river of lava from the volcano.

    c. The canyon forms a boundary between two plains of different ages.

    d. The plains formed first and at one time covered all of map **C**. The canyon was then cut into the plains area by a river in a fashion similar to the Grand Canyon on our Earth.

9. Map **V** shows the area around the volcano Arsia Mons. Use a magnifier to locate several ridges or channels on the side of Arsia Mons. Make sure these channels were made by the volcano. Follow these structures to see if they extend out onto the surrounding plains at its base. Look carefully for any evidence that Arsia Mons has been partially covered by some other geological development.

    From this study choose one of the following historical accounts.

    a. The volcano formed first and was later buried by a lava flow from another volcano.

    b. The volcano formed the plains from its own lava flow and thus the plains and the volcano have the same age.

    Why do you think so?

10. Look at the four volcanoes on the Preliminary Mars Chart. Notice that each volcano has a crater at its peak. Observe the crater density in the surrounding plains. Are the craters at the top of the volcanoes likely to be meteor impacts? _____ Is it possible to determine the age of the area around this volcanic region using crater density as the age indicator? _____ Explain your answer.

11. In the spaces below indicate the relative ages of the six regions you have studied in the exercise. Use 1 for the oldest region and 6 for the youngest.

_____   highlands

_____   Volcano Arsia Mons

_____   region south of canyon near longitudes 45–85°

_____   region south of canyon near longitude 85–100°

_____   Valles Marineris canyon

_____   Tharsis Montes plains

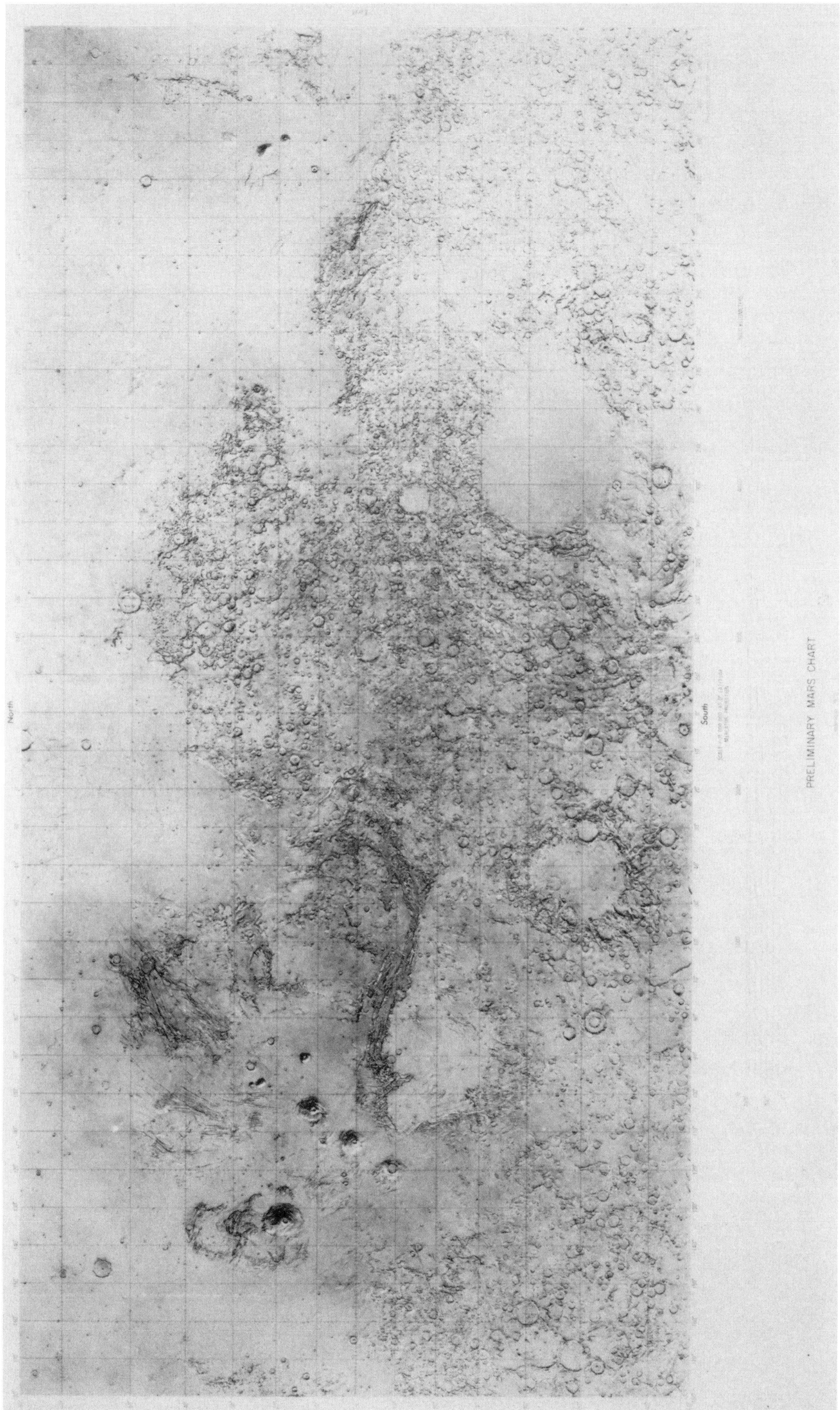

Fig. 1: Mars Chart from Mariner 9 photo mosaics. *(U.S. Geological Survey)*

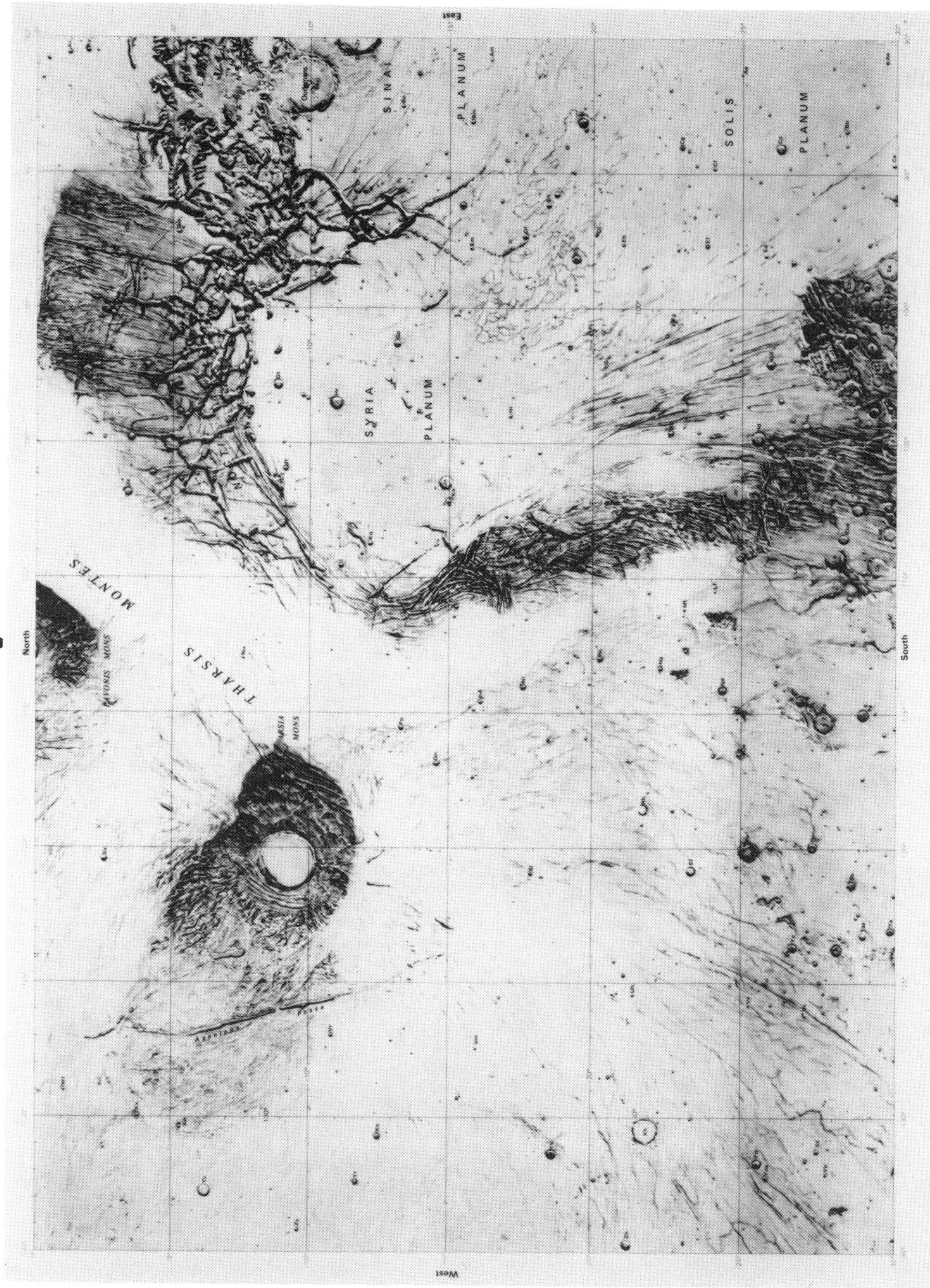

Fig. 2: Map of the Phoenicus Lacus Quadrangle of Mars. *(U.S. Geological Survey)*

C

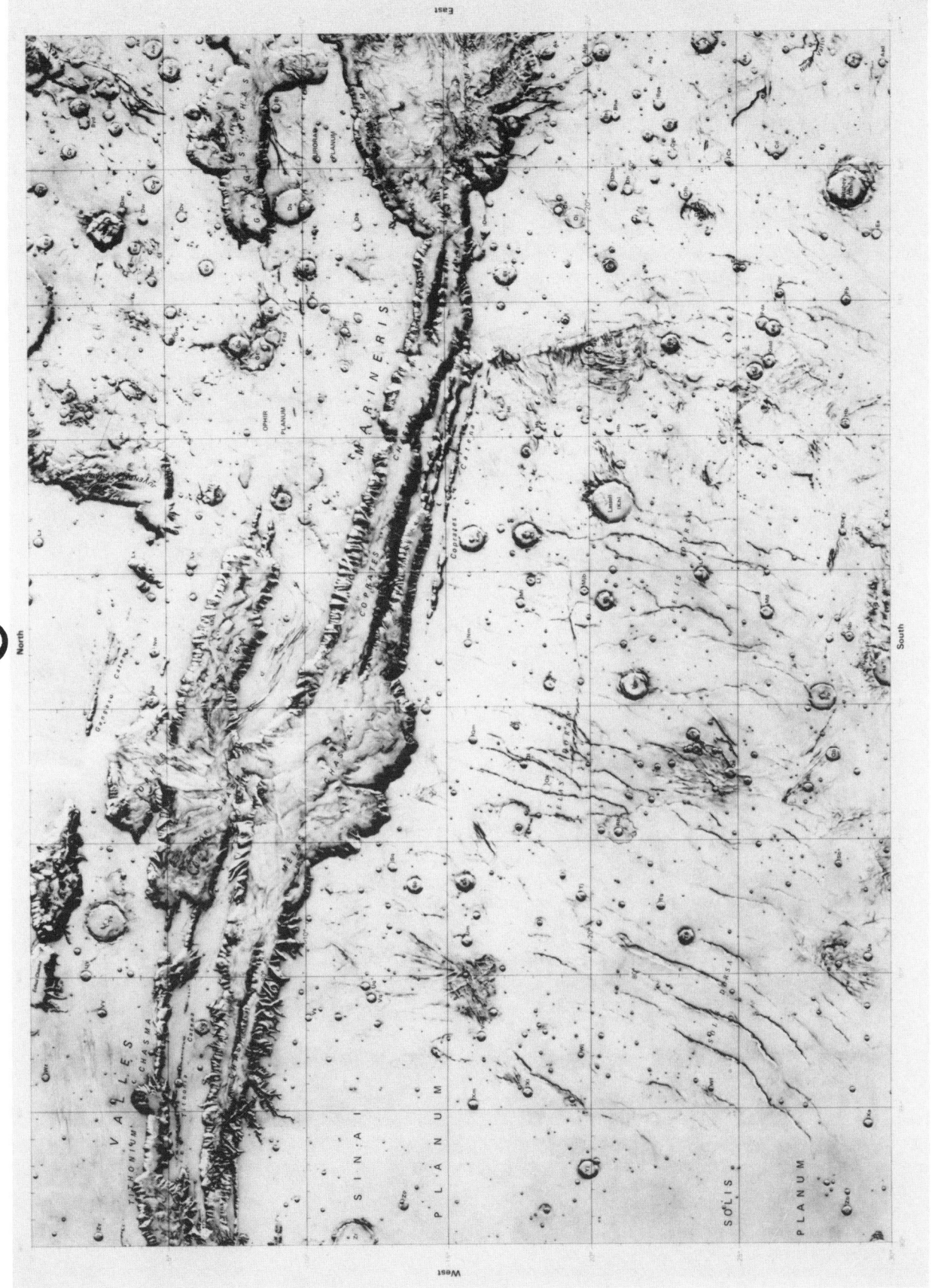

Fig. 3: Map of the Corporate's Quadrangle of Mars. *(U.S. Geological Survey)*

SPECTROSCOPY AND ATOMIC STRUCTURE

OBJECTIVES

After completing this exercise the student should be able to:

1. use a spectroscope to measure the wavelengths of emission-lines produced by a discharge tube.
2. identify unknown gases by comparison of their spectra to known emission-line sources.
3. draw a scale model of a hydrogen atom from measurements of the Balmer emission-lines observed with a laboratory spectroscope.

STUDENT MATERIALS

pencil
compass
mm scale
calculator

LAB MATERIALS

student spectroscopes
spectral emission tubes, including hydrogen
transformers for tubes
a light with electrical socket and lab jacks

Set up ten stations. Each station should be labeled. Station 1 should have a light bulb. Station 2 should have a hydrogen emission tube. Stations 3 through 10 can have assorted emission tubes. All stations need a spectroscope. Stations 2 through 10 need spectral tube transformers. Some stations may need lab jacks to adjust the tube heights to match the spectroscope heights.

STUDENT REQUIREMENTS

Each student is to do individual work, without a lab partner. Turn in answers to the questions, **Table I**, **Fig. 1**, and **Fig. 3**.

INTRODUCTION

Astronomers must obtain most of their information about the stars from observations of the small amount of light received from each star. One of the most useful astronomical instruments is the spectroscope or spectrograph. These use a prism or diffraction grating to spread light into its rainbow of colors. Spectra can be divided into three major groups which depend upon the origin of the spectra. These groups are described by Kirchhoff's Laws of spectral analysis given below:

1st Law: continuous spectrum is produced by a hot, glowing solid.

2nd Law: bright line or emission spectrum is produced from a hot, rarefied gas.

3rd Law: dark line or absorption spectrum is produced when the light from a continuous spectral source passes through a cooler, less-dense gas.

A line spectrum (emission or absorption) can be used to determine the element(s) that are producing the spectrum. The lines are related to the electron orbitals of each element. Since these orbitals are different for each of the elements, the spectral lines act like a set of fingerprints which will identify the element producing them.

In this exercise you will identify several unknown gases by observing their emission-line spectra. Also you will measure the wavelengths of hydrogen emission-lines and use these measurements to construct a model of the hydrogen atom.

PROCEDURE

Spectra

Around the lab room several numbered stations have been set up. Each station has a light source and a spectroscope.

1. At **Station 1** observe the spectrum of an incandescent light bulb, and answer questions 1, 2, and 3 on page 11-3. Move to **Station 2**.

2. Observe the spectrum of the hydrogen gas discharge tube. Sketch the position of each emission line on the scale drawn in **Fig. 1**. Use the spectroscope's scale to determine the wavelength of each line in angstroms, $\mathring{A}$, and record the results in **Table I**.

3. Proceed to each of the stations and sketch the emission-line spectra of each unknown gas in **Fig. 1**. Be sure the station number matches the number of your sketch.

4. Compare your sketches to the standard emission-line spectra in **Fig. 2**. Write the name of each gas in the blank to the right of each sketch in **Fig. 1**.

The Hydrogen Atom

In this lab you viewed a hydrogen emission-line spectrum. This spectrum was produced by applying an electric current to hydrogen gas trapped inside the tube. When the electrons were excited they jumped back and forth between several discrete energy levels or orbits. Because the electrons can only orbit the atoms at particular distances or energy levels, they must give up exactly the energy difference between any two levels in order to drop from a higher orbit down to a lower orbit. The energy is lost in the form of emitted light, which has the correct wavelength (color) for the energy which the electron loses. If this process is repeated many times an emission-line spectrum can be observed.

The hydrogen spectrum observed in lab is called the Balmer Series. Balmer lines are produced when electron transitions are down to or up from the second-smallest orbit. The radii of this orbit and those above it can be calculated from

$$r_n \approx \frac{\lambda}{(0.473)\lambda - 1630} \tag{1}$$

where r_n (n = 2,3,4...) represents the orbital radii of orbits 2,3,4 etc., and λ is the wavelength of the corresponding emission-line in angstroms. The red, blue-green, and violet emission lines observed in the spectroscope came from an electron moving from a high orbit, r_n, down to r_2 as given below:

red	r_3	$\longrightarrow r_2$
blue-green	r_4	$\longrightarrow r_2$
violet	r_5	$\longrightarrow r_2$

1. Use equation **(1)** and your measured values of each emission line in **Table I** to calculate the radius in $\mathring{A}$ units of the 3rd, 4th, and 5th electron orbits for hydrogen. Record your answers in the column labeled "r_n in $\mathring{A}$" of **Table I**.

2. On **Fig. 3** make a scale drawing of the electron orbits for a hydrogen atom for n = 3, 4, and 5. Use a scale of $1 \mathring{A} = 1$ cm. The orbit corresponding to n = 2 has already been drawn to scale and has a radius of 2.1 $\mathring{A}$.

3. On your drawing use arrows to indicate the three electron transitions from levels n = 3, 4, and 5 to level n = 2. Label each arrow with the corresponding color emitted (red, blue-green, violet).

Clean up your lab area and turn in the answers to the questions, **Fig. 1**, **Table I**, and **Fig. 3**.

QUESTIONS

1. Is the spectrum of the light bulb continuous, emission line or absorption line?

2. From Kirchhoff's Laws, describe what causes a light bulb to glow.

3. What is the approximate wavelength of the red light?_____ $\mathring{A}$

    The blue light? _____$\mathring{A}$

TABLE I

Hydrogen Balmer Series

line color	n	λ in Å	R_n in Å
red	3		
blue-green	4		
violet	5		

Station No.	Spectrum	Gas Name

1.   : : | : : : : | : : : : | : : : : | : :   _____
          4000   5000   6000   7000

2.   : : | : : : : | : : : : | : : : : | : :   _____
          4000   5000   6000   7000

3.   : : | : : : : | : : : : | : : : : | : :   _____
          4000   5000   6000   7000

4.   : : | : : : : | : : : : | : : : : | : :   _____
          4000   5000   6000   7000

5.   : : | : : : : | : : : : | : : : : | : :   _____
          4000   5000   6000   7000

6.   : : | : : : : | : : : : | : : : : | : :   _____
          4000   5000   6000   7000

7.   : : | : : : : | : : : : | : : : : | : :   _____
          4000   5000   6000   7000

8.   : : | : : : : | : : : : | : : : : | : :   _____
          4000   5000   6000   7000

9.   : : | : : : : | : : : : | : : : : | : :   _____
          4000   5000   6000   7000

10.   : : | : : : : | : : : : | : : : : | : :   _____
          4000   5000   6000   7000

violet   **blue**   **green**   **yellow**   **red**

Fig. 1: The spectra of a light bulb, hydrogen, and several unknowns.

Standard Spectra

Gas in Tube

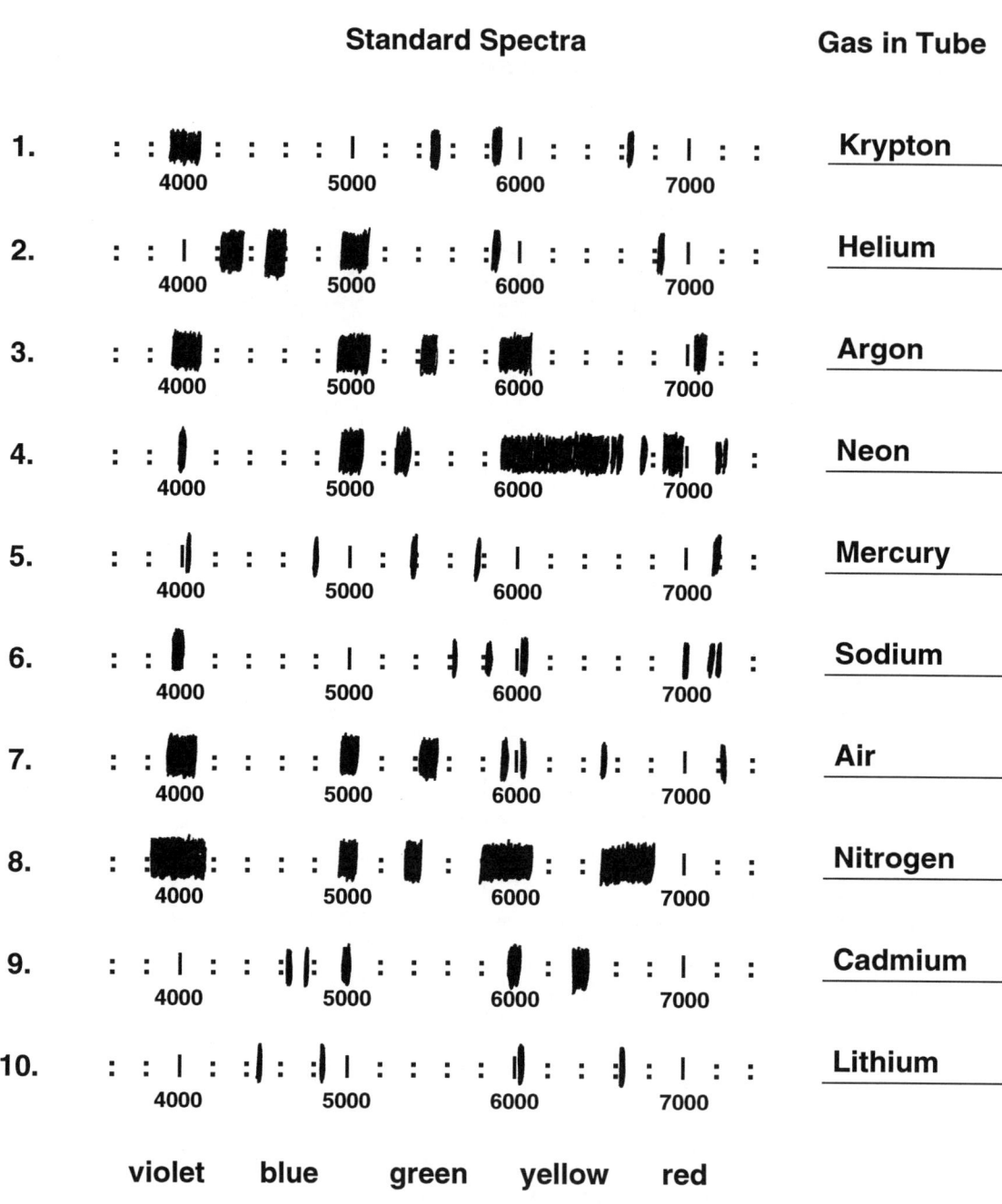

1. **Krypton**
2. **Helium**
3. **Argon**
4. **Neon**
5. **Mercury**
6. **Sodium**
7. **Air**
8. **Nitrogen**
9. **Cadmium**
10. **Lithium**

violet   blue   green   yellow   red

Fig. 2: Standard emission-line spectra for several gas discharge tubes.

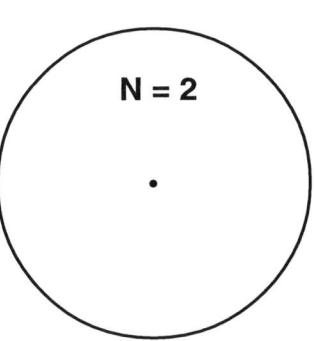

Fig. 3: Scale drawing of the hydrogen atom. Scale is $1\mathring{A} = 1$ cm.

THE INVERSE – SQUARE LAW

OBJECTIVES

After completing this exercise, the student will be able to:

1. measure the brightness of a light bulb with a photoelectric detector.
2. measure the intensity change as the light bulb and detector are moved farther apart.
3. predict the brightness of the light bulb at unmeasured locations.

STUDENT MATERIALS

> pencil
> calculator

LAB MATERIALS

> optical bench
> spherically radiating light source (or light bulb)
> photoelectric detector with meter
> large piece of black or dark grey cardboard

STUDENT REQUIREMENTS

Students may work in pairs during the data collection. Graphing and answering questions are to be done individually, using your own words.

INTRODUCTION

Almost everyone is aware that as a light source gets closer it appears to become brighter. Conversely, as it moves farther away the source appears less bright. It may be tempting to believe that when a light source appears to double in brightness its distance has decreased by one half. In **Fig. 1** it can be seen that light from a spherically radiating source spreads out over an area four times larger when the distance from the source is doubled. Thus, the brightness decreases to one-fourth of the original intensity. Mathematically, this relation can be expressed as ratios

$$\frac{I_2}{I_1} = \left(\frac{d_1}{d_2}\right)^2 \qquad (1)$$

where I_1 and I_2 are the intensities at distances d_1 and d_2 respectively. If d_1 is one distance unit and the

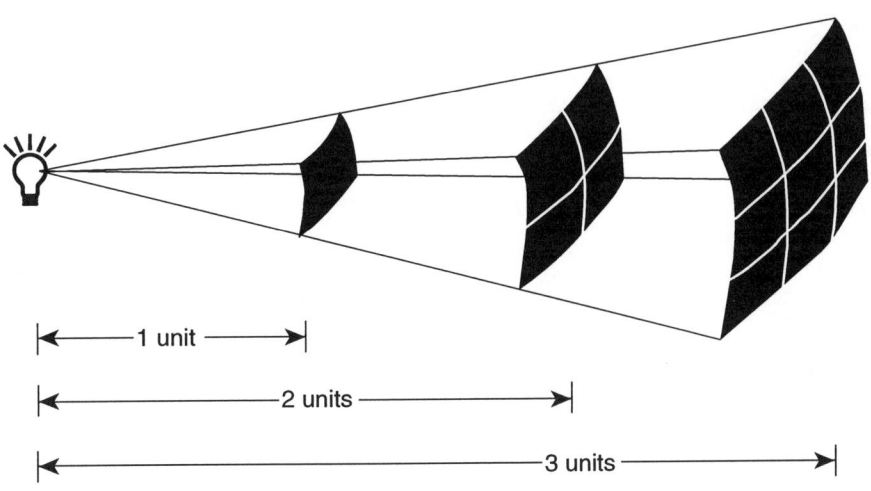

Fig. 1: Pictoral form of the inverse–square law.

initial value of I_1 at d_1 equals one intensity unit, then **eq. (1)** becomes

$$\frac{I_2}{1} = \left(\frac{1}{d_2} \right)^2 \qquad (2)$$

More generally **eq. (2)** can be written as

$$I \propto \left(\frac{1}{d} \right)^2 \qquad (3)$$

PROCEDURE

It is important to keep stray light to a minimum. Reflections and shadows can and do affect your experimental results.

1. Set up an optical bench with a 100-watt bulb and a photoelectric detector with meter, as shown in **Fig. 2**.

2. Place the detector at a distance of 30 cm from the light bulb.

3. Place a large black card in front of the light bulb as shown by the dashed line in **Fig. 2**.

4. With the card blocking the light bulb use the meter to measure the stray background light level reaching the detector. Do *NOT* turn the light bulb off to do this because the bulb itself contributes to the background. Record the background in **Table I**.

5. Measure the light bulb's brightness by removing the black card and recording the result in **Table I** under "source + background."

6. Calculate the bulb's brightness by subtracting the background from the "source + background" columns. This result should be recorded in the source column of **Table I**.

7. Repeat this procedure for distances of 40, 50, 60, 70, 80, 90, 100, and 110 centimeters.

8. Replace the 100-watt bulb with a 60-watt light bulb. Repeat the above procedure with the 60-watt bulb and record the data in **Table II**.

9. Plot the data for both bulbs on the graph given in **Fig. 3**. Use dots for the 100-watt bulb and x's for the 60-watt bulb.

10. Draw a smooth best-fit curve through the data for each bulb. This means to divide evenly the data points with a smooth curve and *not* to connect the dots. Thus your curves may go through some data and above or below other data.

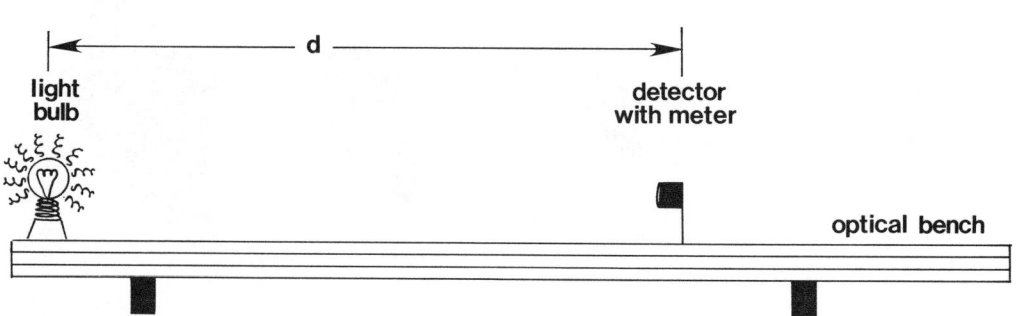

Fig. 2: Laboratory setup for measuring intensities.

TABLE I

Data for the 100-watt bulb

d (cm)	background (footcandles)	source + background (footcandles)	source (footcandles)
30			
40			
50			
60			
70			
80			
90			
100			
110			

TABLE II

Data for the 60-watt bulb

d (cm)	background (footcandles)	source + background (footcandles)	source (footcandles)
30			
40			
50			
60			
70			
80			
90			
100			
110			

QUESTIONS

1. Use the smooth curve you drew for the 100-watt bulb and determine the intensity at each of the distances, **d**, listed below. (For example, at 30 cm go straight up the graph to the curve. At the point where the line intersects the curve, read the value for **I** from the y axis.)

   $d_1 = 30$ cm $I_1 =$ _____

   $d_2 = 60$ cm $I_2 =$ _____

   $d_3 = 90$ cm $I_3 =$ _____

   Does $I_2 \approx \frac{1}{4} I_1$? _____

   Does $I_3 \approx \frac{1}{9} I_1$? _____

   Do your data for the 100-watt bulb confirm the Inverse–Square Law? _____

2. Repeat question 1 for the 60-watt bulb.

   $d_1 = 30$ cm $I_1 =$ _____

   $d_2 = 60$ cm $I_2 =$ _____

   $d_3 = 90$ cm $I_3 =$ _____

   Does $I_2 \approx \frac{1}{4} I_1$? _____

   Does $I_3 \approx \frac{1}{9} I_1$? _____

   Do your data for the 60-watt bulb confirm the Inverse–Square Law? _____

3. Use the intensity at 30 cm for the 100-watt bulb and equation (1) to predict the intensity at 15 cm and 120 cm. (**Hint:** $I_1 =$ intensity at 30 cm and $d_1 = 30$ cm.) Be sure to **show your work**.

   I_{15} = _____

   I_{120} = _____

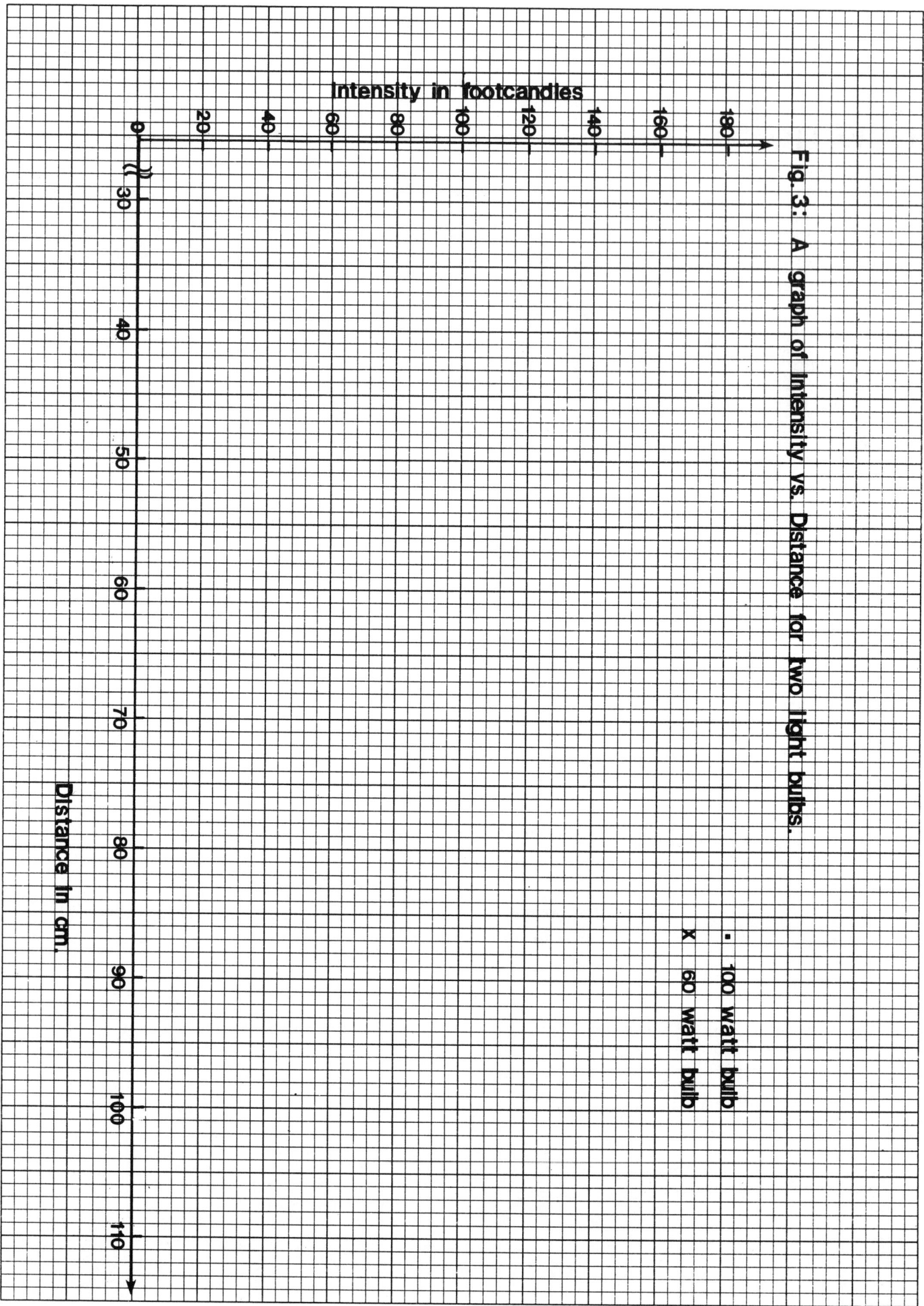

Fig.3: A graph of Intensity vs. Distance for two light bulbs.

Intensity in footcandles

Distance in cm.

■ 100 watt bulb

× 60 watt bulb

ROTATION OF THE SUN

OBJECTIVES

After completing this exercise the student will be able to:

1. follow the linear path of a sunspot across the solar disk.
2. convert this path to a circular arc on the spherical Sun.
3. calculate the synodic and sidereal rotation period of the Sun based on sunspot observations.

STUDENT MATERIALS

mm scale
protractor
compass
calculator

LAB MATERIALS

There is no setup needed. It is handy to have some spare pages of tracing paper and some *Sky and Telescope* reprints to give to students who have lost theirs.

STUDENT REQUIREMENTS

This lab is to be done individually, without lab partners. Turn in **Fig. 1** and your tracing paper drawing.

INTRODUCTION

Galileo Galilei first observed sunspots and solar rotation in 1611. Since that time astronomers have determined that our Sun rotates differentially. In other words, the rotation period is slightly shorter near the equator than at higher latitudes.

In this exercise you will use a series of solar photographs to determine the average rotation rate of the Sun. These photos were obtained at the U.S. Naval Observatory in Washington, D.C. This particular series was taken during a time interval when the Earth was crossing the equatorial plane of the Sun. Therefore, the sunspots appear to move across the solar disk in straight lines. These linear displacements will be transferred to a drawing of the spherical Sun so that an angular velocity can be obtained. From this velocity the synodic and sidereal rotation periods can be calculated.

All photos are from the *Sky and Telescope* reprint "The Rotation of the Sun," that is in the packet at the back of this manual.

PROCEDURE

I. Tracing the Apparent Motion of Sunspots

1. On each photo of the Sun locate the north and south indicator marks. Make these marks darker, if necessary, in order to see them through the tracing paper.

2. Measure to the nearest millimeter the diameter of the Sun in the photo taken on May 22.71.

3. On the tracing paper (in the packet in the back of this manual), draw a circle which has a diameter equal to the above millimeter measurement.

4. Place your circle over the May 22nd image and trace the north and south indicator marks on your circle.

5. On one of the first few photos locate a sunspot near the eastern edge of the Sun and label it as **A**.

6. Locate spot **A** previously identified in step 5 and label it on the next four or five photos in the sequence.

7. On the first photo you labeled with sunspot **A**, carefully overlay your circular drawing onto the solar image. Be sure the center of your circle lies over the center of the Sun's image. Also be sure that your north and south markers are aligned with the solar north and south indicator marks.

8. Trace around sunspot **A** and label this position with the photograph's date. Be sure to include the fractional portion of the date.

9. Move the tracing paper to the next photo and repeat steps 7 and 8. Follow this procedure until spot **A** has disappeared around the Sun's western limb.

10. On your tracing paper use a ruler to draw a line which passes through your plotted sunspot positions. This line should begin and end on the east and west edges of the Sun (the edge of your circle). If some spot positions are not on the line check to see if you traced the correct positions.

11. On the same circle repeat steps 5 through 10 for sunspots at two different latitudes than **A**. Label them as spots **B** and **C**. You may need to start **B** and **C** on photos taken at later dates than the ones used for spot **A**. When you have finished you should have a piece of tracing paper that has one circle with three chords passing across the circle.

II. Finding the Sun's Rotation

If you examine the sunspot paths made in **part I** you will notice that they appear to move more rapidly when near the center of the Sun's disk than when near the limb. This foreshortening is caused by the fact that the Sun is spherical and the linear paths are projections onto a flat surface. In order to determine the Sun's rotation a simple graphical procedure can be used to eliminate errors caused by foreshortening. Imagine the Sun to be a globe with a circle drawn around it at the latitude of a sunspot. Slice through

the globe at this latitude. Now if you look down on the Sun from above the rotation axis you should see a disk whose edge represents the circular path of the sunspot. The line drawn through the linear path of each sunspot on your tracing paper represents such a circle seen edge-on.

You will now draw such a circle from your tracing paper overlay. A completed example is shown in the figure on page 4 of your *Sky and Telescope* reprint.

1. Measure to the nearest millimeter the length of the straight line for spot **A**'s apparent motion across the solar disk. Be sure your measurement goes from the Sun's east limb to its west limb.

2. Draw a horizontal line on **Fig. 1**, for spot **A**, which is exactly this length.

3. Find the midpoint of this line and use a compass to draw a semicircle connecting the two ends. This half circle represents the Earth-facing surface of the Sun at spot **A**'s latitude, and the baseline is its projection onto a flat surface.

4. Use a ruler and transfer the sunspot positions from the tracing paper to the baseline of this semicircle. Be sure to label each position with the dates. When completed you should be able to overlay the tracing paper onto the baseline of the semicircle and get a very close match.

5. Pick two widely spaced positions for spot **A** and draw a vertical line from each position up to the semicircle representing the Sun's surface. Be sure this line makes a 90° angle to the baseline. The intersections of the vertical lines and the semicircle represent two actual positions of spot **A** at two separate times.

6. From the baseline's midpoint (the hole made by the compass) draw lines up to the semicircle which pass through both sunspot positions. These two lines will form an angle at the midpoint.

7. Use a protractor to measure the angle you just made in step 6. It may be necessary to extend the lines so that your protractor can be used prop-

erly. Record the angular measurement on your diagram.

8. Subtract the dates of the two sunspot positions to find the elapsed time between them. Record the result beside the diagram. (For spot photos taken in June, you should think of June 1.65 and June 5.58 as May 32.65 and May 36.58 respectively.)

9. Calculate the Sun's angular velocity, the number of degrees it rotates each day, by dividing the angular measurement by the time interval. Record this value beside your diagram.

10. Repeat steps 1 through 9 for sunspots **B** and **C**.

11. Calculate the average angular velocity of the Sun and record your answer at the bottom of **Fig. 1**.

12. To find out how long it takes the Sun to make one full rotation, its synodic period, divide 360° (the number of degrees in one rotation) by your angular velocity. Record your answer at the bottom of **Fig. 1**. If you have done things carefully you should get a synodic rotation period near 27.3 days ± 2 days.

13. The synodic period is the Sun's rotation as observed from the moving Earth. To get the Sun's sidereal rotation period, its true rotation period, as observed with respect to a stationary observer, you must use the equation

$$P = \frac{(365.25)S}{365.25 + S}$$

where **S** is your synodic period in days. Calculate the sidereal period **P** and record your answer at the bottom of **Fig. 1**.

Staple your tracing paper drawing onto **Fig. 1** and turn them in together.

NAME: ____________________

SECTION: ____________________

TIME INTERVAL ____________________

ANGULAR VELOCITY ____________________

Spot A

TIME INTERVAL ____________________

ANGULAR VELOCITY ____________________

Spot B

Fig. 1: Conversion of each sunspot's linear path into a circular arc on the spherical sun.

TIME INTERVAL _____

ANGULAR VELOCITY _____

Spot C

AVERAGE ANGULAR VELOCITY _____

SYNODIC ROTATION PEROID _____

SIDEREAL ROTATION PERIOD _____

Fig. 1: (continued)

ECLIPSING AND SPECTROSCOPIC BINARY STARS

OBJECTIVES

After completing this exercise the student will be able to:

1. determine graphically the observed contact time for primary eclipse of an eclipsing binary.
2. determine the spectroscopic and photometric orbital elements of a double-line spectroscopic eclipsing binary star.
3. calculate the masses and radii of the two stars in the binary system from the orbital elements.

STUDENT MATERIALS

pencil
ruler
calculator

LAB MATERIALS

photometric and spectroscopic data for several eclipsing binaries (optional)

STUDENT REQUIREMENTS

This lab is to be done individually, without lab partners. After completion, turn in answer sheet, **Fig. 3**, and **Fig. 4**.

INTRODUCTION

When a binary star's orbit is nearly edge-on to our line of sight, the two stars will periodically pass in front of each other and eclipse as shown in **Fig. 1a**. It can be seen that two eclipses occur during the complete orbital cycle. The deeper of these two eclipses is called primary eclipse and occurs when the hotter star is eclipsed by the cooler star. Secondary eclipse is the shallower of the two eclipses and occurs when the cooler star is eclipsed by the hotter

star. Note that these eclipses are designated according to the relative temperatures of the two stars and not according to their relative sizes or brightness. When the stars are not eclipsing, the light from both stars is observed and causes the constant light level seen during the out-of-eclipse phases of the light curve.

Some eclipsing binaries are also spectroscopic binaries, and their orbital motion can be observed as a periodic Doppler shift of their spectral lines. Single-line spectroscopic binaries show only the spectral lines of the brighter star. The spectral lines of the fainter star are not visible because they have been flooded out by the intense light of the brighter star. Double-line spectroscopic binaries show spectral lines from both stars in the system. This can only occur if the two stars of the system have about the same brightness. Usually one star will be no more than about twice as bright as its companion. **Fig. 1b** shows a hypothetical double-line spectroscopic binary which has circular orbits along with the resulting radial-velocity curves. The measured radial-velocity is composed of two parts; the center-of-mass radial velocity is usually called the γ-velocity and occurs where the two curves intersect. In **Fig. 1b** the γ-velocity of the system is +25 km/sec. A positive radial velocity indicates that the system is moving away from the Sun and a negative radial velocity indicates that the system is approaching the Sun.

It can be seen that the light curve in **Fig. 1a** and the radial-velocity curve in **Fig. 1b** are interrelated. At positions 1 and 3 both stars are moving across our line of sight. At these positions neither star has a radial-velocity component which is produced by the orbital motion of the stars. The light curve shows that either primary or secondary eclipses must be occurring. At position 2, Star A has the maximum possible orbital component of its radial velocity away from the Sun and Star B has the maximum possible orbital component of its radial velocity toward the Sun. At position 4, these conditions are reversed. From the light curve it can be seen that near positions 2 and 4, the full amount of light from both stars is seen and thus the light curves are flat and show the maximum light of the system.

Now let's examine in detail a hypothetical central eclipse of two spherical stars. **Fig. 2** shows the light curve of such a system during primary eclipse and the relative positions of the two stars as the cooler star passes in front of the hotter star. At position A, just before the eclipse begins, the light from both stars is seen to be constant and is defined to be equal to 1 (100%). First contact occurs at position B when the light level begins to fade as the hotter star is eclipsed. At position C, second contact occurs when the hotter star becomes totally eclipsed. The light level remains constant until third contact is reached at position E. It should be noted that between second and third contact only light from the cooler star can be observed since the hotter star is completely hidden from view. From third contact at position E until fourth contact at position F the light steadily increases until it is again equal to 1 (one) at position F, when the light from both stars is observed once again. The two stars have now reversed their original orientation from that seen before first contact.

PROCEDURE

I. Photometric Elements of the Totally Eclipsing Binary SS Bootis

During the spring of 1980 the RS Canum Venaticorum type eclipsing binary SS Bootis (SS Boo) was observed photoelectrically using the 24-inch Seyfert telescope at Dyer Observatory of Vanderbilt University and the No. 4 16-inch telescope of Kitt Peak National Observatory near Tucson, Arizona. The eclipse data obtained are shown in **Fig. 3**. (The data

shown have been corrected for the effects of star spots, reflection, and ellipticity.) The time axis (horizontal) is calibrated in fractional Julian Day units. The Julian Day (H.J.D.) is the number of days in a consecutive count starting at noon on January 1, 4713 B.C., as described in the April 1981 issue of *Sky and Telescope*. The light-level axis (vertical) is calibrated so that the light out-of-eclipse, when the light from both stars is seen, is equal to 1 or 100%. Thus the light seen throughout the eclipse is expressed as a fractional part of the total light of the system or as a percent of the system's total brightness. For this exercise we shall assume the stars in the system are spherical and in circular orbits.

A. Relative Luminosity

The brightness, or luminosity, of each star relative to its companion can be determined from the light level along the bottom of the eclipse. From spectroscopic data it has been determined that the cooler star is a K-type subgiant and the hotter star is a G-type main-sequence star. Since the primary eclipse is the eclipse of the hotter star by the cooler star, and since the cooler star is the larger, it can be seen from **Fig. 2** that all the light observed during totality must originate only from the cooler star. Therefore, the relative luminosity, L_C, of the cooler star in the SS Boo system can be directly determined by extending the eclipse bottom in **Fig. 3** toward the left until it intersects the light-level axis. Read off the light level of this intersection to determine the value of L_C. Record your answer in the space provided on the answer sheet. Recall that the total light of the system, outside eclipse when both stars are fully visible, was defined to be equal to 1 (one). Therefore the relative luminosity L_h of the hotter star must be given by

$$L_h = 1 - L_C \qquad (1)$$

From your value of L_C and equation (1) calculate the value of L_h. Record your answer in the space provided.

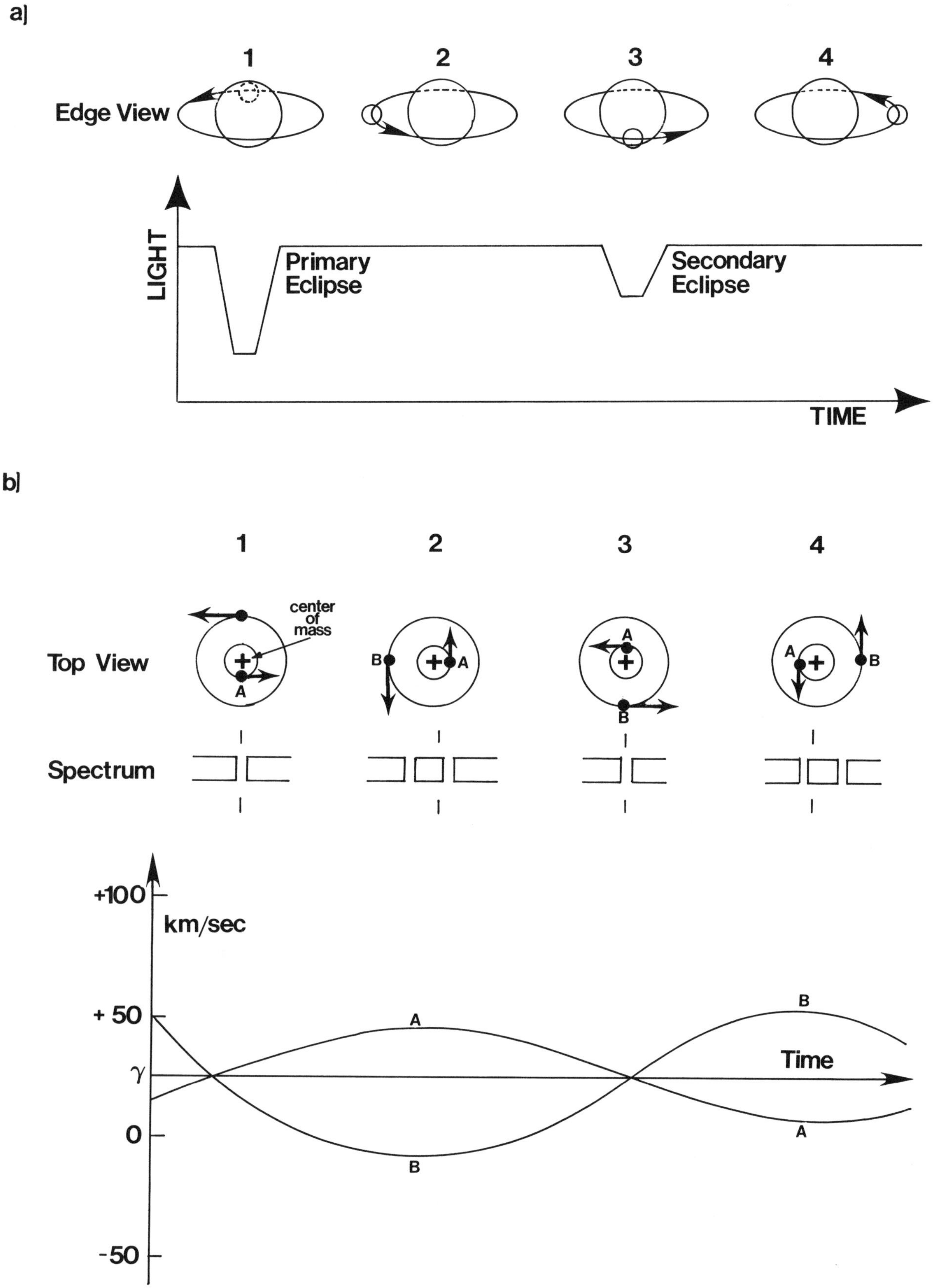

a]

Edge View

1   2   3   4

LIGHT

Primary Eclipse

Secondary Eclipse

TIME

b]

1   2   3   4

Top View

center of mass

B • ⊕ •A

A ⊕ B

A ⊕ B

Spectrum

km/sec

+100

+ 50

γ

0

-50

A

B

B

A

Time

Fig. 1: Comparison of photometric **(a)** and spectroscopic **(b)** data for a hypothetical eclipsing binary with spherical stars and circular orbits.

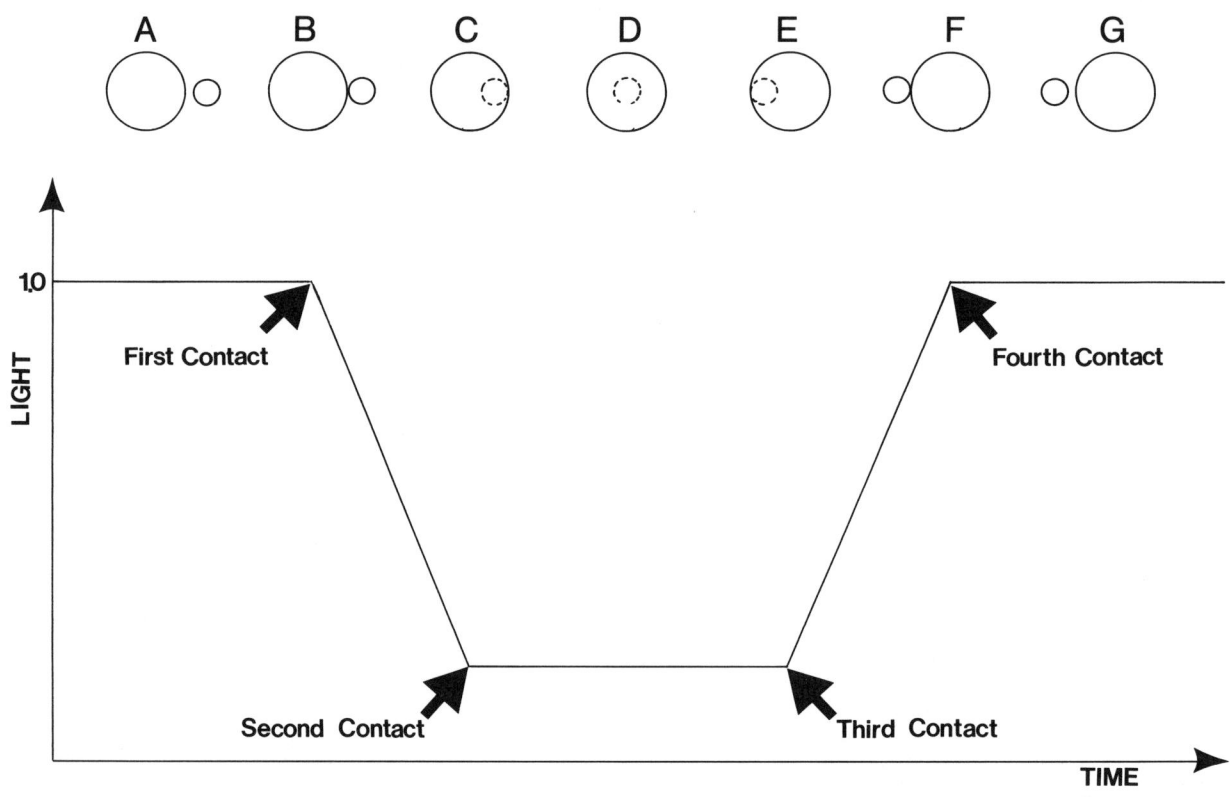

Fig. 2: An expanded view of primary eclipse for the hypothetical binary in **Fig. 1**.

B. Relative Stellar Radii

The location of the first, second, third and fourth contacts was described in the last part of the introduction. With the aid of this description locate the first, second, and third contacts of the SS Boo eclipse shown in **Fig. 3**. Fourth contact was not observed and will not be used for any orbital calculations. From each of these three contacts drop a vertical line to the Julian-Day axis and read off the time each contact occurred. Write your answer in the space on the answer sheet. Be careful and do not forget about the 2444000+ on the H.J.D.

These contact times can be used to determine the radii of the two stars relative to the orbit's circumference. From **Fig. 2** it can be seen that during the interval of time between the first and second contact the smaller star has moved a distance equal to its own diameter. Similarly, during the time interval between first and third contacts the smaller star has moved a distance equal to the diameter of the larger star. The ratio of these time intervals to the orbital period is the same as the ratio of each star's diameter to the circumference of its orbit. Therefore the relative radii of the cooler star, r_c, and the hotter star, r_h, can be calculated from

$$r_c = \frac{\pi(t_3 - t_1)}{P} \qquad (2)$$

$$r_h = \frac{\pi(t_2 - t_1)}{P} \qquad (3)$$

where P = orbital period = 7.60614 days

t_1 = time of first contact

t_2 = time of second contact

t_3 = time of third contact

π = 3.1416

With the above value for the period and the previously determined contact times, use equations (2) and (3) to calculate the relative radii of the two stars in the SS Boo system. Is the hotter or cooler star the larger star in this system?

II. Spectroscopic Elements for SS Bootis

SS Boo is also a double-line spectroscopic binary as described in the introduction and as shown in **Fig. 1b**. From 1934 to 1945, Roscoe Sanford observed SS Boo spectroscopically at Mount Wilson Observatory. His data and a radial-velocity curve for SS Boo are shown in **Fig. 4**. The scatter in these data is caused by the faintness of the star which is about 9th magnitude. The vertical axis represents the radial-velocity of the system in km/sec and the horizontal axis represents the orbital phase, or the fractional orbital position. The phases begin with 0 (zero) at mid-primary eclipse. Thus one-quarter of the way around the orbit corresponds to 0.25 phase units, halfway around the orbit corresponds to 0.5 phase units, and three-quarters of the way around corresponds to 0.75 phase units.

A. Center of Mass Velocity

The radial velocity of the center of mass for SS Boo can be determined by drawing a line which connects the intersections of the two curves in **Fig. 4**. Determine the γ-velocity for SS Boo. Record your answer on the answer sheet.

B. Mass Ratio

The mass ratio of the two stars in the SS Boo system can be determined by measuring the semi-amplitudes of the radial-velocity curves in **Fig. 4**. At phase 0.25 and 0.75 draw a vertical line from the top curve to the bottom curve. Measure in units of km/sec from the center-of-mass radial-velocity line to the top of each curve at phases 0.25 and 0.75, and record these lengths as α_c and α_h respectively. Repeat the above procedure, except this time measure down to the bottom of the curves and record as β_h and β_c respectively. These measurements give us a method of determining the mass ratio of the two stars but not their actual masses. With equation (4) below and your measured values of α and β, determine the mass ratio for the stars in SS Boo.

$$\textbf{\textit{Mass Ratio}} = \frac{M_h}{M_C} = \frac{\alpha_C + \beta_C}{\alpha_h + \beta_h} \qquad (4)$$

III. Dimensions of the SS Bootis System

By combining both the spectroscopic velocities with the photometric properties, the actual dimensions of an eclipsing binary such as SS Boo can be calculated. Thus it will be possible to calculate the absolute masses, in solar mass units, for each star in the system, and to calculate the absolute radius of each star in solar radius units.

A. Stellar Masses

Since SS Boo is a totally eclipsing binary it can be assumed that the orbital inclination is 90° (edge-on). Thus, the separation, a, between the two stars can be calculated from

$$a = \frac{(0.211 \ V)(P/365.25)}{2\pi} \qquad (5)$$

where V is the maximum relative velocity of the two stars in km/sec and where P is the orbital period in days. The factor 0.211 converts the velocity from units of km/sec to units of AUs/year. It should be obvious that the factor 365.25 converts the orbital period from units of days into years. Therefore, a will be in astronomical units. From your previously determined values of α_h and β_c, calculate V from the relation

$$V = \alpha_h + \beta_c \qquad (6)$$

Use this value of V and the known value of P to calculate the stellar separation, a, using equation 5. Record your answer on the answer sheet. The sum of

the stellar masses can now be calculated from the values of a and P using Kepler's Third Law, which states

$$M_h + M_c = \frac{a^3}{(P/365.25)^2} \qquad (7)$$

Use the mass sum and the mass ratio previously determined to estimate the individual masses of each star in the SS Boo system. Record these values on the answer sheet.

B. Stellar Radii

We can now calculate the absolute radius for each star in terms of the Sun's radius with the equations

$$R_c = r_c \, a(214.95) \qquad (8)$$

and

$$R_h = r_h \, a(214.95) \qquad (9)$$

where r_c, r_h, and a have previously been determined.

The factor 214.95 is the number of solar radii in one astronomical unit and converts the radii obtained from astronomical units to solar radius units. Calculate the values R_c and R_h for SS Boo. Record the results on the answer page. Stop and think about your answers. Do they make sense? Recall that one star is a K-type subgiant and the other star is a G-type main-sequence star. The above procedure is one of the few methods by which astronomers can obtain information about the masses and sizes of stars. Thus it is very important to modern astronomy.

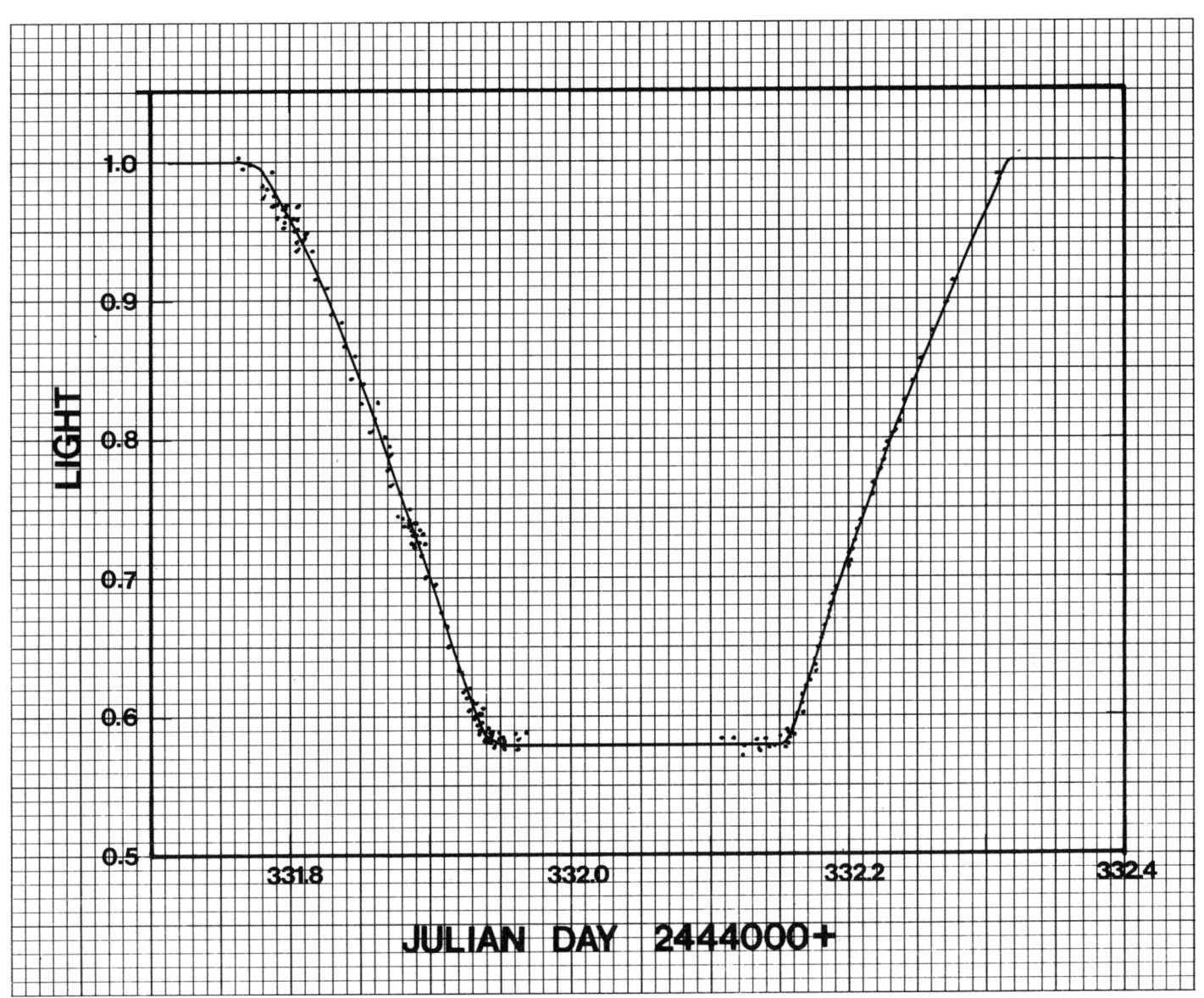

Fig. 3: Primary eclipses of SS Boo.

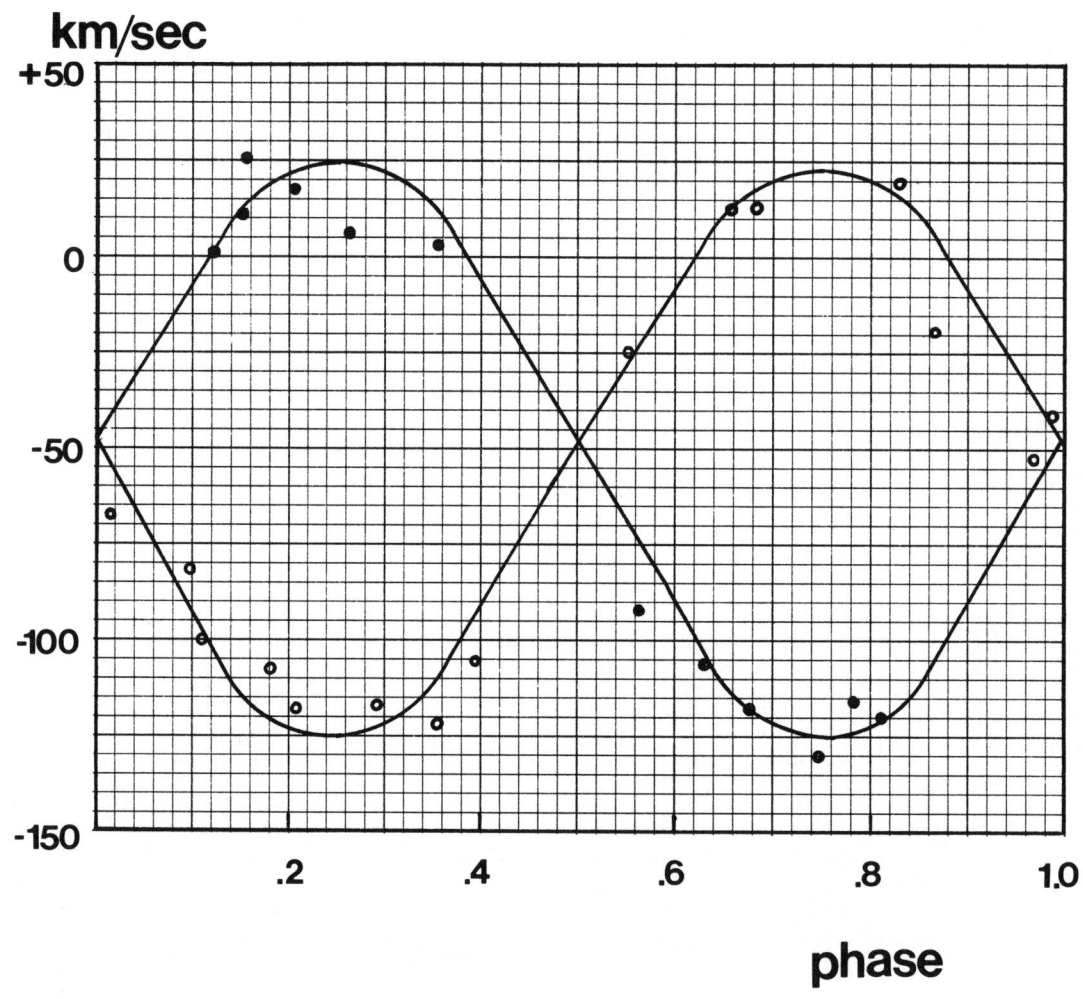

Fig. 4: Radial-velocity curve for SS Boo. Filled circles represent cooler star and open circles represent hotter star.

Eclipsing and Spectroscopic Binary Stars

I. **Photometric Elements for SS Bootis**

    A. **Relative Luminosity**

        $L_c =$ _____ $L_h =$ _____

    B. **Relative Stellar Radii**

        J.D.(hel.) of 1st contact = $t_1 =$ _____

        J.D.(hel.) of 2nd contact = $t_2 =$ _____

        J.D.(hel.) of 3rd contact = $t_3 =$ _____

        $r_c =$ _____ $r_h =$ _____

II. **Spectroscopic Elements for SS Bootis**

    A. **Center of Mass Velocity**

        $\gamma =$ _____   **km/sec**

    B. **Mass Ratio**

        $\alpha_c =$ _____ km/sec $\beta_c =$ _____ km/sec

        $\alpha_h =$ _____ km/sec $\beta_h =$ _____ km/sec

        Mass ratio = _____

III. **Dimensions of the SS Bootis System**

    A. **Stellar Masses**

        Total relative velocity = V = _____ **km/sec**

        separation $a =$ _____ **AUs**

        $M_c + M_h =$ _____ $M_\odot$

        $M_c =$ _____ $M_\odot$ $M_h =$ _____ $M_\odot$

    B. **Stellar Radii**

        $R_c =$ _____ $R_\odot$ $R_h =$ _____ $R_\odot$

AGES AND DISTANCES OF STAR CLUSTERS

15

OBJECTIVES

After completing this exercise the student will be able to:

1. estimate the distance to a cluster using main sequence fitting.
2. correct the distance for interstellar reddening and absorption.
3. estimate the age of a cluster from the main sequence turn-off point.

STUDENT MATERIALS

pencil
calculator

LAB MATERIALS

extra transparent overlays

STUDENT REQUIREMENTS

This lab is to be done individually, without lab partners. After completion, turn in data table and the answers to the questions.

INTRODUCTION

Much of our understanding of the characteristics of individual stars is resultant from an application of our knowledge about clusters of stars. While investigating various types of clusters, we make certain reasonable assumptions about the stars found in each specific cluster. For instance, if we assume all of the stars in a given cluster began to form at approximately the same time, and that a given cluster formed from the same cloud of gas and dust, we can assume that the composition of these component stars will be alike. Also, relative to the size of the cluster and its distance away from us, all of the stars within a cluster

can be considered to be approximately the same distance from us. Thus, if interstellar reddening is present, all of the stars in a given cluster should be affected to the same degree. We can also determine the approximate evolutionary age of a star cluster, and further, we can compare clusters to final differences in their ages and compositions.

This lab exercise will be concerned with determining the approximate ages of various star clusters, determining the distances to them, and noting the effects that interstellar reddening has on the distance estimate made for each.

PROCEDURE

Example: The cluster M45 (Pleiades) has been plotted in **Fig. 1** as a color magnitude diagram, which is similar to an H-R diagram (except for the use of different scales). **V** represents the apparent magnitude of each star and **B – V** represents the color index of each star, and is equivalent to temperature of spectral class. The main sequence of this cluster should be evident from the plot.

The transparency overlay provided is a graph of absolute magnitude, **M**, versus the corrected color index (**B – V**). On it is plotted the theoretical Zero Age Main Sequence (ZAMS) line of unevolved stars, and also a series of isochrones (lines of equal time) with their respective age estimates. For instance, if a star cluster is approximately 20 million years old (2×10^7 yrs.), the upper main sequence stars in the cluster will appear to lie along this line evolving away from the main sequence and going toward the red giant region. The remaining stars in the cluster below this turn-off point will be on or near the main sequence. This is because the upper main sequence stars (more massive) evolve faster than the lower main sequence stars (less massive).

STEP 1: Alignment

Place the overlay (overlay is in packet at the back of this book) on top of the Pleiades plot, lining up the corrected color index (**B** – **V**) scale of the overlay with the corrected (**B** – **V**) scale printed along the top of the Pleiades diagram. Note that the 0.0 points at the bottom of the overlay and on the cluster diagram do not necessarily coincide. This will be discussed later.

The overlay can now be moved only in the *vertical direction* along the corrected 0.0 (**B** – **V**) line. In order to align the cluster main sequence stars with the ZAMS line, move the overlay along this 0.0 line until the ZAMS line falls approximately one-third of the way from the bottom side of the plotted main sequence stars of the cluster. In other words, slide the transparent overlay up or down until its ZAMS is running along the middle of the Pleiades main sequence; then lower the transparency's ZAMS until more main sequence is above than below it.

STEP 2: Distance Modulus and Distance

Now that the position of the overlay has been established it is possible to determine the difference in magnitude between the observed apparent magnitudes **V** of the cluster and their theoretical absolute magnitudes, **M**. Look at where the overlay's value of **M** = 0.0 crosses the **V** axis of the cluster diagram directly under it. This should be around 5.6 or so. Thus, the distance modulus to the Pleiades is **V** – **M** = 5.6 – 0.0 = 5.6, approximately. Look up the distance modulus value of 5.6 on the graph of distance vs. distance modulus in **Fig. 11** and estimate the distance to the Pleiades. Record both the distance modulus and the distance to the Pleiades in the data table.

STEP 3: Cluster Age Estimate

With the ZAMS still aligned with the cluster's main sequence, find where the stars in the cluster's main sequence appear to be turning away from the ZAMS. Where they turn off is an indication that they are completing their main sequence lifetime. If we

assume that all the stars formed at the same time then an estimate of the lifetimes of these massive stars gives an age estimate for the cluster as a whole. Follow the cluster's main sequence until it starts following one of the age isochrones to the right. Read off the age estimate for this isochrone. Selected ages have been given, so a cluster will not necessarily fall exactly on one of these isochrones. Estimate the cluster age using the selected isochrones as a guideline only. Record your answer in the table.

STEP 4: Interstellar Reddening

On some of the cluster graphs it is apparent that the (**B** – **V**) corrected color index scale on top and the (**B** – **V**) uncorrected color index scale on the bottom do not coincide with each other. The overlay zero point will either be aligned or shifted to the right on the bottom scale. You are to determine how much, if any, the scales have been shifted with respect to each other (a positive decimal number). The shift in the two scales is called the *color excess* (CE), or difference between the observed and actual color index of the star in the cluster. Record this number in your table.

The interstellar absorption factor **A** (the number of magnitudes absorbed by dust) is simply three times the color excess, which you have just recorded. Find the interstellar absorption factor **A** = (3 × CE) and record this in the table. If interstellar absorption is present, **A** will be some positive number; if not, **A** will be zero. If there is interstellar absorption, the distance to the cluster will have to be corrected. This is very easily done by subtracting the value **A** from the distance modulus previously found and written in column one of the data table. In other words,

corrected distance modulus = (V – M$_V$) – A

Record the corrected distance modulus in your table; refer again to the graph of distance vs. distance modulus and find the corrected distance to the cluster. Record this new distance in your table for the cluster. Repeat steps 1 - 4 for the remaining clusters, recording your answers as you go along on the accompanying answer sheet.

AGES AND DISTANCES OF STAR CLUSTERS

CLUSTER	distance modulus $V - M_v$	estimated age (years)	distance d(pcs)	color excess CE	absorption factor $A = 3 \times CE$	corrected distance modulus $(V - M_v) - A$	corrected distance d(pcs)
M45 Pleiades							
NGC 6791							
NGC 6705							
NGC 2632 M-44 Praesepe							
NGC 2682 M67							
NGC 457							
IC 4725 M25							
NGC 752							
Mel 20 α Per							
Orion OB-1							

M45 (Pleiades)

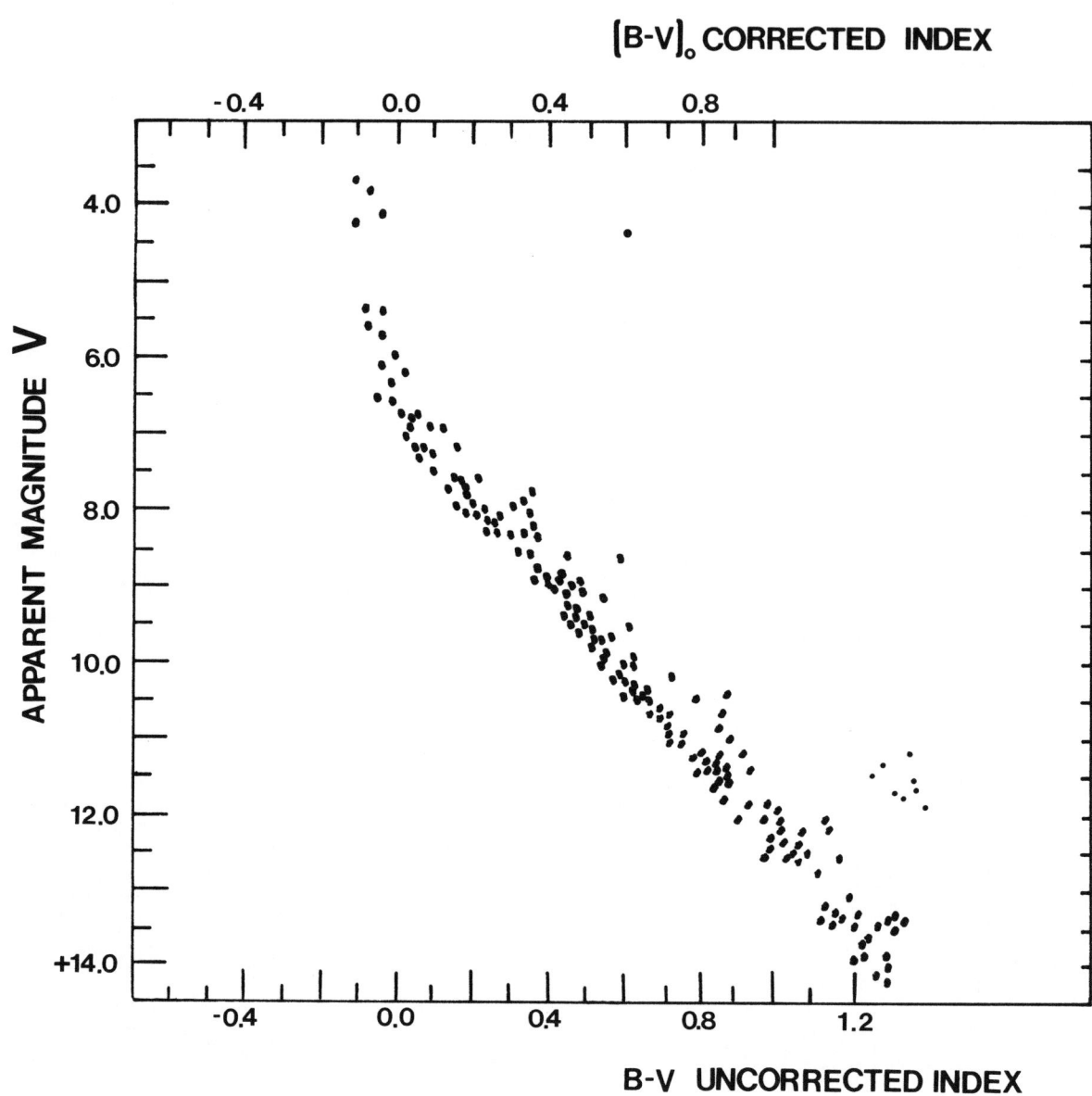

Fig. 1: H-R diagram for the Pleiades.

NGC 6791

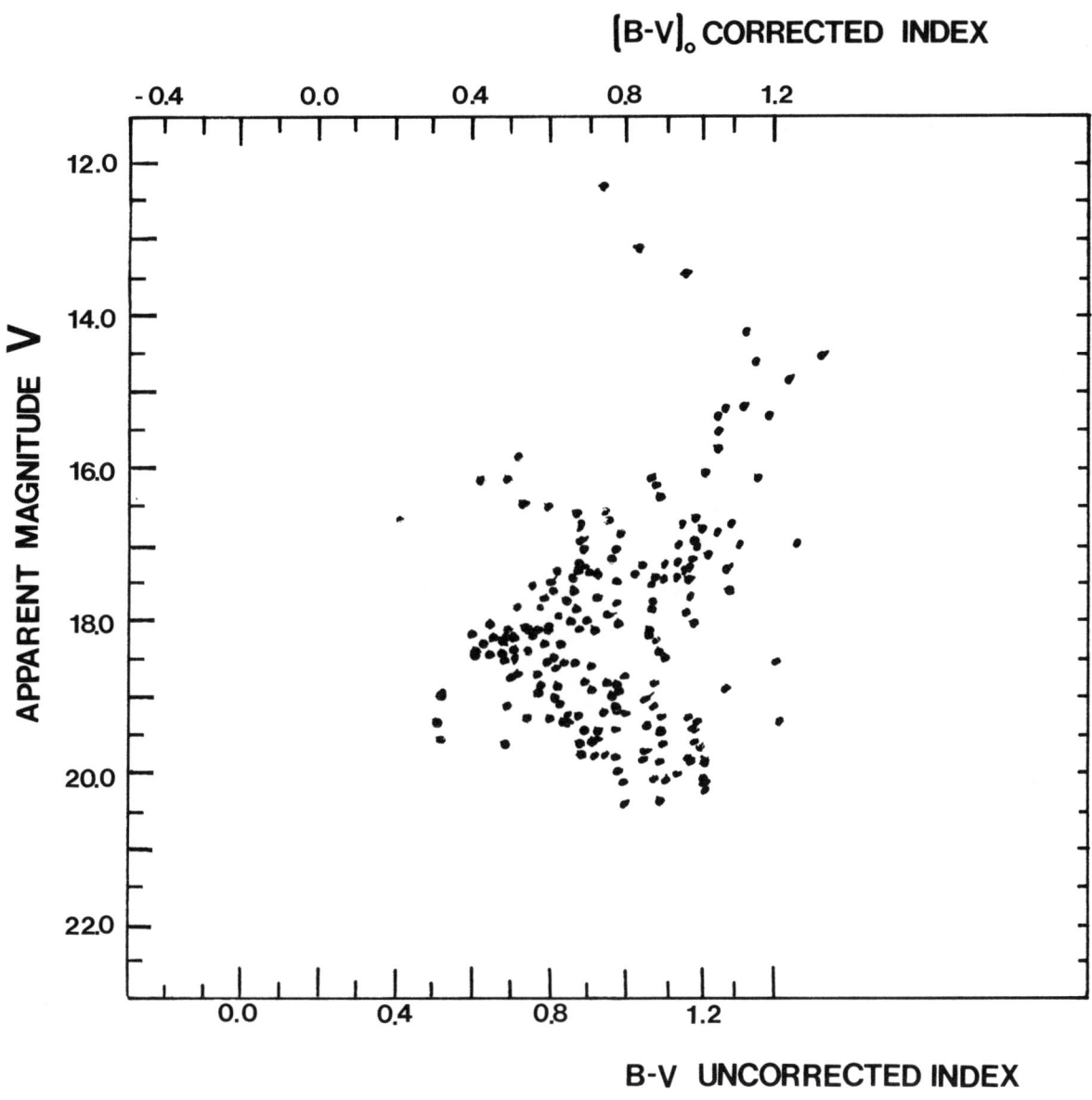

Fig. 2: H-R diagram for NGC 6791.

NGC 6705 [M 11]

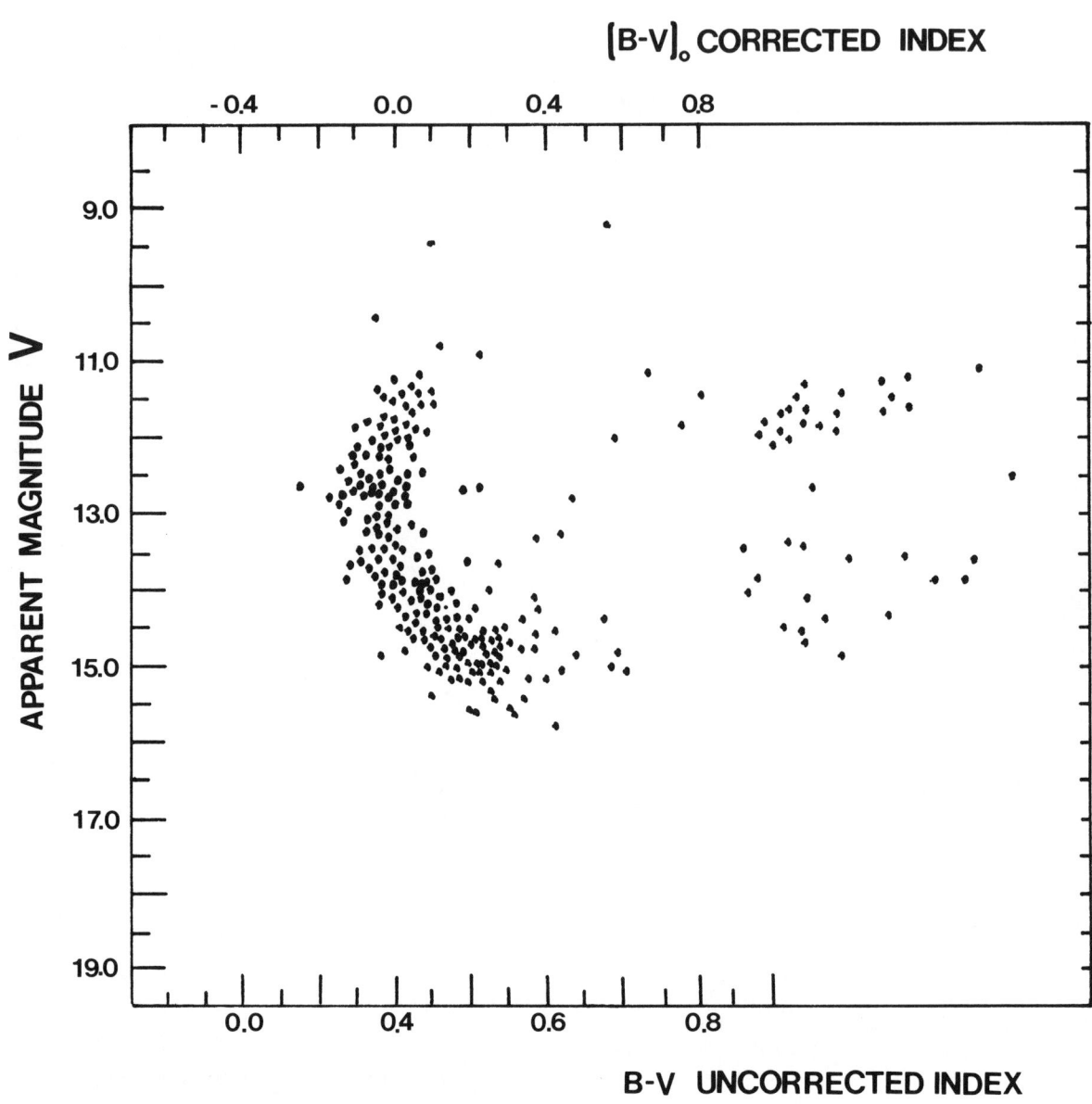

Fig. 3: H-R diagram for NGC 6705.

NGC 2632 (M44-Praesepe)

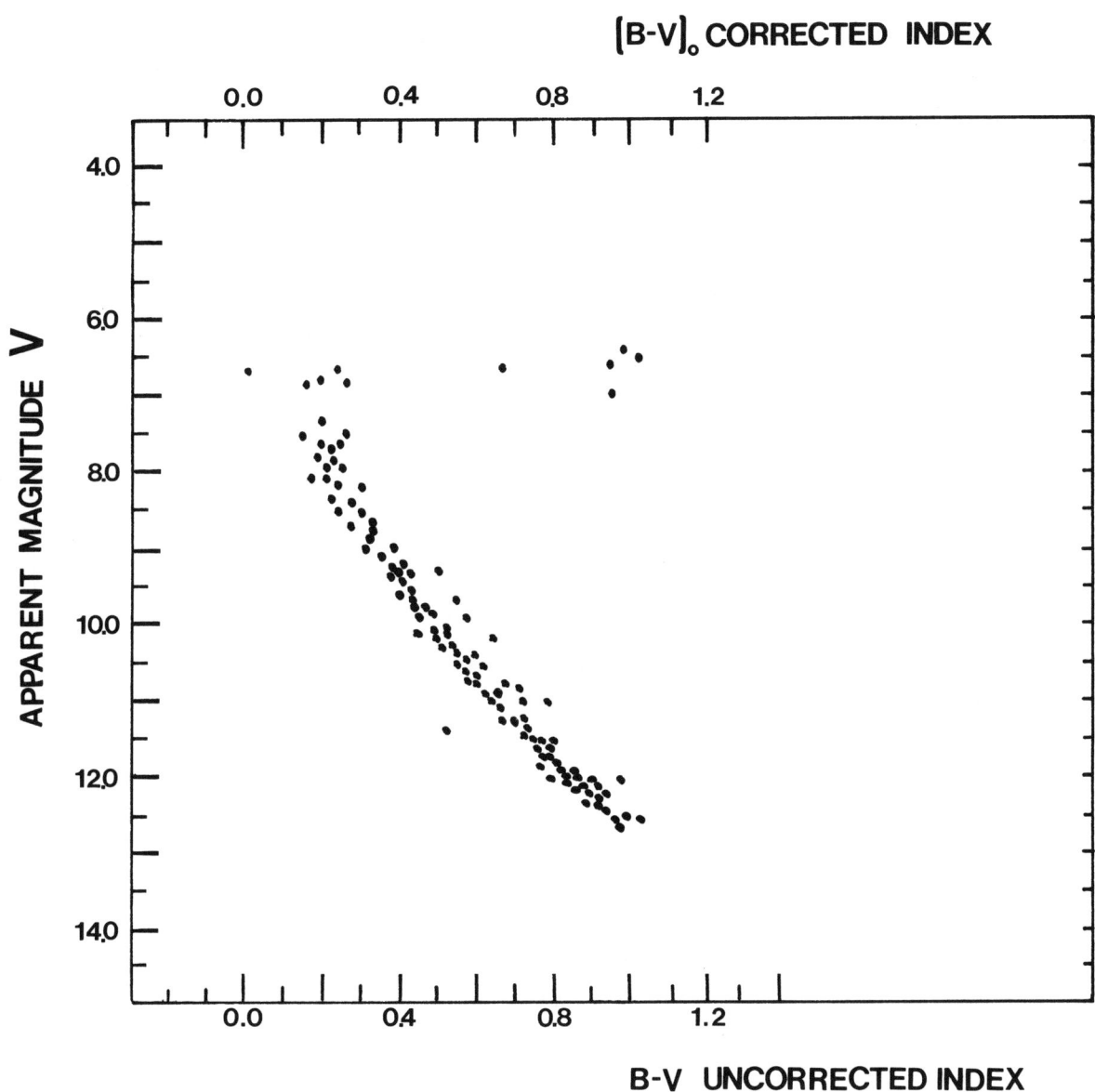

Fig. 4: H-R diagram for the Praesepe.

NGC 2682 (M 67)

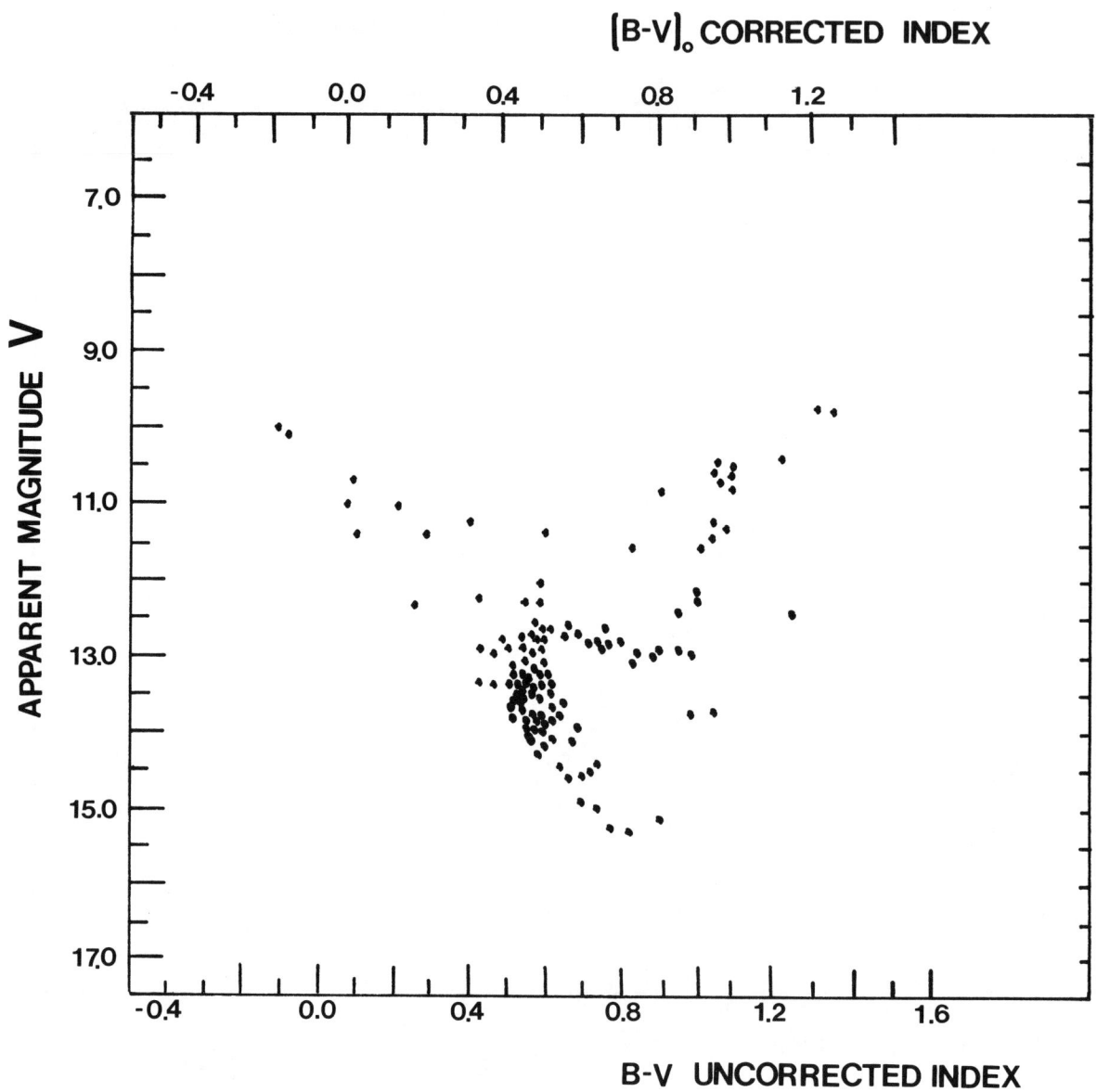

Fig. 5: H-R diagram for M67.

NGC 457

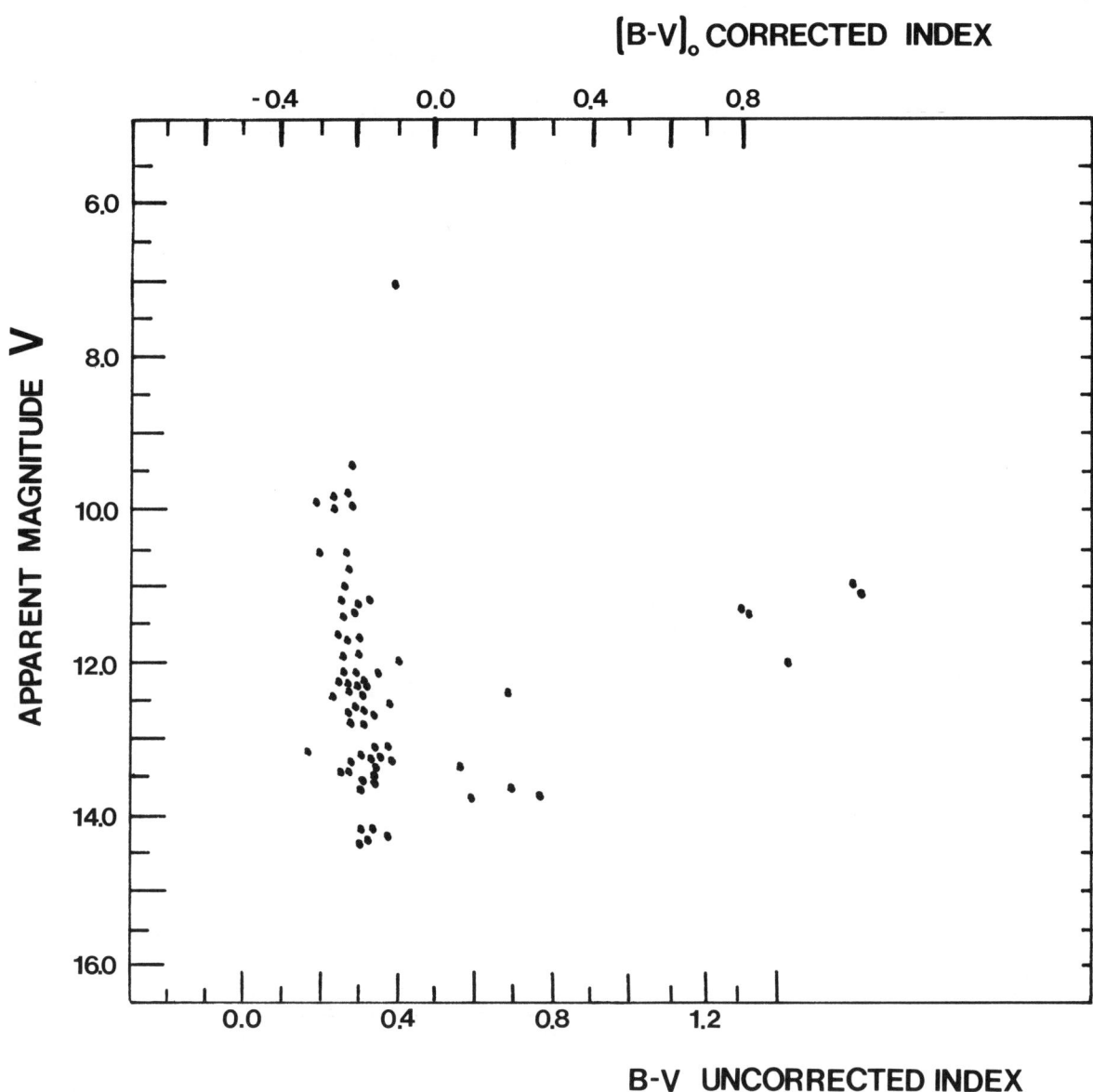

Fig. 6: H-R diagram for NGC 457.

IC 4725 (M 25)

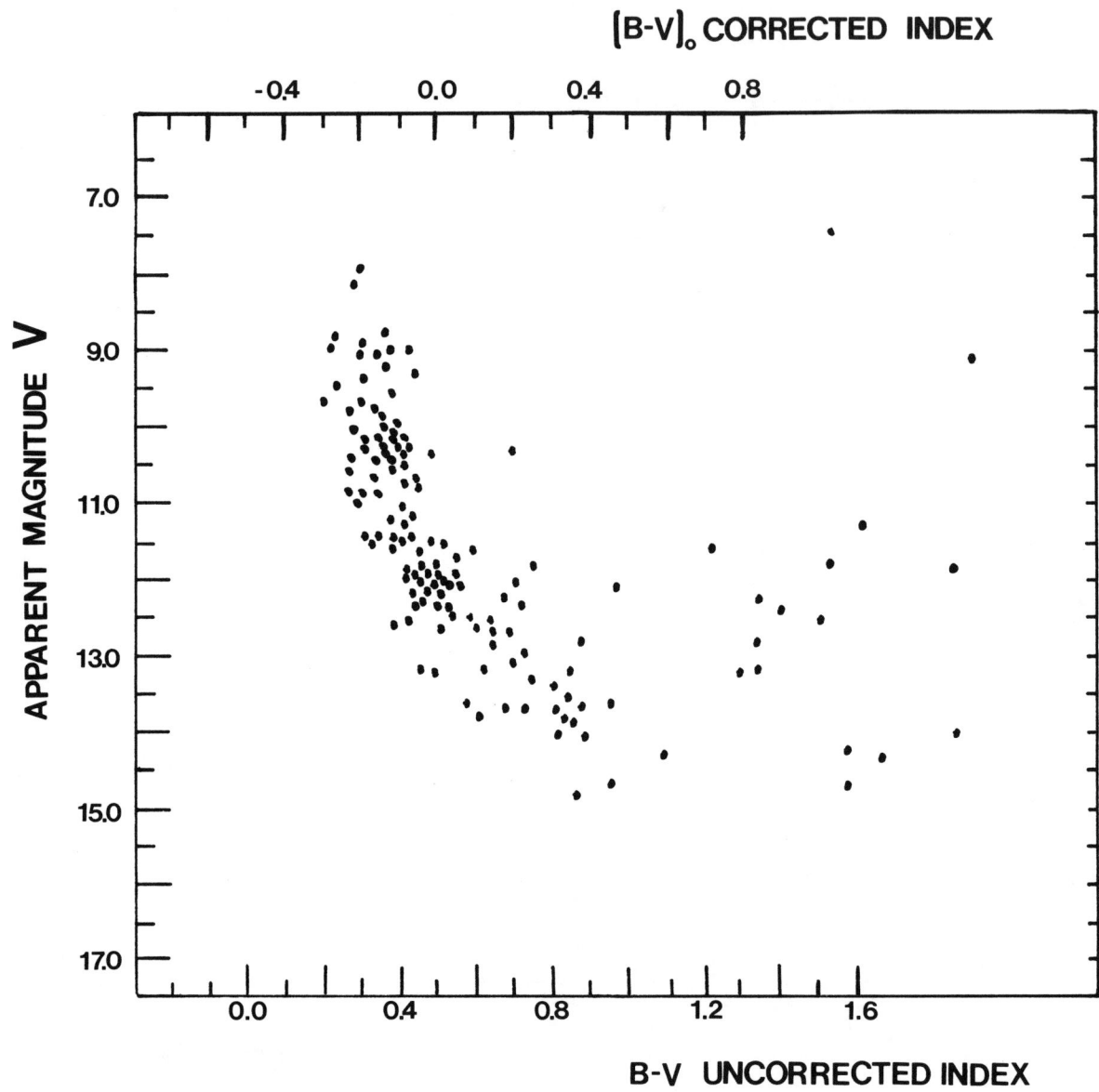

Fig 7: H-R diagram for M25.

NGC 752

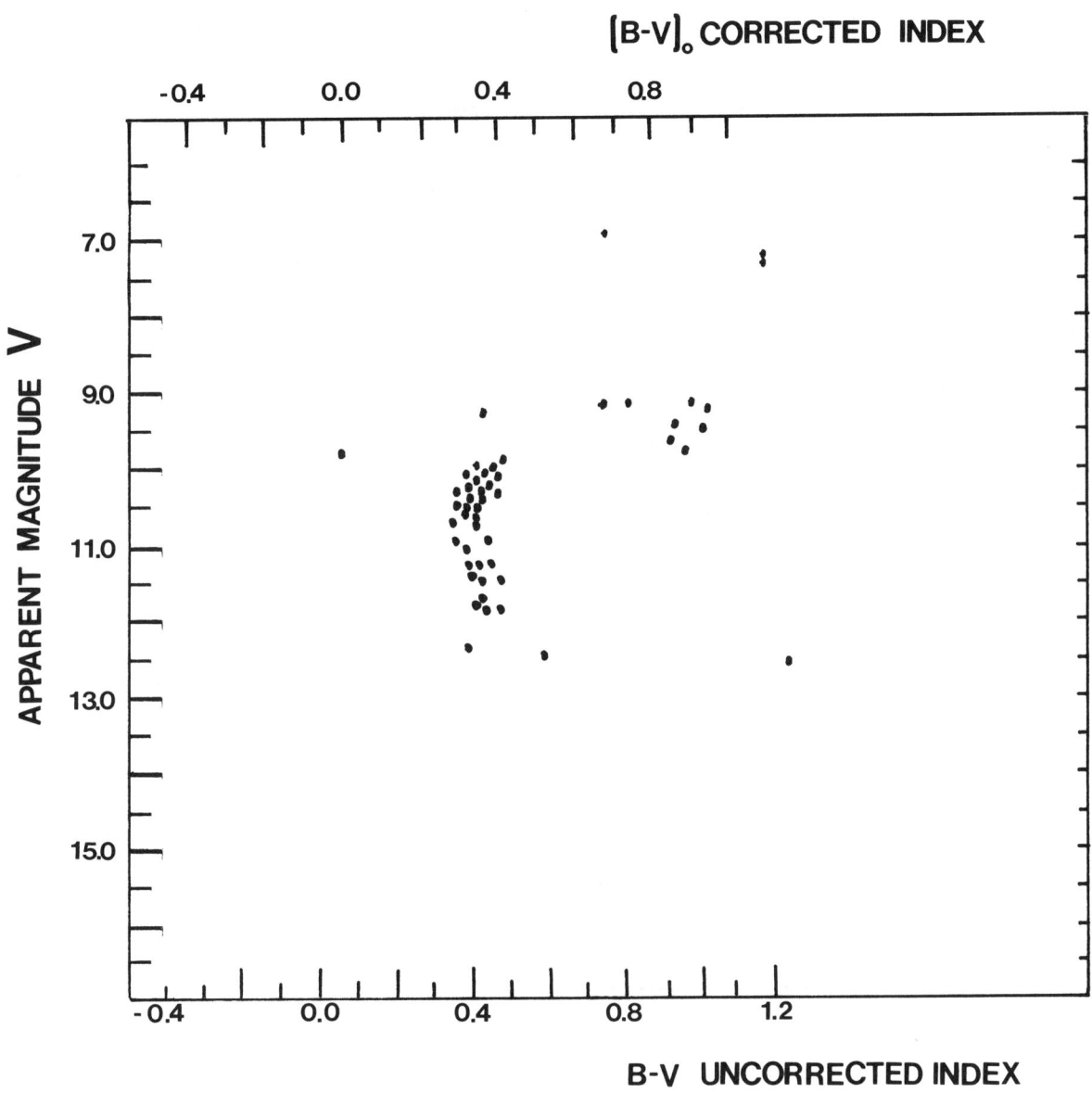

Fig 8: H-R diagram for NGC 752.

MEL 20 (∝ Per)

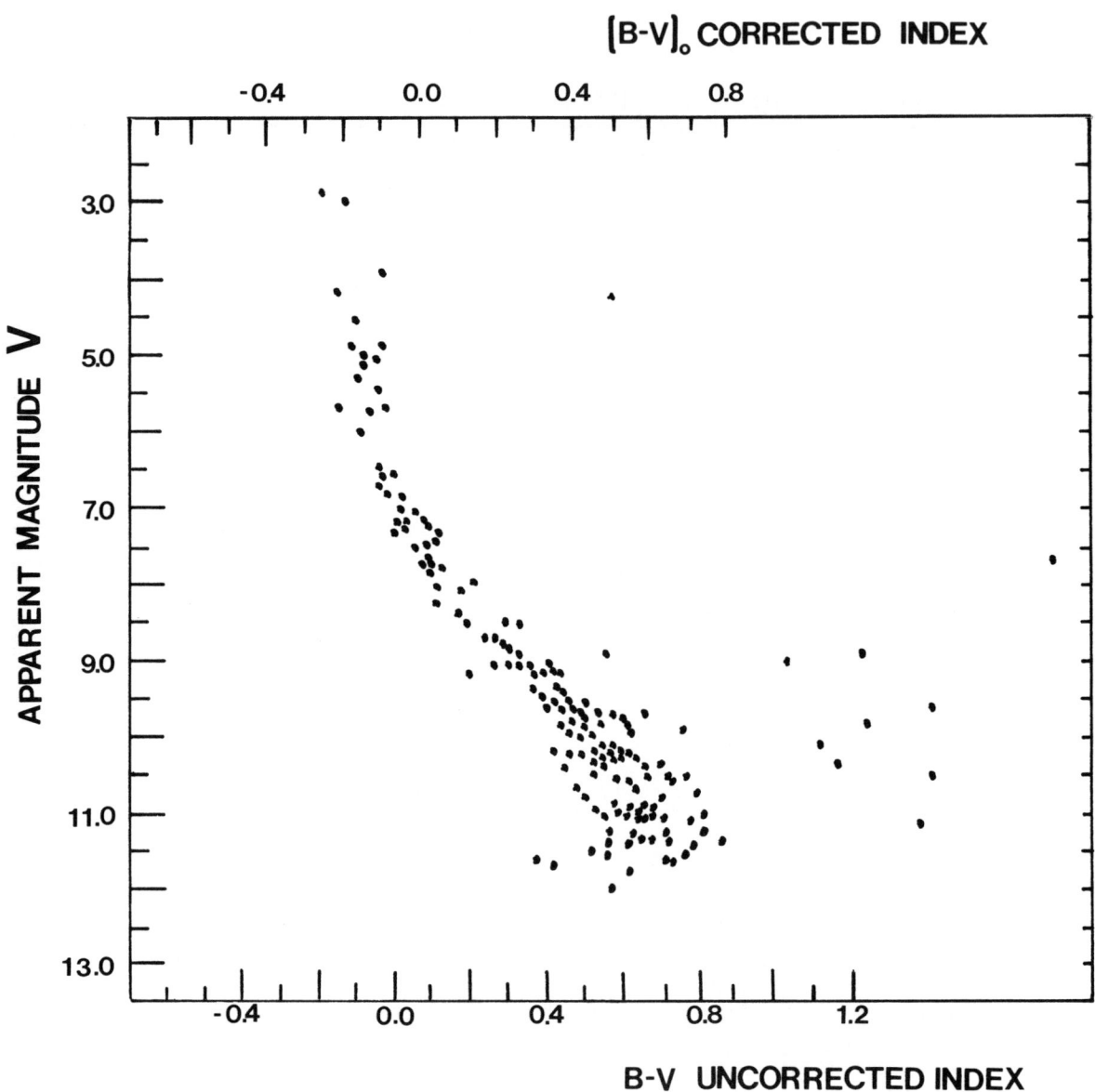

Fig 9: H-R diagram for α Persei.

Orion OB-1

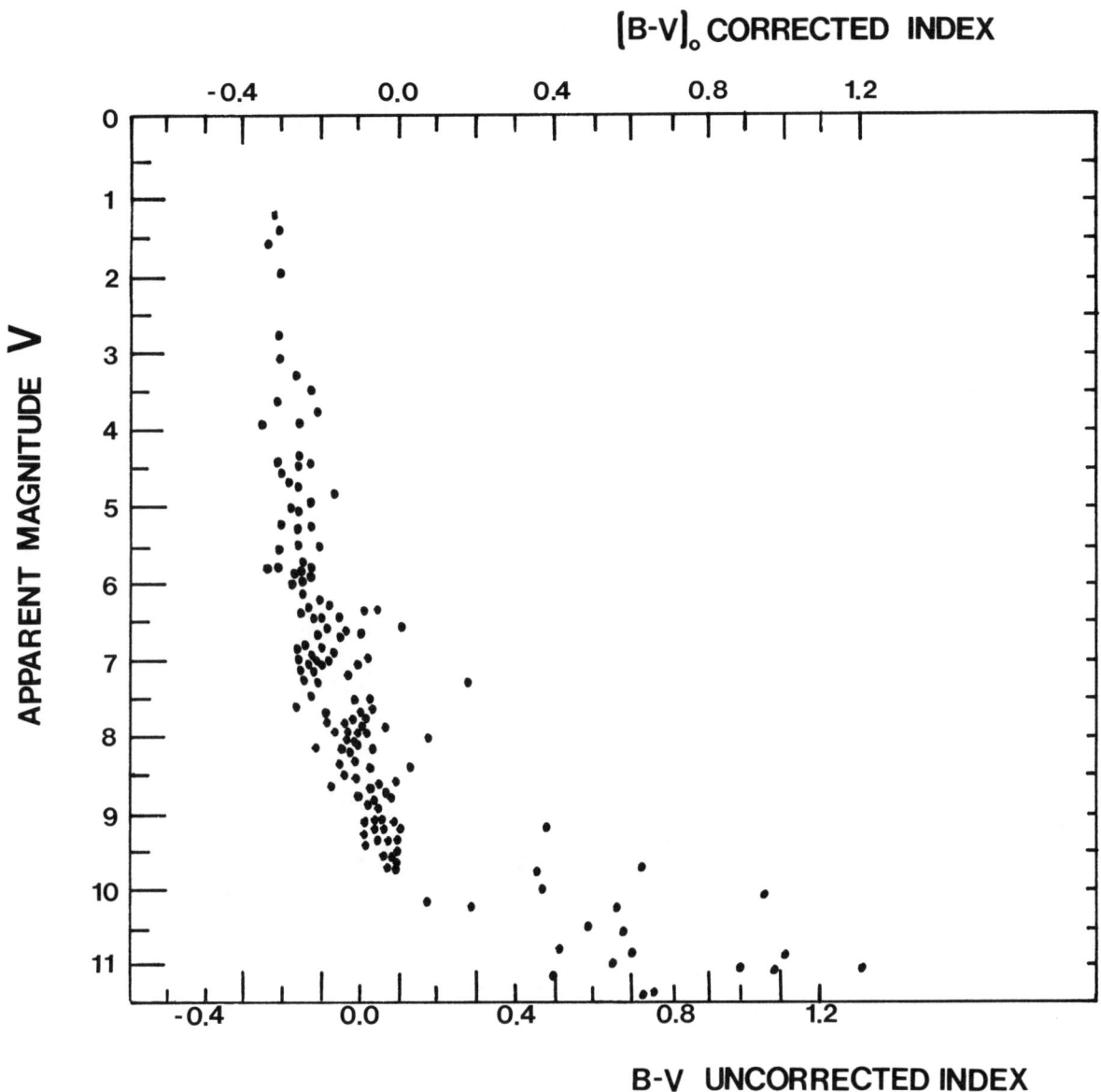

Fig 10: H-R diagram for Orion OB-1.

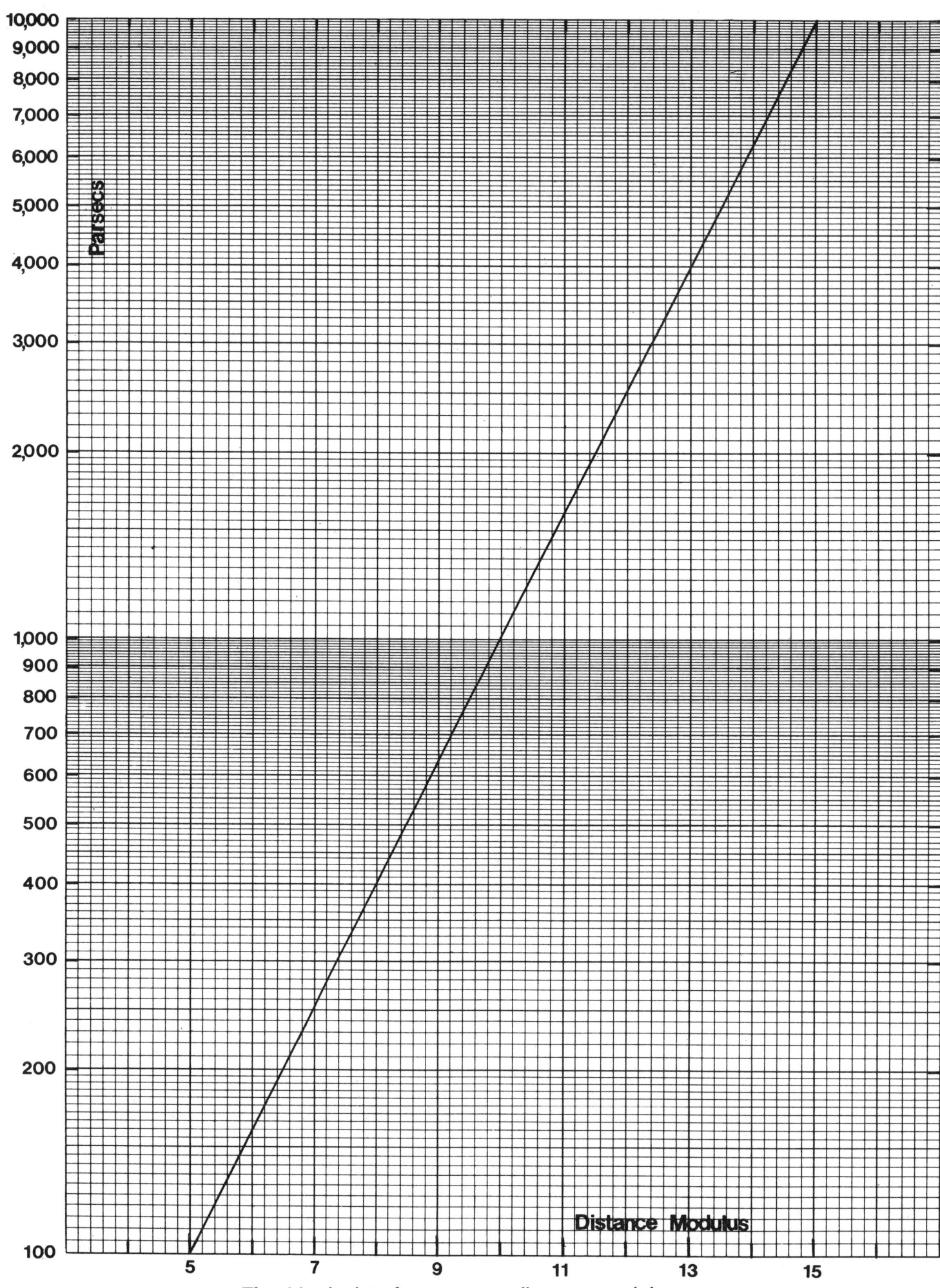

Fig. 11: A plot of parsecs vs. distance modulus.

THE PERIOD–LUMINOSITY RELATION

16

OBJECTIVES

After completing this exercise the student will be able to:

1. calculate the absolute magnitude for a cepheid variable with a known distance.
2. plot a period-luminosity diagram for classical cepheids.
3. use the period-luminosity relation to determine the distance to another galaxy.

STUDENT MATERIALS

mm ruler
calculator

LAB MATERIALS

photometric data for several cepheids (optional)

STUDENT REQUIREMENTS

This lab is to be done individually, without lab partners. After completing the exercise, turn in **Table I**, **Fig. 1**, and **Fig. 2**.

INTRODUCTION

In the previous lab the technique of main sequence fitting is used to determine the distance of several star clusters. Thus, if an astronomer can determine the distance to a star cluster which contains one or more cepheid variable stars they also know the distance to these cepheids. From the observed average magnitude of these stars and their known distance it is possible to calculate their absolute magnitudes. If this can be done for several cepheids a plot of absolute magnitude vs. log(**P**) can be made. This graph represents the period-luminos-ity relation for cepheids. Thus, if astronomers can observe a cepheid's pulsation period they can use this relation to find its absolute magnitude.

Since the apparent magnitude can be observed and the absolute magnitude is determined by observing the star's period, it is possible to determine the distance-modulus (m-M) for cepheids. The distance to any cepheid can be determined using the relation

$$log(D) = \frac{(m - M) + 5}{5}$$

The beauty is that by simply observing a cepheid's average apparent magnitude and period, its distance can be calculated. Because cepheids are giant yellow stars, they are extremely bright and can be observed over large distances. In fact, they are observed in several nearby galaxies. By using the period-luminosity relation the distance to these galaxies can be determined from observations of their cepheid variable stars.

During this exercise you will make a period-luminosity relation for cepheids in our galaxy. From this relation you will estimate the distance to another galaxy.

PROCEDURE

I. Calibration of Period-Luminosity Relation

1. In **Table I** some observations of cepheids in the star cluster χ Persei are listed. The technique of main sequence fitting gives a distance to χ Persei of about 2600 parsecs. Use this distance and the relation **M = m + 5 – 5 log(D)** to calculate the absolute magnitude, **M**, for each of these stars. Complete **Table I** with the results.

2. On **Fig. 1** make a plot of the absolute magnitude against the log(**P**) values for the four cepheids in **Table I**.

3. In **Table II** are data on eight additional cepheids which are found in six other star clusters. Their absolute magnitudes have been determined by the same method you just used in part 1, above. Plot their **M**s against their log(**P**)s on **Fig. 1**.

4. In order to best represent the period-luminosity relation, use a ruler to draw a best-fit straight line through the data points plotted on **Fig. 1**. This line should divide the data equally so that you have about the same number of data points above it as below it. Also, notice that the point in the upper right of this figure will help you obtain the proper slope for your line.

II. Distance Determination Using the P-L Relation

Table III gives data obtained for a cepheid in the Large Magellanic Cloud, a nearby irregular galaxy. Column 1 lists the time in fractional days of each observation. The second column gives the apparent magnitude measured at each time.

1. On **Fig. 2**, plot a light curve for the cepheid data in **Table III**. Notice that "maximum" refers to maximum brightness. Thus, the magnitude scale seems to be backwards from most other graphs you have seen.

2. Draw a free-hand best-fit curve that represents the data plotted. Make sure that your curve reaches the same maximum and minimum values for each cycle. From the light curve determine the time for each maximum. The difference in time is the pulsation period, **P**. Record your value of **P** in the space provided in **Fig. 2**.

3. Use a calculator to determine the value of log(**P**), and record the answer in **Fig. 1**. Look up this value of log(**P**) on the x-axis of **Fig. 1**. From the best-fit line determine the cepheid's absolute magnitude. In other words, at your log(**P**) value,

go straight up the graph to the best-fit line of the P-L relation and read off the corresponding absolute magnitude on the vertical axis. Record your answer in the space provided in **Fig. 2**.

4. From **Table III** calculate the average apparent magnitude, **m**. Record your results in the space provided in **Fig. 2**.

5. Use the apparent and absolute magnitudes to compute the distance modulus, **m-M**. Record your answer in **Fig. 2**.

6. Use the Distance vs. Distance Modulus graph in **Fig. 3** to determine the distance, **D**, to this cepheid. This is the distance to the Large Magellanic Cloud. Currently, the distance to the LMC is believed to be 57000 parsecs and 65000 parsecs. Record your answer in the space provided in **Fig. 2**.

TABLE I

Cepheids in χ Per

Star	Period (days)	log P	m	M
VY Persei	5.37	0.73	8.36	
V Persei	5.53	0.74	7.99	
VX Persei	10.89	1.04	7.56	
SZ Cassiopeiae	13.61	1.13	7.19	

TABLE II

Other Galactic Cepheids

	Period (days)	log P	M
EV Scuti	3.09	0.49	−2.90
CE Cassiopeiae A	5.14	0.71	−3.84
CF Cassiopeiae B	4.48	0.65	−3.78
DL Cassiopeiae	4.86	0.69	−3.64
U Sagittarii	6.73	0.83	−3.63
DL Cassiopeiae	8.00	0.90	−3.86
S Normae	9.75	0.99	−4.27
RS Puppis	41.40	1.62	−6.25

TABLE III

A Cepheid in the LMC

Time (days)	mag
1.28	15.83
1.37	15.95
1.56	15.59
1.84	15.26
2.16	15.20
2.33	15.23
2.67	15.32
3.20	15.41
3.98	15.51
4.17	15.56
4.22	15.63
4.54	15.70
5.20	15.84
5.38	15.84
5.94	15.85
6.04	15.93
6.31	15.61
6.50	15.30
6.92	15.19
7.45	15.33
7.88	15.39
8.65	15.53
8.83	15.56
8.88	15.64
9.21	15.70

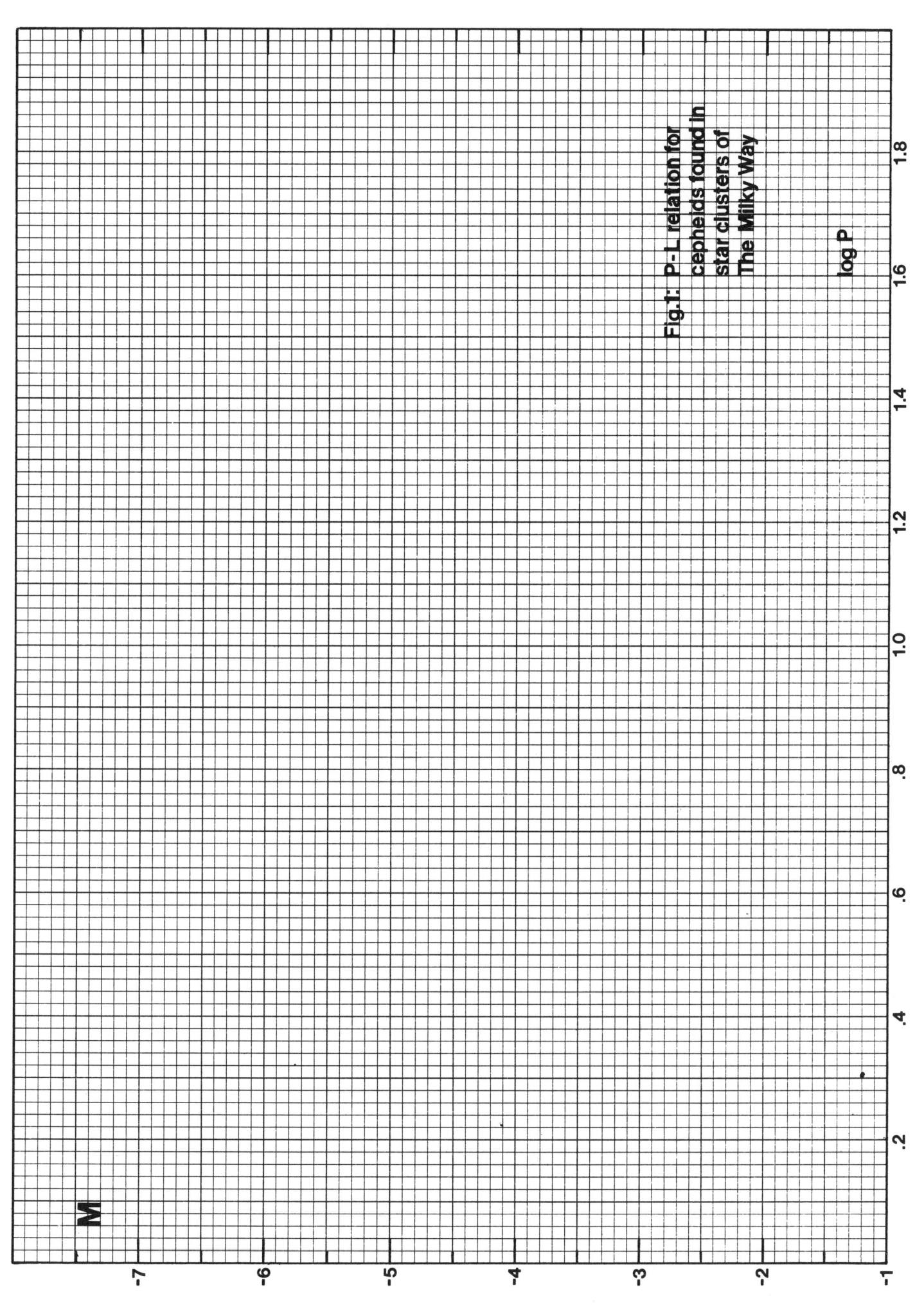

Fig.1: P - L relation for cepheids found in star clusters of The Milky Way

log P

M

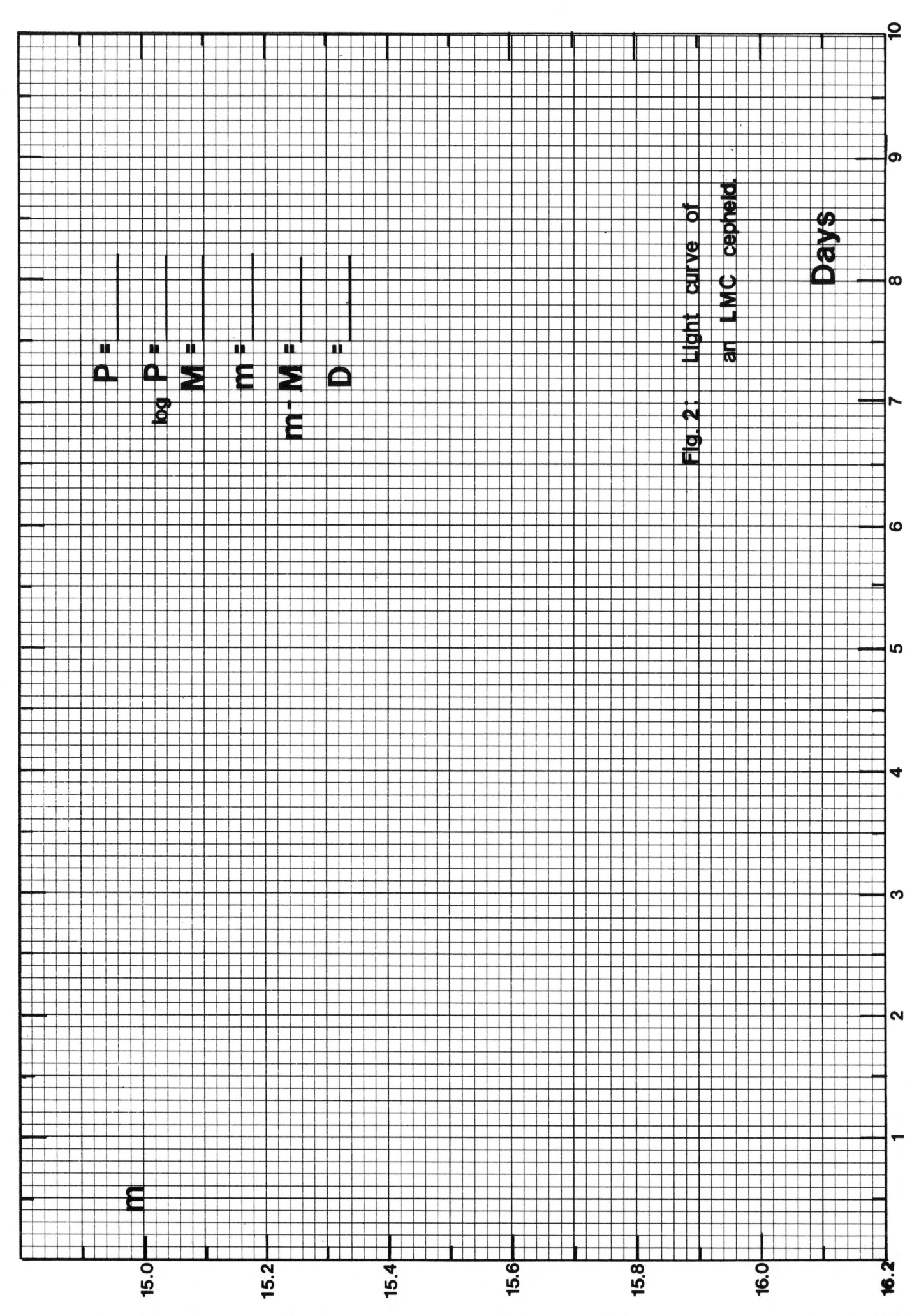

m

P =
log P =
M =
m =
m - M =
D =

Fig. 2: Light curve of
an LMC cepheid.

Days

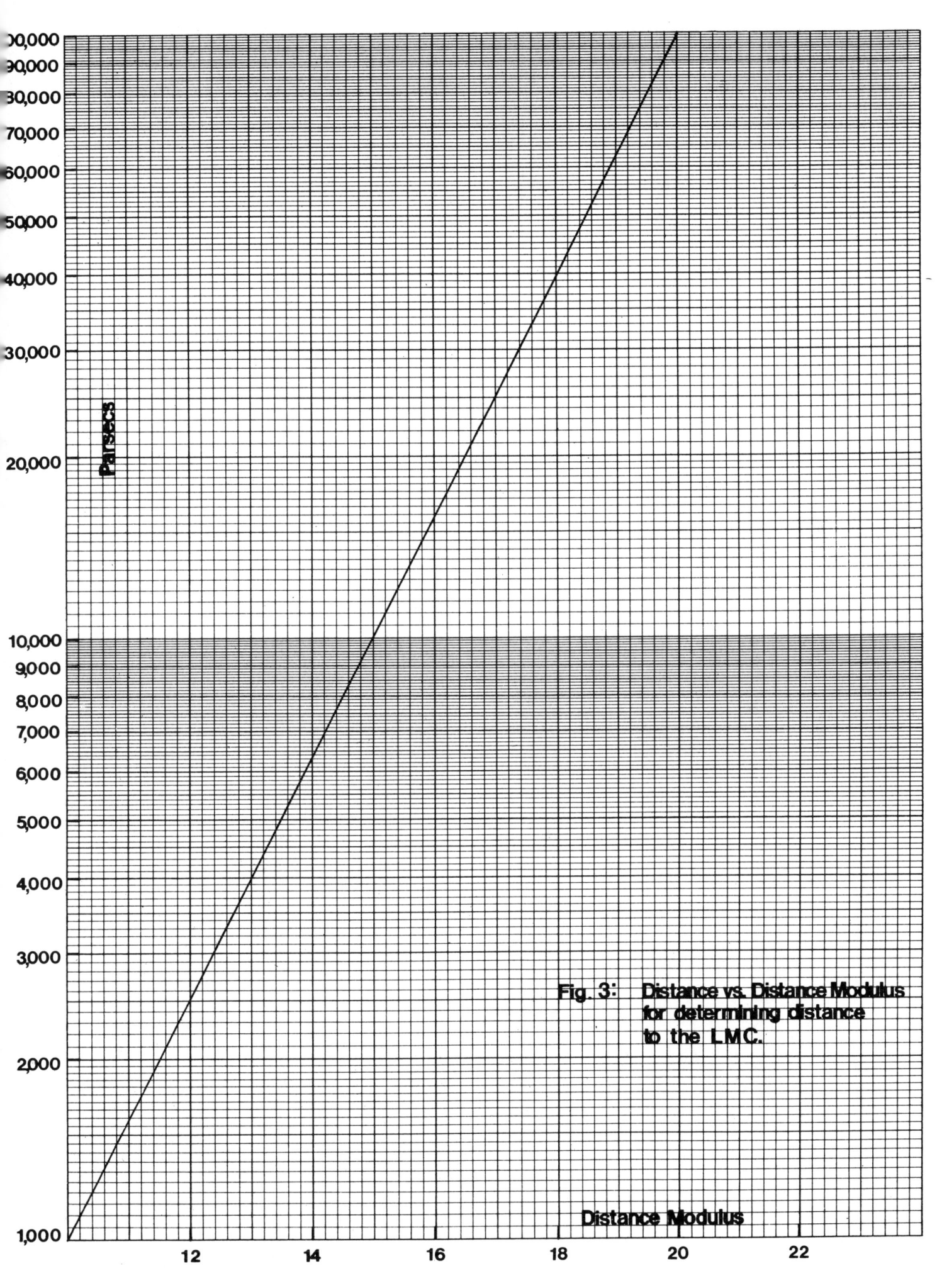

Fig. 3: Distance vs. Distance Modulus for determining distance to the LMC.

Parsecs

Distance Modulus

GALAXY CLASSIFICATION

OBJECTIVES

After completing this exercise the student will be able to:

1. classify galaxies into the major classes of spiral, elliptical, irregular, and peculiar.
2. estimate the distance to a cluster of galaxies given the distance to another cluster of galaxies.

STUDENT MATERIALS

pencil
calculator

LAB MATERIALS

Palomal Sky Survey Prints 0-1563 and 0-83
magnifying lens

STUDENT REQUIREMENTS

This lab is to be done individually, without lab partners. After completing the exercise, turn in **Table I**, **II**, **III**, and the answers to the questions.

INTRODUCTION

In this exercise you will learn to recognize spiral and elliptical galaxies along with a few less common types. This requires looking at a lot of different galaxies and making comparisons between them. You will examine galaxies in both the Virgo and Hercules galaxy clusters. Prints from the Palomar Sky Survey which contain photographs of these two clusters will be used for this purpose. *THESE PHOTOGRAPHS ARE EXPENSIVE AND EASILY DAMAGED. DO NOT WRITE ON THEM OR ON PAPER THAT IS ON TOP OF A PHOTOGRAPH* because an impression of your writing comes through the paper and appears on the print

below. It should be obvious that stray marks will become confused with the black star and galaxy images on the prints. When looking at a print do not have a pen or pencil in your hand because it will be tempting to place the pencil point on the print in order to point to a particular image.

PROCEDURE

1. Use a magnifier to examine all the galaxies on print number 0–1563. Classify each galaxy as an elliptical (**E**), spiral (**S**), irregular (**I**), or galaxies in collision (**C**) and place the letter designation of your answer in the column labeled *classification* in **Table I**.

2. The galaxies 1, 7, 8, and 23 are all spiral galaxies in the Virgo cluster. Since they are in the same cluster we can assume that they are all at the same distance from us. Any differences seen when comparing these galaxies to each other must be real effects.

   a. Estimate to a tenth of a mm the diameters of these three galaxies. Place your answer in **Table II** under the column labeled *Diameter*.

   b. Inspect these galaxies for relative brightness. Under the column labeled *rel. bright* place the number 1, 2, 3, or 4 by each galaxy, with 1 indicating the brightest galaxy and 4 representing the faintest galaxy.

   c. Rate the dominance of the nucleus on the scale of 1 to 4, with 1 being placed beside the galaxy which has the most dominant nucleus.

   d. Use the 1 to 4 scale again and note the strength of the spiral arms for each galaxy. Place your ratings in **Table II**.

3. Galaxies 1, 7, 8, 15, and 16 should have the same classification. Are they spiral or ellipticals?

4. Do galaxies 5, 9, 10, 11, 12, 13, and 14 have the same classification as the galaxies in 3? If so, why do they look different?

5. Sketch below the general form of a spiral galaxy viewed face-on (from above), and edge-on (from the side).

face-on   **edge-on**

6. Examine galaxies 17, 18, 19, and 20. These are specifically called **barred spirals**, because they have a central bar of stars with the arms extending from the bar's ends. Sketch below the face-on and edge-on views of barred spirals.

face-on   **edge-on**

7. The Hercules cluster of galaxies is located at the center of print 0-83. Since this cluster is farther away than the Virgo cluster the galaxies all look smaller. If it can be assumed that the large spiral galaxies in both clusters have the same average size, then the change in angular size (diameter) is an indicator of distance.

   a. Estimate to the nearest tenth of a mm the largest diameter of galaxies 1, 7, and 8 in the Virgo cluster. Record your measurements in **Table III**.

   b. Make the same type of measurements for three large spirals in the Hercules cluster and record your results in **Table III**.

   c. Calculate the average diameter of the large spirals in each cluster and record your answer at the bottom of each column. Let's assume that the average size of large spiral galaxies is the same throughout the universe. Thus, the difference between the average sizes in Virgo and Hercules must be caused by a difference in distance.

   d. Calculate how many times farther away the Hercules cluster is than the Virgo cluster by dividing the average diameter of the Virgo spirals by that of the Hercules spirals. Record your answer in the space provided below **Table III**.

   e. If the distance to the Virgo cluster is independently found to be 7×10^7 light years, what is the distance to the Hercules cluster? Write your answer in the space provided below **Table III**.

TABLE I

Classification of some galaxies in the Virgo Cluster.

GALAXY	CLASSIFICATION
1	
2	
3	
4	
5	
6	
7	
8	
9	
10	
11	
12	
13	
14	
15	

GALAXY	CLASSIFICATION
16	
17	
18	
19	
20	
21	
22	
23	
24	
25	
26	
27	
28	
29	
30	

TABLE II

GALAXY	DIAMETER (mm)	REL. BRIGHTNESS	DOMINANCE OF NUCLEUS	STRENGTH OF ARMS
1				
7				
8				
23				

TABLE III

Distance to Hercules Cluster.

VIRGO (mm)	HERCULES (mm)

average = _____   average = _____

distance ratio = _____

distance to Hercules Cluster = _____

HUBBLE'S LAW

OBJECTIVES

After completing this exercise the student will be able to:

1. measure the value of Δl for the calcium K and H lines with respect to a known reference line.
2. calculate the redshift velocity from the Δl values.
3. measure the angular size of a galaxy and use this to estimate its distance.
4. make a plot of velocity *vs* distance and determine the value of the Hubble constant.

STUDENT MATERIALS

pencil
mm scale
calculator

LAB MATERIALS

magnifying lenses
spare copies of *Sky and Telescope* reprint "Hubble's Law"
list of other galaxies' diameters and velocities (optional)

STUDENT REQUIREMENTS

This lab is to be completed individually, without lab partners. After completing the exercise, turn in **Tables I** and **II** and the Hubble's Law graph.

INTRODUCTION

In the previous lab the distance to the Hercules Cluster of galaxies was estimated based on the average angular size of large spiral galaxies. Similarly, it is possible to estimate the distances to large elliptical galaxies. Distance to the five galaxies in this lab exercise is calculated based on their average angular diameter.

Most astronomers believe that the universe began as a huge explosion called the "**Big Bang**." This explosive birth was first indicated from observations of galactic spectra. Absorption lines observed in these spectra were seen to be shifted to the red side of the positions expected for these lines. Astronomers interpret this as a Doppler shift caused by the galaxies racing away from the observer. The faster the galaxy recedes, the greater is the observed redshift. Hubble discovered that the redshift velocities were related to the distance of each galaxy in a linear fashion. In today's lab, you will make estimates of redshift velocities and galactic distances for several elliptical galaxies. These data will be used to confirm "**Hubble's Law**."

PROCEDURE

This lab uses photographs in the "*Sky and Telescope*" reprint "Hubble's Law" found inside the packet at the back of this manual. Please estimate all measurements in this lab to a tenth of a millimeter.

I. Scale of the Spectra

In one of the spectra, draw a line vertically through the centers of each of the two spectral lines labeled *a* (3888.7Å) and *g* (5015.7Å). These two spectral lines will serve to determine the scale of the photograph and as reference lines for measuring the Doppler shift.

Measure the distance in the spectrum, in mm, between the lines labeled *a* and *g*. Determine the wavelength difference, in angstroms, between these two lines by subtracting the wavelengths given above.

Finally, calculate the scale on the photograph in Å/mm by dividing the difference in Å by the separation in mm. Record this scale on **Table I**.

II. The Doppler Shift and the Recessional Velocities

1. The Doppler shift of the K and H lines of calcium in each galactic spectrum will give us the recessional velocity for each galaxy. Using the reference line labeled *a* in each spectrum, measure the distance to a tenth of a mm, from *a* to each K and H absorption line, and record these measurements in **Table I** for the column labeled $\Delta\lambda$ in mm.

2. Using the scale factor for each spectrum as determined in Part I, convert each K and H measurement from $\Delta\lambda$ in mm to $\Delta\lambda$ in Å by multiplying each K and H number by the scale factor. Record your values in **Table I**.

3. Since each of the K and H line shifts were measured from the reference line *a* (3888.7Å) and not the true rest wavelengths for K(3933.7Å) and H(3968.5Å), then $\Delta\lambda$ determined in step 2 needs a zero-point correction to get to the proper wavelengths. To do this, subtract 45.0Å from each $\Delta\lambda$ for the K line, and 79.8Å from each $\Delta\lambda$ for the H line, and record these new values in the corrected $\Delta\lambda$ in Å columns for K and H in **Table I**.

4. Calculate the recessional velocity of each galaxy according to the Doppler formula

   $V = (\Delta\lambda / \lambda)c$, where $c = 300,000$ km/sec.

   Do this for each K and H line measured. The rest wavelength λ in the denominator will either be 3933.7Å, if $\Delta\lambda$ for K is used in the numerator, or 3968.5Å, if $\Delta\lambda$ for H is used. Record your answers in **Table I**.

5. Finally, average the two velocities determined for each galaxy and record this average value in the last column in **Table I**. You should notice

that the two individual determinations of **V** do not agree perfectly. This disagreement indicates the approximate error in the averaged **V** values. So you can write **V** as 1200, or 52000, etc.

III. Scale of the Photograph

1. Measure the length of the line at the bottom of the galaxy photographs to the nearest tenth of a millimeter.

2. This line is known to be 150 seconds-of-arc long. Calculate the scale of the galaxy photographs in seconds-of-arc/mm by dividing 150 seconds-of-arc by your millimeter measurement obtained in step 1 above. Record the result at the top of **Table II**.

IV. Galaxy Distances

We will assume that the galaxies in each cluster as illustrated here are about the same average size; that is, they measure about 0.03 megaparsecs or about 100,000 light years in diameter. If we know their actual diameters, which we just assumed, their distances, *D*, can readily be determined from the following:

$$D = \frac{(0.03)\,(206,265)}{d} \qquad (1)$$

where *d* is the angular size in arc seconds, and 206,265 is the number of second-of-arc in a radian.

1. Measure the linear diameter, *d*, of each image accurately to tenths of a millimeter. If the image is elliptical, use the average of its shortest and longest diameters. Record your answer in **Table II**.

2. Convert each diameter, *d*, from mm to seconds-of-arc by multiplying by the scale factor as determined in part III and record your results in **Table II**.

3. Use equation **1** and determine the distance, *D*, in megaparsecs (Mpc) for each galaxy. Record these values in **Table II**.

V. Plotting the Velocity-Distance Relationship and Determining Hubble's Constant

1. On the graph paper provided on page 16-9, plot the average redshift velocities (**V**) *vs* the calculated distances (**D**) for each cluster of galaxies.

2. Starting from the origin of the graph draw a best-fit straight line through the plotted points. This straight line will represent the Hubble relationship **V = HD**, where **V** = recessional velocity, **H** = Hubble's constant, and **D** = distance. Notice this is the equation of a straight line **y = mx + b**, where **b** = 0. Thus **H** is the slope of the line you drew on the graph. Find the slope of the line to determine the value of Hubble's constant in km/sec/Mpc units. Record your value of **H** in the space provided at the bottom of **Table II**.

3. Because the Hubble constant represents the present-day rate of the universe's expansion, we can determine, to a first approximation, the age of the universe by taking the reciprocal of Hubble's constant,

$$\textbf{\textit{Age of Universe}} = \textbf{\textit{T}} = \frac{\textbf{\textit{1}}}{\textbf{\textit{H}}} \times \textbf{\textit{10}}^{12} \qquad (2)$$

    where the 10^{12} converts the time units from seconds to years.

    From your value of **H** calculate the age of the universe in years using **eq. (2)**. Record your results in the space provided at the bottom of **Table II**.

4. A very simple approximation of the universe's radius can be obtained from the following relationship,

$$\textbf{\textit{R = c/H}} \qquad (3)$$

    This represents the distance at which the straight-line Hubble Law would predict a radial velocity equal to the speed of light. Using $c = 3 \times 10^5$ km/sec and your value for **H**, calculate the radius of the universe in Mpc and record your answer in the space provided at the bottom of **Table II**.

TABLE I

Scale of Galaxy Spectra = _____

GALAXY in	$\Delta\lambda$ in mm		$\Delta\lambda$ in Å		corrected $\Delta\lambda$		recessional velocities		average velocity in km/sec.
	K	H	K	H	K	H	V_K	V_H	V
Virgo									
Ursa Minor									
Corona Borealis									
Bootes									
Hydra									

TABLE II

Scale of Galaxy Photographs = _____

GALAXY PHOTOGRAPH	d in mm	d in arcsec	D in Mpc
Virgo			
Ursa Major			
Corona Borealis			
Bootes			
Hydra			

H = _____

Age of Universe = _____

Radius of Universe = _____

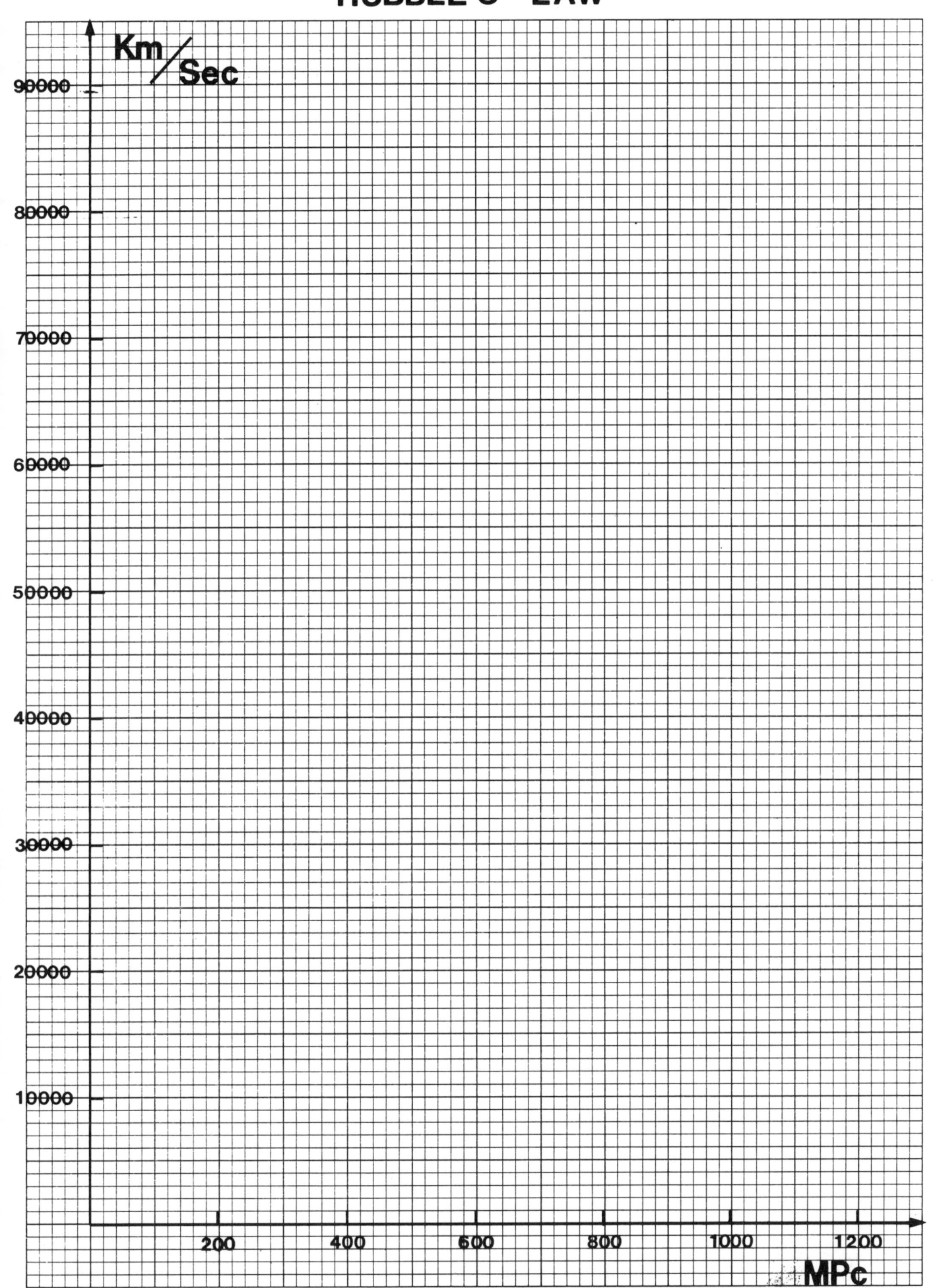

HUBBLE'S LAW

OBSERVING EXERCISE— STAR TRAIL PHOTOGRAPHY

OBJECTIVES

After completing this exercise the student will be able to:

1. locate the celestial north pole and equator.
2. use a camera to photograph star trails.

STUDENT MATERIALS

a camera which can take time exposures
roll of 400-speed color print film
tripod
cable release
clipboard (or some other writing surface)
flashlight

OBSERVATORY MATERIALS

same as above (minus the film, for students who do not have photo equipment)

STUDENT REQUIREMENTS

This observing laboratory is to be completed at an observing session or under the supervision of a lab instructor. After making the observations, turn in the answers to the questions, your observation data table, and **Figs. 1** and **2** with photographs attached.

INTRODUCTION

As the Earth rotates on its axis it gives the stars an apparent motion from east to west. If a camera is used to make a time exposure of the night sky the star images appear as short lines or curves. Stars near the celestial equator will move in straight lines and stars nearer to the celestial poles will move in a circle centered on one of the celestial poles.

In this project you will take photographs of star trails in two different areas of the sky, the celestial north pole, and the celestial equator.

PROCEDURE

Be sure to choose a moonless night because bright moonlight will fog your film. It is also best to find an observing site which is relatively dark. However, some students have successfully taken star trail photographs from suburban locations.

1. Load the camera with a roll of 400-speed color print film.

2. Mount the camera to a tripod. If a tripod is not available, set the camera on a portable table or a car roof and prop it up with some books or magazines.

3. Use a street map or compass to locate north.

4. Set shutter speed on **B** (bulb) to take a time exposure.

5. Set the f-stop ring to its smallest number (1.5, 1.8, 3.5, etc.) so that the lens is wide open. If you are in a suburban location set the f-stop at 5.6.

6. Focus for infinity.

7. Attach the cable-release to the camera.

8. Point the camera to the north and aim the lens so that the northern horizon is along the bottom edge of the viewfinder. The camera should now be pointing more or less toward the celestial north pole.

9. Fill out the information requested in the data table.

10. Start the exposure and record the starting time.

11. Expose the film for about 20 minutes. During this time, make sure stray light does not strike the camera and do not touch the camera. If you are in a suburban location, expose the film for only 10 minutes.

12. Close the shutter and record the time and exposure length in the Data Table. Also record comments, such as clouds passed by during exposure, car lights may have shone into camera, etc. You may want to try several more exposures in this area of the sky to be sure you have a good photo of the polar region.

13. Repeat steps 5 through 12 with the camera aimed at the celestial equator. To locate the equator turn the camera to the south and aim it about 50° or 55° above the southern horizon.

14. Mount a photo from each area of the sky in the spaces provided on **Figs. 1** and **2**. Fill in the requested information about each photo.

Turn in the **Data Table**, **Figs. 1** and **2**, and your answers to the questions on page 17-3 by the end of the lab.

Questions

1. If you look carefully at your photographs you can see that the stars have color. List below the stellar colors seen on your star trail photographs.

2. Compare your photographs of the north celestial pole and the celestial equator. Below make a sketch of how the star trails should appear on a photo taken with your camera pointed at the zenith.

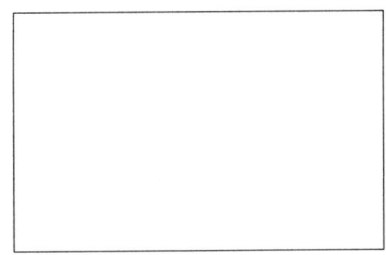

3. If you pointed your camera at the southern horizon, how would the trails appear?

4. Would the south celestial pole be in the photo of the southern horizon? Why or why not?

DATA TABLE

Star Trail Photography

Date: _____   Lens Focal Length: _____

Film Type: _____   Film Speed: _____

frame number	subject	f-stop	start time	stop time	exposure length	comments
1						
2						
3						
4						
5						
6						
7						
8						
9						
10						
11						
12						
13						
14						
15						
16						
17						
18						
19						
20						
21						
22						
23						
24						

WILSON

NAME: ______________________________

SECTION: ______________________________

Place photo of

North Celestial Pole

in this space

Date taken: ______________________

Exposure time: ______________________

Lens focal length: ______________________

Fig. 1: Student photograph of circumpolar star trails.

Place photo of

Celestial Equator

in this space

Date taken: _____

Exposure time: _____

Lens focal length: _____

Fig. 2: Student photograph of equatorial star trails.

OBSERVING EXERCISE— LUNAR PHOTOGRAPHY

OBJECTIVES

After completing this observational project the student will be able to:

1. point a telescope at the moon.
2. photograph the moon and keep records of each exposure.
3. identify by name some lunar features visible on their photograph.
4. measure the actual diameter of lunar features visible on the photograph.

STUDENT MATERIALS

one roll of 400 speed 35mm color print film (12- or 24-exposure) **or** one 3-½ floppy disk — (call instructor to see whether film or disk will be used)

OBSERVATORY MATERIALS

equatorial telescope with clock drive and eyepieces
35mm camera with cable release, T-ring, and other telescope mounting hardware

STUDENT REQUIREMENTS

These observations are to be made at a photographic observing session under the direction of a lab instructor. After getting the photos developed, turn in the **Photographic Data Table** and **Fig. 1** with one of your lunar photos attached.

PROCEDURE

1. Buy a roll of color print 35mm film with 12- or 24- exposures and a speed of 400 (ISO = 400) **or** one 3-½ floppy disk .

2. Load your camera with film (camera provided by the instructor).

3. Fill out information at the top of the Photographic Data Table.

4. Mount a T-ring onto the camera body. (**Note:** Each camera company has different lens mounts and your T-ring must be made for the camera model you are using.)

5. Screw an extension tube onto the T-ring of the camera and mount the camera to the telescope.

6. Aim the telescope at the moon. Be sure to lock the declination and right ascension axis after the moon is centered. This will help keep the telescope aimed at the object and make it more difficult to accidentally bump it off.

7. Focus the telescope very carefully. If the moon is not well focused you cannot get good photographs. This is not trivial and may take some practice.

8. Mount a cable release in the threaded hole provided on the camera. This is usually in the center of the shutter-release button.

9. So that you can concentrate on what you are doing, let a partner record your exposures on the log sheet.

10. Cock the camera and depress the plunger at the end of the cable release to expose the film. Make an exposure with each of the shutter speeds the camera provides. Record each exposure in the data table.

11. Remove the camera from the telescope. Rewind the film and remove it from the camera.

12. Let your partner take photographs while you record their exposures.

13. Have your film developed at a commercial photographic lab.

LUNAR FEATURES AND THEIR SIZE

1. You will need to use the Lunar Map in the packet at the back of this manual. In order to learn how to use the selenographic coordinate grid, refer to its description in part A of the lab *Lunar Features* in this book on page 7-1 .

2. Orient your photograph so that it corresponds to the map. The best method is to try and match the large maria and the heavily cratered southern hemisphere. Usually the south is located at the top and the illuminated portion of the moon is to the left.

3. Tape, staple, glue, or in some other reasonable way attach the photo to **Fig. 1** with the moon's south pole at the top and its eastern limb to the left.

4. On the bottom of **Fig. 1** state the phase of the moon in the photograph, the date it was taken, the telescope and eyepiece used, and the exposure time.

5. Locate on your photo as many of the features listed in **Table I** as you can. Use a ballpoint pen and place these feature numbers (given in the table) beside them or on top of them on your photograph. Although this makes the photo look ugly, you will enjoy finding these features on a photo you have personally taken.

6. Determine the scale of your photograph by measuring the north and south diameter of the moon's image in millimeters. Record this measurement in the space provided on **Fig. 1**.

7. The scale of your photo can be calculated in units of km/mm by dividing the moon's actual diameter of 3476 km by your millimeter measurement. Thus

$$SCALE = \frac{3476\ km}{d},$$

where d is the diameter of the moon in millimeters on your photograph.

Record the scale of your photo in the space provided in **Fig. 1**.

This scale factor is like a map scale. If you measure some distance in millimeters between two points on your photograph, you can determine their actual separation on the moon by multiplying the measured distance by the scale factor.

8. Now determine the diameter of one mare and one crater which you identified in step 5 above. State the names of the mare and crater you have chosen in the spaces provided in **Fig. 1**. Use a millimeter scale to measure the average diameter of these two features and record the results in the blanks. Multiply your scale factor by the millimeter measurements and estimate their actual diameters in kilometers. Record your answers in the spaces in **Fig. 1**.

Turn in **Table II** and **Fig. 1** within two weeks after you take your photos or by the last day of lab, whichever comes first.

TABLE I

Table of Lunar Features

1. Mare Crisium
2. Mare Frigoris
3. Mare Serenitatis
4. MareTranquillitatis
5. Mare Nectaris
6. Mare Nubrium
7. Mare Imbrium
8. Oceanus Procellarum
9. Appennine Mountains
10. Albalegnium
11. Aristoteles
12. Eudoxus
13. Copernicus
14. Archimedes
15. Plato

TABLE II

Photographic Data Table

Name: _____   Film type: _____

U. T. Date: _____   Film speed: _____

Telescope and camera used: _____

FRAME	EXPOSURE	SUBJECT	EYEPIECE
1			
2			
3			
4			
5			
6			
7			
8			
9			
10			
11			
12			
13			
14			
15			
16			
17			
18			
19			
20			
21			
22			
23			
24			

NAME: ____________________

SECTION: ____________________

Place photo
in this space

Phase of Moon: ____________________

Date: ____________________

Exposure time: ____________________

Telescope used: ____________________

Diameter of Moon: ____________________

Scale: ____________________

Mare: ____________________

Diameter in mm = ____________________

Diameter in km = ____________________

Crater: ____________________

Diameter in mm = ____________________

Diameter in km = ____________________

Fig. 1: Student photograph of the moon.

OBSERVING EXERCISE— PLANETARY PHOTOGRAPHY

OBJECTIVES

After completing this observational project the student will be able to:

1. point a telescope at a bright star or planet using a finder scope.
2. focus a telescope and camera combination.
3. load a 35mm camera.
4. photograph a bright planet and keep records of each exposure.

STUDENT MATERIALS

one 12- or 24-exposure roll of 400 speed 35mm color print film

OBSERVATORY MATERIALS

equatorial telescope with clock drive and eyepieces
35mm camera with cable release, T-ring, and other telescope mounting hardware

STUDENT REQUIREMENTS

These observations are to be made at a photography observing session under the direction of a lab instructor. After getting the photos developed, turn in your **Photographic Data Table** and **Fig. 1** with one of your planetary photos attached.

PROCEDURE

1. Buy a roll of color print 35mm film with 12 exposures. This film should have an ISO (speed number) of 400 or faster.

2. Load your camera with film (camera provided by the instructor).

3. Fill out information at the top of the Photographic Data Table.

4. Mount a T-ring onto the camera body. (**Note:** Each camera company has different lens mounts and your T-ring must be made for the camera model you are using.)

5. Place an eyepiece into the eyepiece holder of the telescope and lock it in place with the little set screw. This will prevent the eyepiece from falling out when you are using the telescope.

6. Place an extension tube over the eyepiece and screw it into place using the threads on the outside edge of the eyepiece holder and the inside edge of the extension tube.

7. Aim the telescope at the chosen planet. Be sure to lock the declination and right ascension axis. This will help keep the telescope aimed at the object and make it more difficult to accidentally bump it off.

8. Focus the telescope very carefully. If the planet is not well focused you cannot get good photographs. This is not trivial and may take some practice.

9. Mount a cable release in the threaded hole provided on the camera. This is usually in the center of the shutter-release button.

10. So that you can concentrate on what you are doing, let a partner record your exposures on the log sheet.

11. Cock the camera and depress the plunger at the end of the cable release. Expose the film for 5 seconds and release the plunger.

12. Repeat step 11 for the following exposure times: 4 sec, 3 sec, 2 sec, 1 sec, ½ sec, ¼ sec, ⅛ sec, 1/30 sec, 1/60 sec. Be careful to have your partner

record each exposure, even mistakes, so that you will be able to figure out later which exposure was the best.

13. Remove the camera from the telescope. Rewind the film and remove it from the camera.

14. Let your partner take his photographs while you record his exposures.

15. Have your film developed at a commercial photographic lab. Be sure to tell them that the photos are astronomical and the little dots are important.

HOW TO FIND THE BEST EXPOSURE

When your prints come back from the photo lab, you need to find the best one and its exposure time. This should be done using the negatives instead of the prints.

1. Locate the frame numbers along the bottom edge of each frame (1, 1A, 2, 2A, etc.).

2. Since your first exposure was for 5 seconds, the first dark black blob near frame 1 or 2 should be your first shot. Use your data table to identify each exposure on the negatives.

3. Compare the negatives to the prints to correlate which prints come from which frames. You may find that not all frames were printed.

4. When the best print is identified, look up its exposure time in the Photographic Data Table.

Turn in the **Data Table** and **Fig. 1** within two weeks after you take the photos or by the last day of lab, whichever comes first.

NAME: _____

SECTION: _____

Photographic Data Table

U. T. Date: _____   Film type: _____

Telescope and camera used: _____   Film speed: _____

FRAME	SUBJECT	EXPOSURE	EYEPIECE
1			
2			
3			
4			
5			
6			
7			
8			
9			
10			
11			
12			
13			
14			
15			
16			
17			
18			
19			
20			
21			
22			
23			
24			

NAME: ______________________________

SECTION: ______________________________

Place photo

in this space

Planet photographed: ______________________

Exposure time: ______________________

Telescope used: ______________________

Eyepiece focal length: ______________________

Fig. 1: Student photograph of a planet.

OBSERVING EXERCISE— STELLAR MAGNITUDES AND COLORS

22

OBJECTIVES

After completing this observational project the student will be able to:

1. identify in the sky the constellations used in this lab.
2. estimate stellar magnitudes.
3. observe the colors of bright stars.

STUDENT MATERIALS

current issue of *Sky and Telescope* or *Astronomy* magazine
small flashlight or penlight
binoculars (optional)

OBSERVATORY MATERIALS

same as above

STUDENT REQUIREMENTS

These observations are to be made individually or with partners (two people, not groups). Observing is to be done during an observing session under the direction of a lab instructor. After completing the observations, turn in your five constellation pages on which you made the observations.

INTRODUCTION

A basic knowledge of the constellations gives you a sense of satisfaction and an appreciation of the night sky. Learning the names of stars and constellations makes them seem more friendly and less confusing.

The first thing you will notice about the stars is that they are of different brightness. A Greek astronomer named Hipparchus classified the stars according to their apparent brightness. All the brightest stars were considered first class or first magnitude. The next fainter group was called second magnitude. This ranking continued to sixth magnitude, which are stars barely visible in a dark sky. This scheme became so common in astronomical writings that modern-day astronomers still use the magnitude system of Hipparchus.

Modern astronomers have developed a mathematical relation for calculating apparent magnitudes. This equation is stated as follows:

$$m_1 - m_2 = -2.5 \log \frac{b_1}{b_2}$$

The equation above states that the magnitude difference between two stars of different brightness is related to the logarithm of their brightness ratio. This relation allows astronomers to calculate fractional magnitudes such as 2.6 or 5.1, and they are not restricted to a whole-number magnitude scale of 1, 2, 3, etc. Also, a mathematical formula allows the determination of magnitudes brighter than first magnitude and fainter than sixth. In fact, very bright objects can have negative magnitudes. Venus can be as bright as –4.4 magnitude. The faintest stars visible in large telescopes have a brightness of about 23rd magnitude. As you can see, a mathematical expression of the magnitude scale is extremely useful to astronomers.

In addition to stellar brightness an observer can also see that some stars appear blue while others seem more yellow or red in color. This color difference is best seen in the brightest stars or with some optical aid such as binoculars or a small telescope. Astronomers use star colors to classify stars according to their surface temperature. Blue stars have temperatures greater than 10,000K°. Stars similar to the Sun appear to be yellow and have temperatures around 5000K° to 6000K°. The coolest stars have temperatures around 3000K° and appear red in color. By simply making careful observations of the stars, their brightness and temperature can be determined.

In this observing project you will attempt to estimate the magnitude and color for several naked-eye stars. To locate these stars you will be required to learn the constellations in which they can be found. This is not difficult but it may require making several attempts at constellation identification.

PROCEDURE

I. Using a Star Map

You may need to buy a current copy of *Sky and Telescope* or *Astronomy* magazine. In the center of these magazines is a star map for the sky currently visible to someone in the northern hemisphere. These charts are drawn for the early evening sky. The actual times are given on the chart itself. However, you should have no problem using the chart at any convenient time between sunset and about 11:00 P.M. or so.

All star charts are made to be held overhead with north on the chart oriented toward the observer's northern horizon. The chart is now in a position such that the actual stars in the sky match their respective positions on the chart. One last reference point is the observer's zenith, or the point directly overhead. On the chart, the zenith is the center of the chart. **Note:** this does *not* correspond to the north celestial pole.

At the back of this lab you have several star charts of individual constellations. Use the magazine chart to locate the current seasonal constellations as listed in **Table I**. This may take several attempts on different nights. You will probably be most successful if you pick a night when the moon is not bright (i.e., waxing crescent phases, or any time after full moon).

II. Estimating Magnitudes and Colors

After you can locate each of the constellations for which you have been given a chart, it is time to take a more detailed look at each constellation. Each chart at the back of this lab is oriented like the all-sky chart used already. You now hold it overhead with north to the north horizon. Each chart has a magnitude limit of 5th magnitude. Stars brighter than 4.5 have their proper names or Greek-letter names labeled.

At the bottom of each chart is a list of several stars within the constellation. Find each of these stars in the sky. If it is hazy, or the sky is too bright, you may not be able to see the faintest stars shown.

By now you have noticed that some of these stars do not have a magnitude and/or a color listed. It is your job to complete the listings by filling in the blanks from your own observations. Magnitude estimates are made by comparing the unknown star's brightness to the brightness of the stars whose magnitudes are listed. If the unknown seems to have a brightness that is between two known magnitudes, then give it a magnitude value that is between the two known values.

Observation of stellar color can only be done for the brightest stars. You are only expected to give a qualitative color such as red, yellow, or blue. Again, you must compare the colors of known stars to the unknowns in order to determine their color. A pair of binoculars may be useful for color estimates but they are not necessary.

Turn in your completed charts on or before the last day of lab.

Seasonal List of Constellations

SEASON	CONSTELLATION
Autumn	Lyra Cygnus Aquila Cassiopeia Pegasus
Winter	Taurus Orion Canis Major Auriga Gemini
Spring	Gemini Leo Corvus Ursa Major Bootes
Summer	Bootes Scorpius Lyra Cygnus Aquila

Lyra

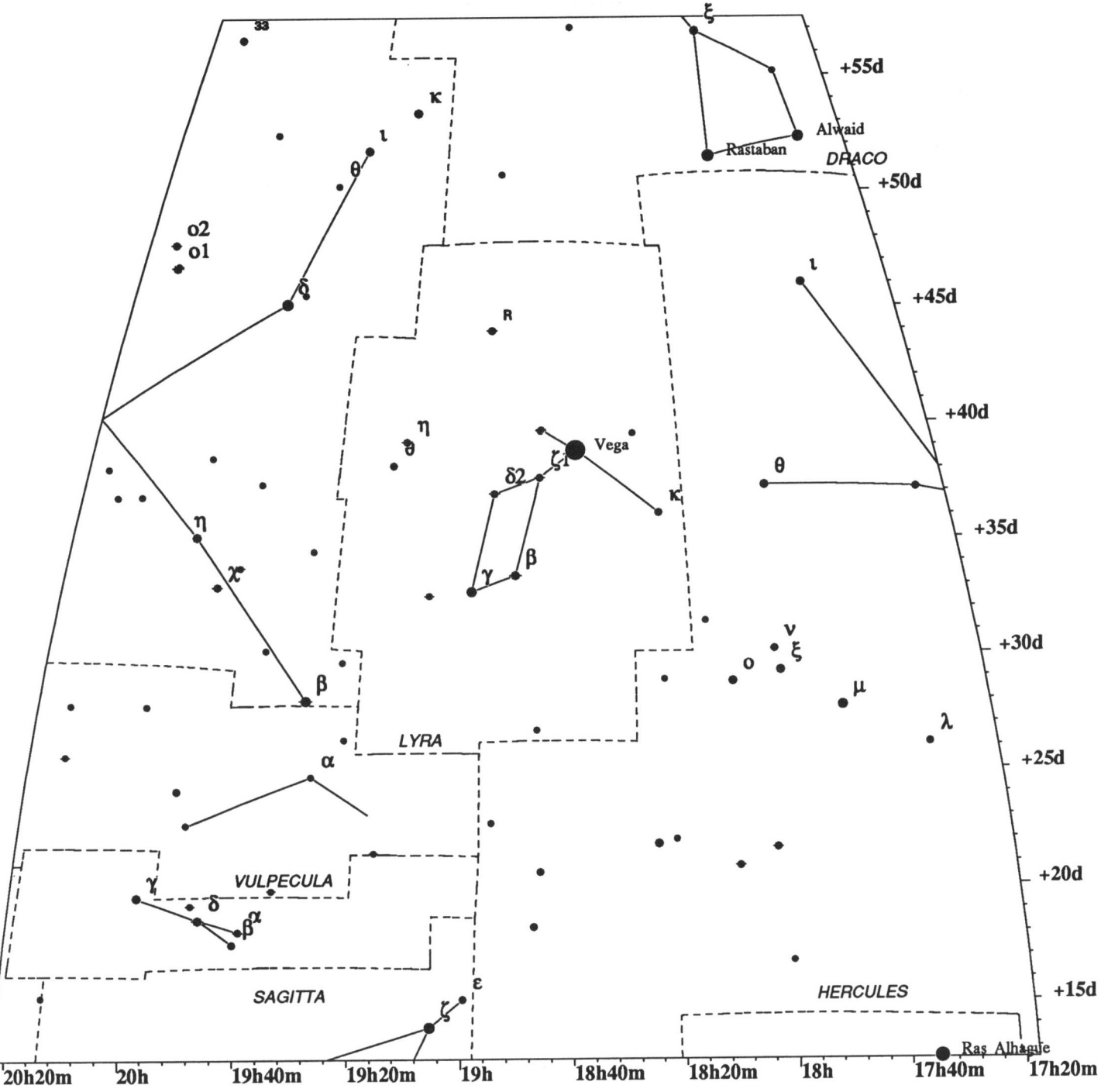

Observe the constellation and fill in the missing magnitudes and colors.

Star	Mag	Color
Vega	0.0	
ζ¹ Lyr	4.4	blue
δ² Lyr	4.3	red
α Lyr	3.2	blue
β Lyr		blue

Star	Mag	Color
κ Lyr	4.3	red
η Lyr		blue
θ Lyr	4.4	yellow
β Cyg	3.2	blue

Cygnus

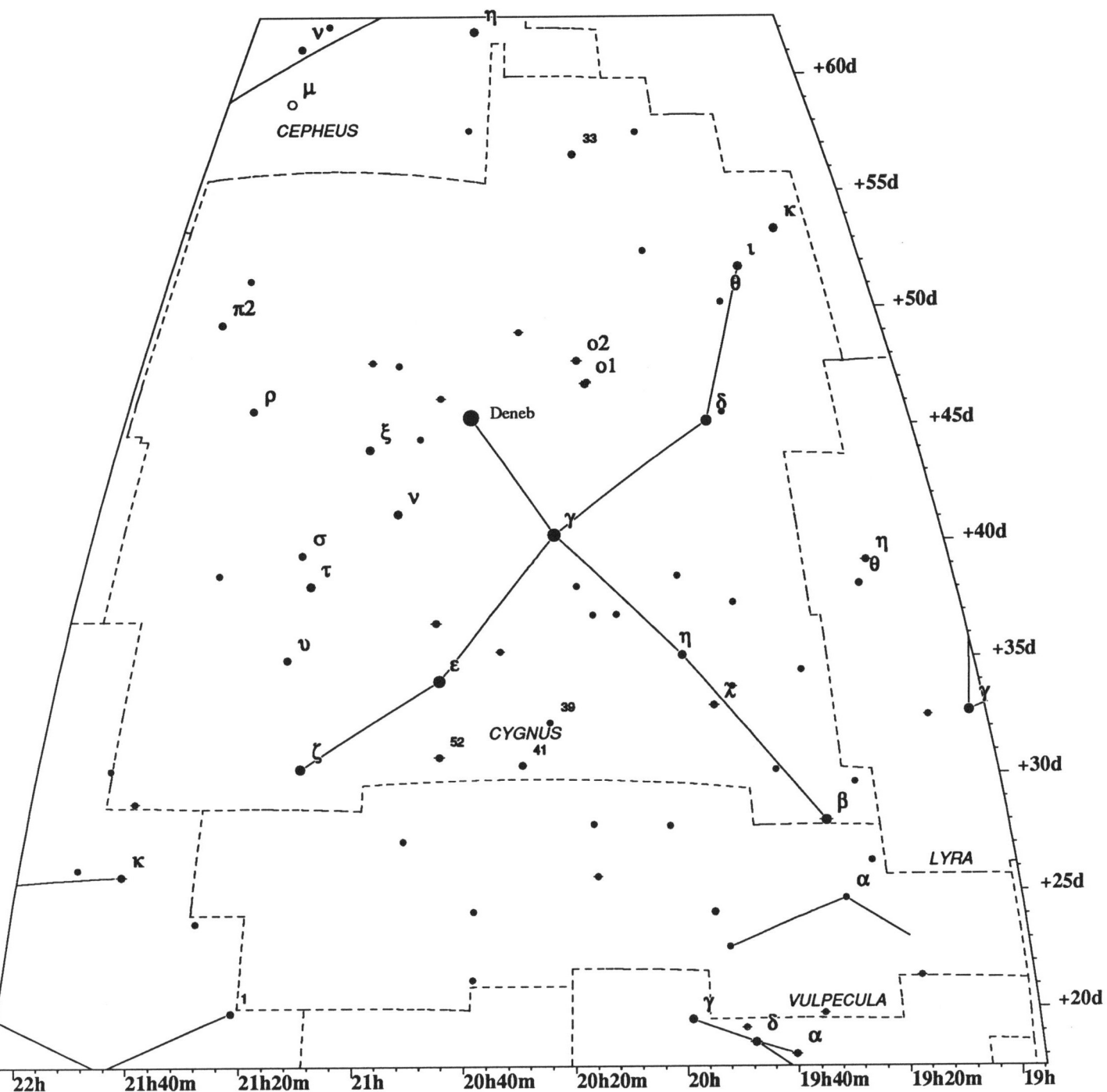

Observe the constellation and fill in the missing magnitudes and colors.

Star	Mag	Color	Star	Mag	Color	Star	Mag	Color
Deneb	1.2		η Cyg	3.9	red	o² Cyg	4.0	blue
β Cyg	3.2		θ Cyg	4.5	blue	υ Cyg	4.4	blue
γ Cyg		yellow	ι Cyg		blue	τ Cyg	3.7	blue
ε Cyg	2.5	yellow	κ Cyg	3.8	yellow	σ Cyg	4.2	blue
ζ Cyg	3.2	yellow	δ Cyg	2.9	blue	ν Cyg		blue

Aquila

NAME: _____

SECTION: _____

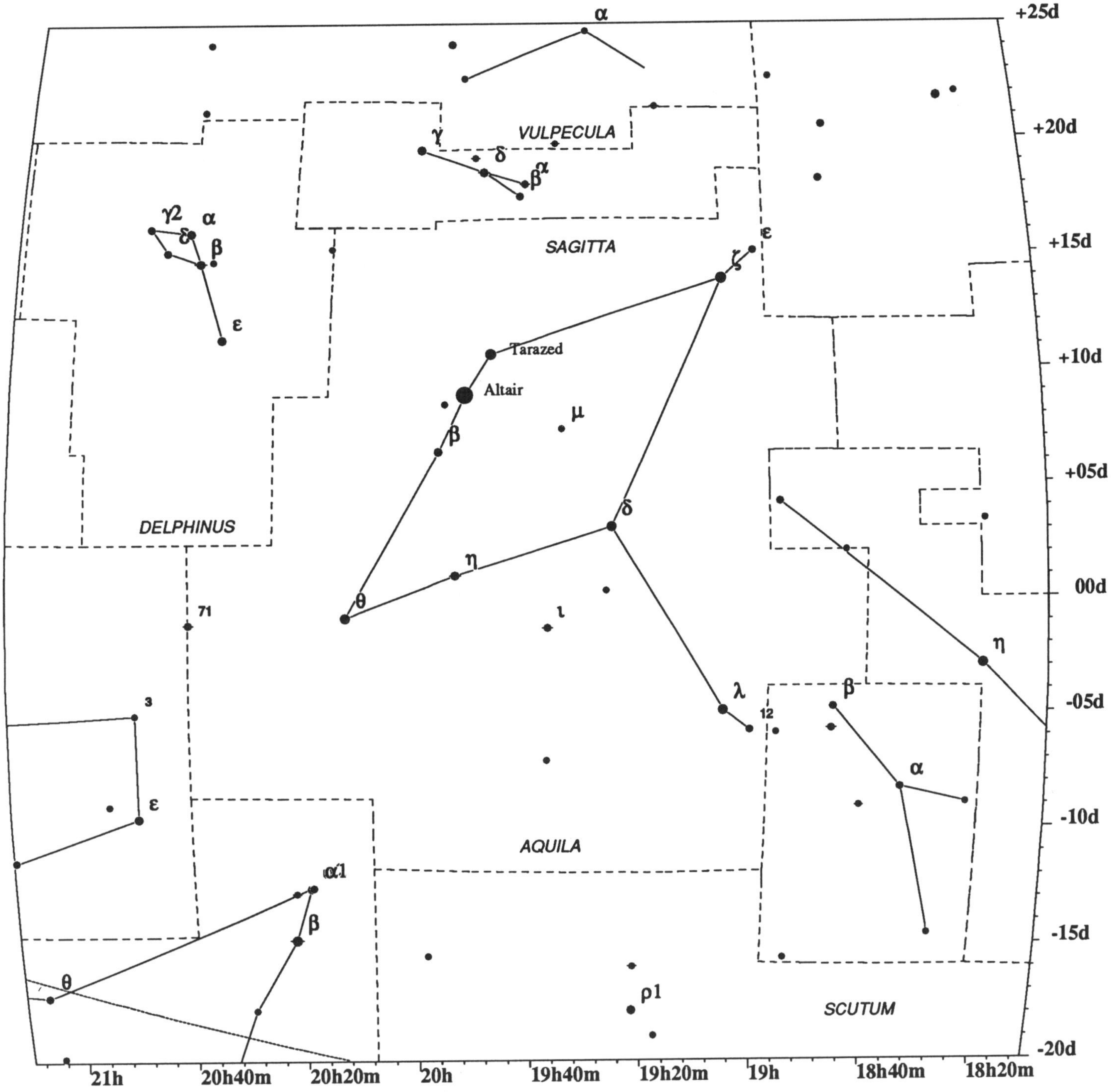

Observe the constellation and fill in the missing magnitudes and colors.

Star	Mag	Color		Star	Mag	Color
Altair	0.8			ζ Aql		blue
Tarazed	2.7	yellow		ε Aql	4.0	yellow
β Aql	3.7	yellow		δ Aql	3.4	blue
θ Aql		blue		λ Aql	3.4	blue
η Aql	3.5	blue		ι Aql	4.4	blue
μ Aql	4.5	red				

Cassiopeia

NAME: _____

SECTION: _____

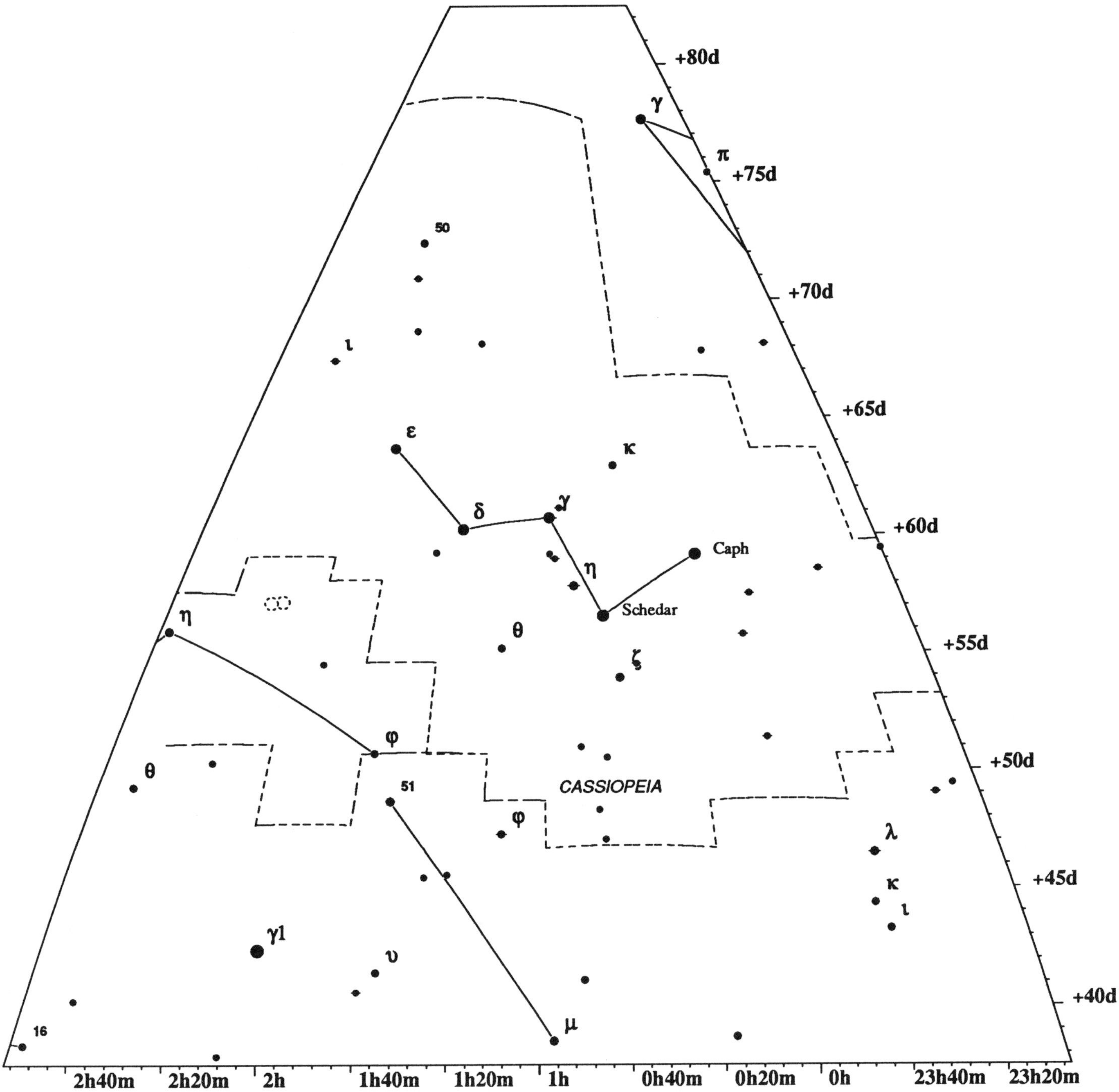

Observe the constellation and fill in the missing magnitudes and colors.

Star	Mag	Color
Schedar	2.2	yellow
Caph	2.3	blue
η Cas	3.4	yellow
γ Cas		blue
δ Cas	2.7	blue

Star	Mag	Color
ε Cas		blue
θ Cas	4.3	blue
κ Cas	4.2	blue

Pegasus

NAME: ______________________________

SECTION: ____________________________

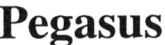

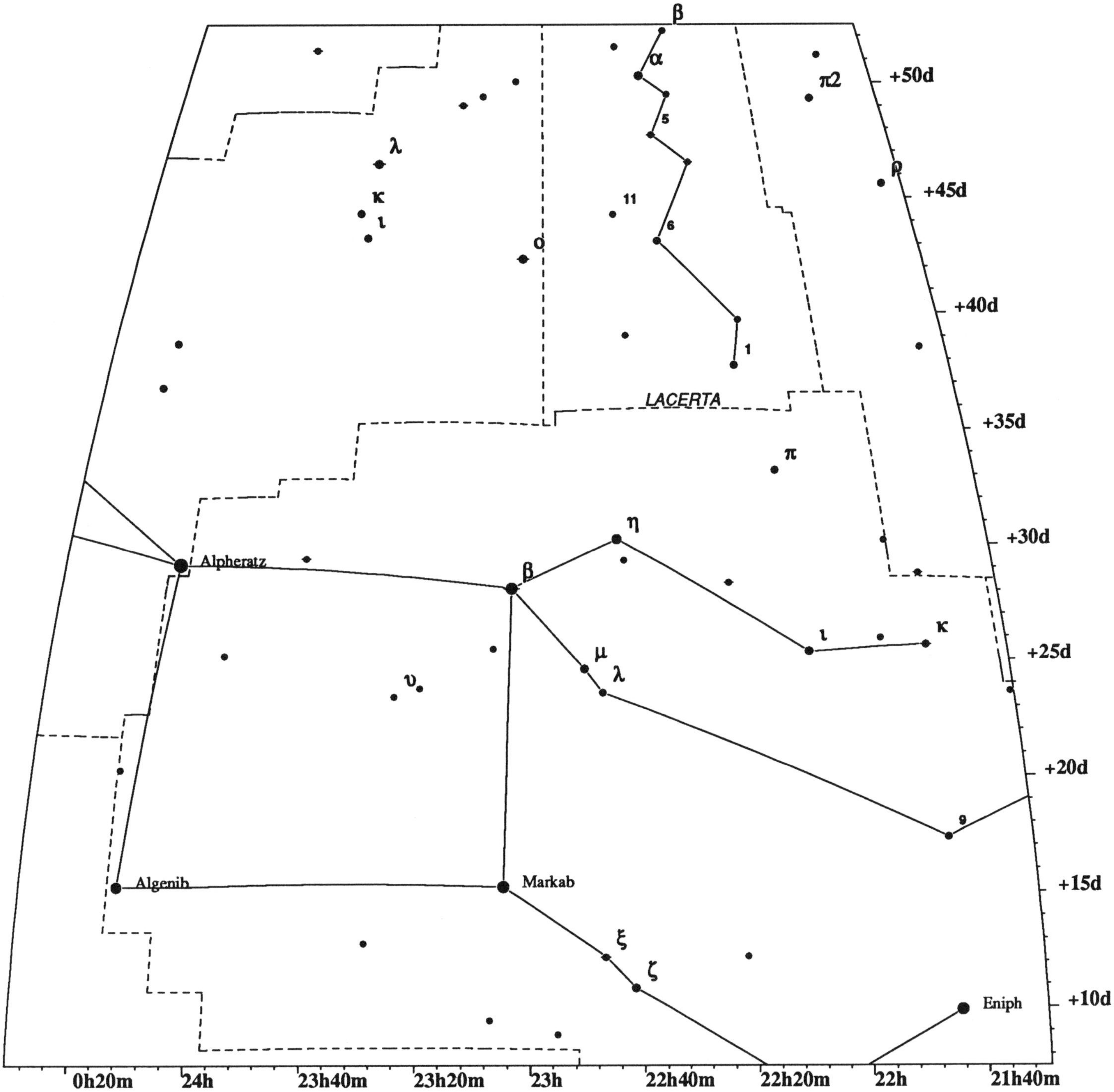

Observe the constellation and fill in the missing magnitudes and colors.

Star	*Mag*	*Color*
Alpheratz	2.1	blue
Algenib	2.8	blue
Markab	2.5	blue
β Peg		red
η Peg	2.9	yellow

Star	*Mag*	*Color*
μ Peg	3.5	yellow
λ Peg		yellow
υ Peg	4.4	yellow
Eniph	2.4	red

Taurus

NAME: _____

SECTION: _____

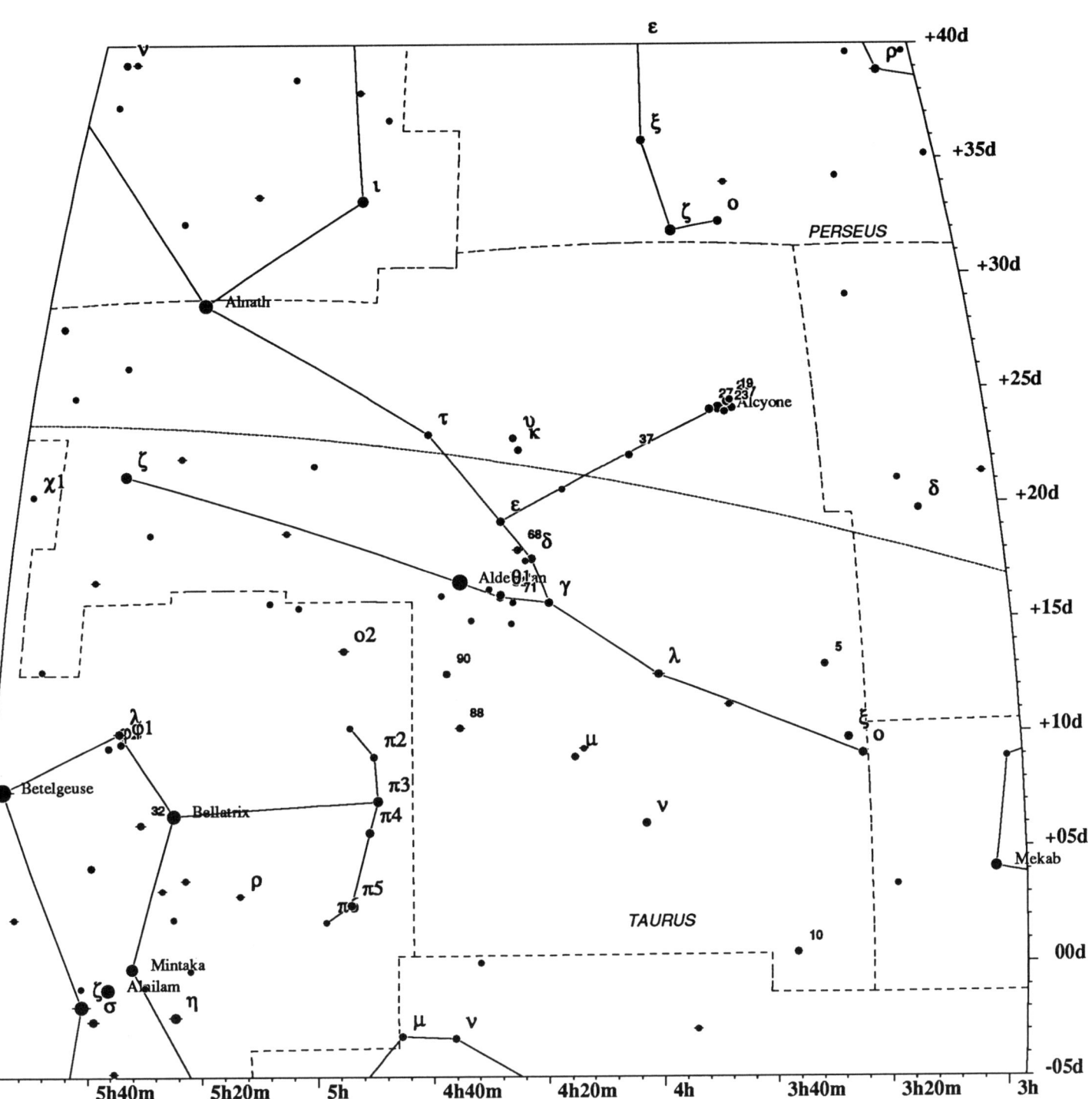

Observe the constellation and fill in the missing magnitudes and colors.

Star	*Mag*	*Color*
Aldebaran	0.9	
ε Tau	3.5	red
λ Tau	3.5	blue
γ Tau		red
δ Tau	3.8	red

Star	*Mag*	*Color*
κ Tau		blue
υ Tau	4.3	blue
τ Tau	4.3	blue
Alnath	1.7	blue
ζ Tau	3.0	blue

Orion

NAME: _____

SECTION: _____

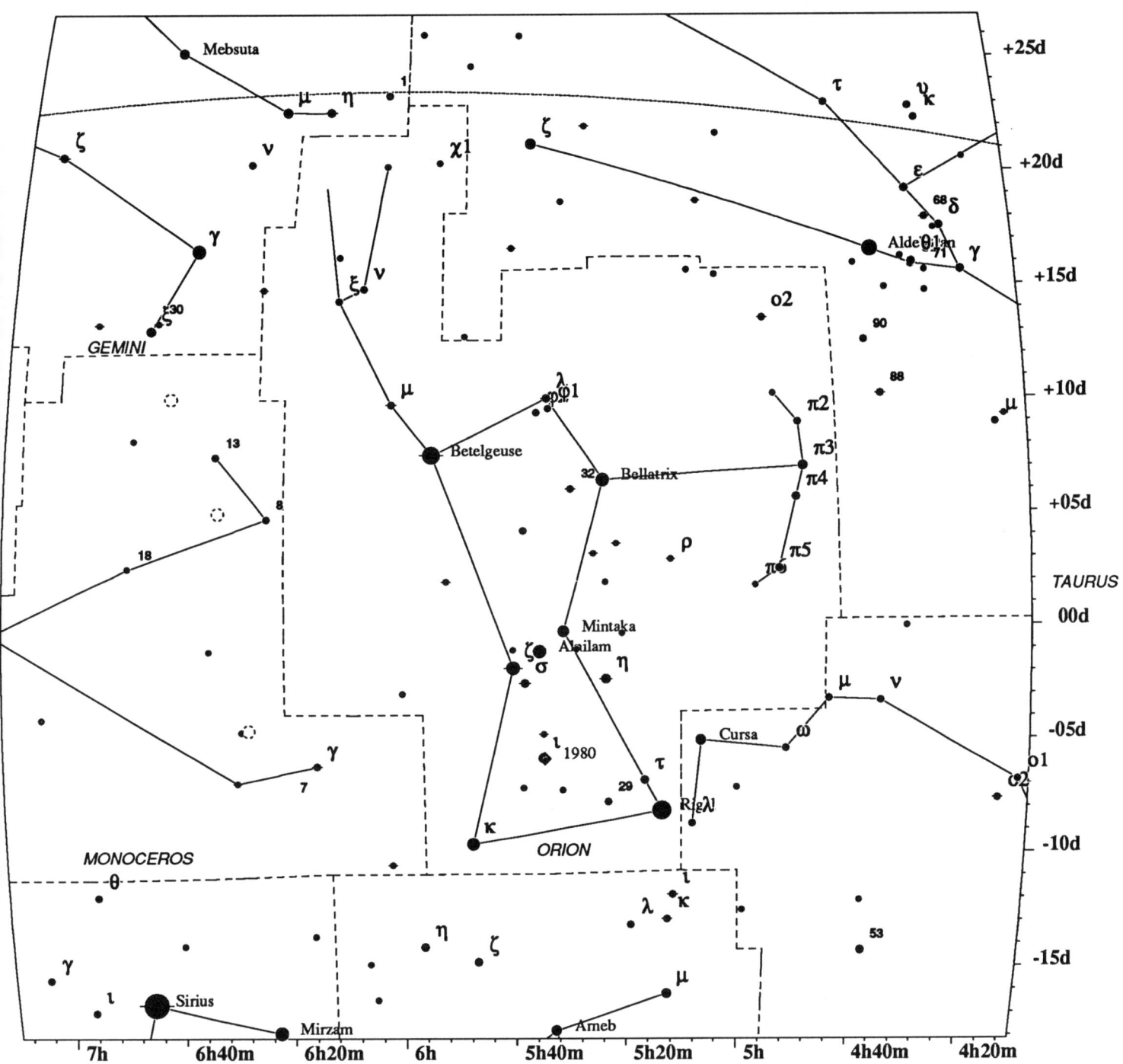

Observe the constellation and fill in the missing magnitudes and colors.

Star	Mag	Color
Rigel	0.1	
Bellatrix	1.6	blue
η Ori	3.4	blue
Mintaka		blue
Alnilam	1.7	

Star	Mag	Color
ζ Ori	2.0	blue
σ Ori	3.8	blue
κ Ori	2.1	blue
Betelgeuse	0.5	

Canis Major

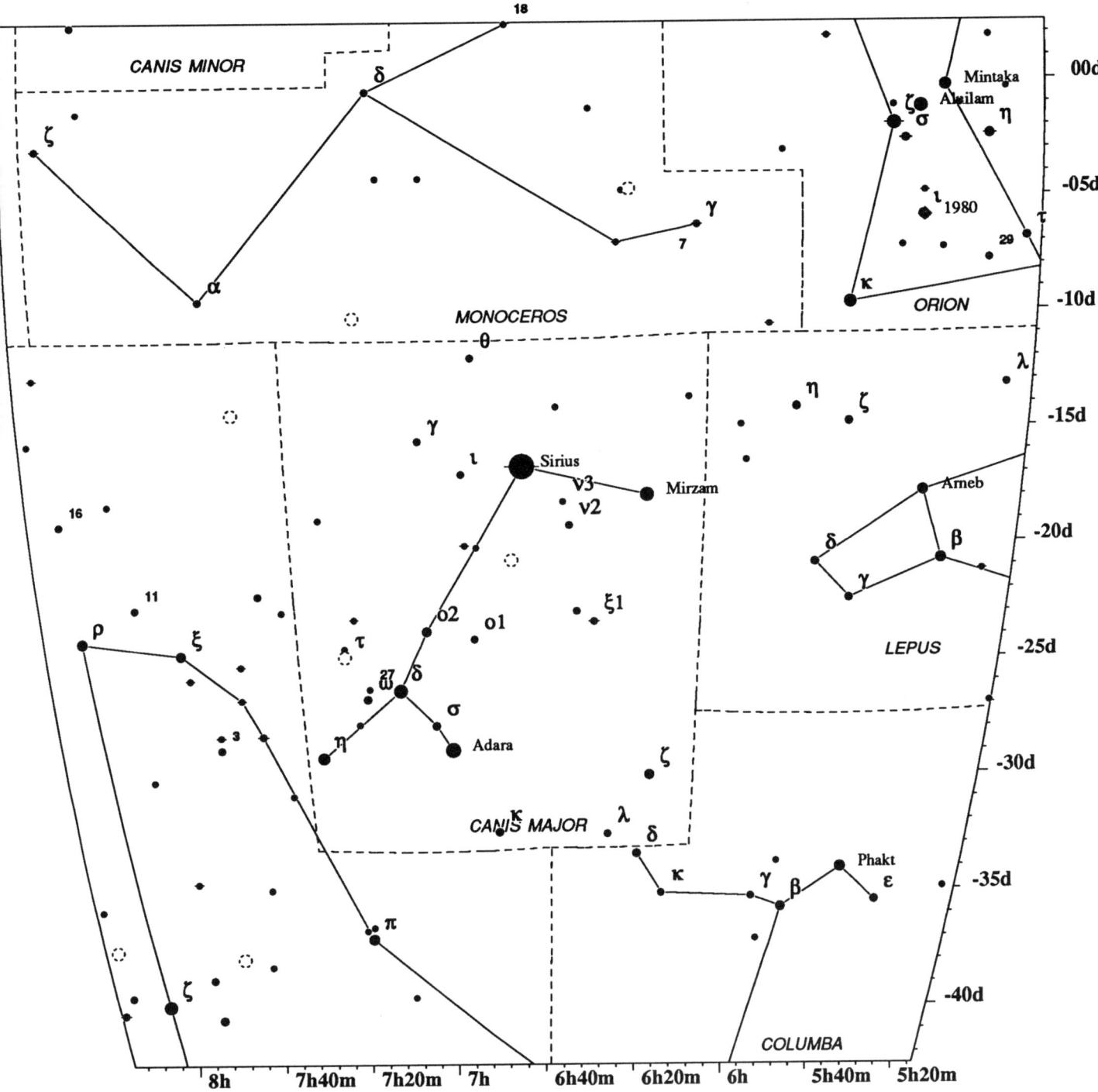

Observe the constellation and fill in the missing magnitudes and colors.

Star	Mag	Color
Mirzam	2.0	blue
Sirius	-1.5	
o² CMa		blue
o¹ CMa	3.9	red

Star	Mag	Color
δ CMa	1.9	yellow
σ CMa	3.5	red
Adara		blue
η CMa	2.4	blue

Auriga

NAME: _____

SECTION: _____

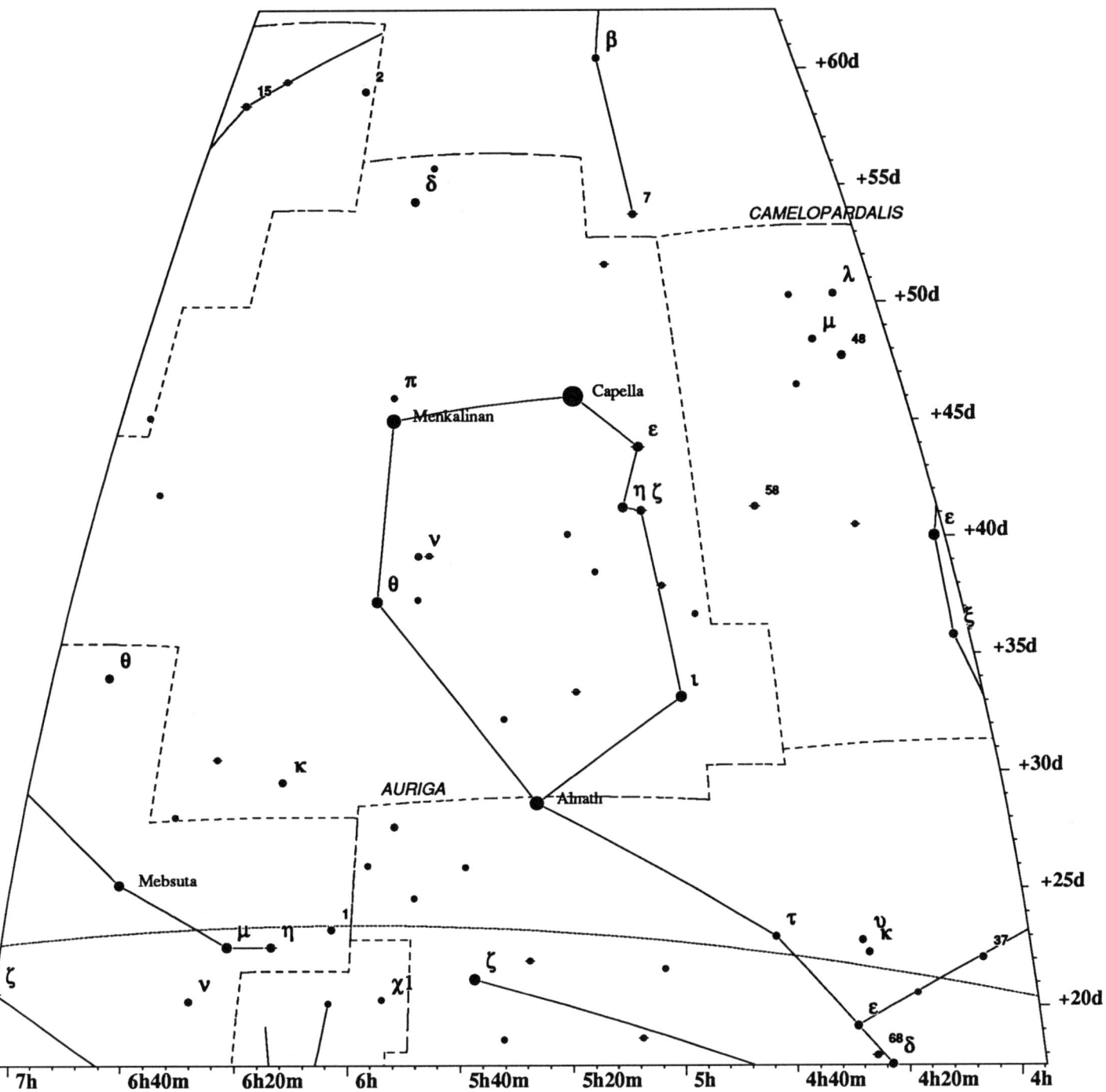

Observe the constellation and fill in the missing magnitudes and colors.

Star	Mag	Color
Capella	0.8	
ε Aur	3.0	blue
η Aur		blue
ζ Aur	3.8	red
ι Aur	2.7	red

Star	Mag	Color
Menkalinah	1.9	blue
π Aur	4.3	red
θ Aur		blue
Alnath (β Tau)	1.7	blue
ν Aur		yellow

Gemini

NAME: _____

SECTION: _____

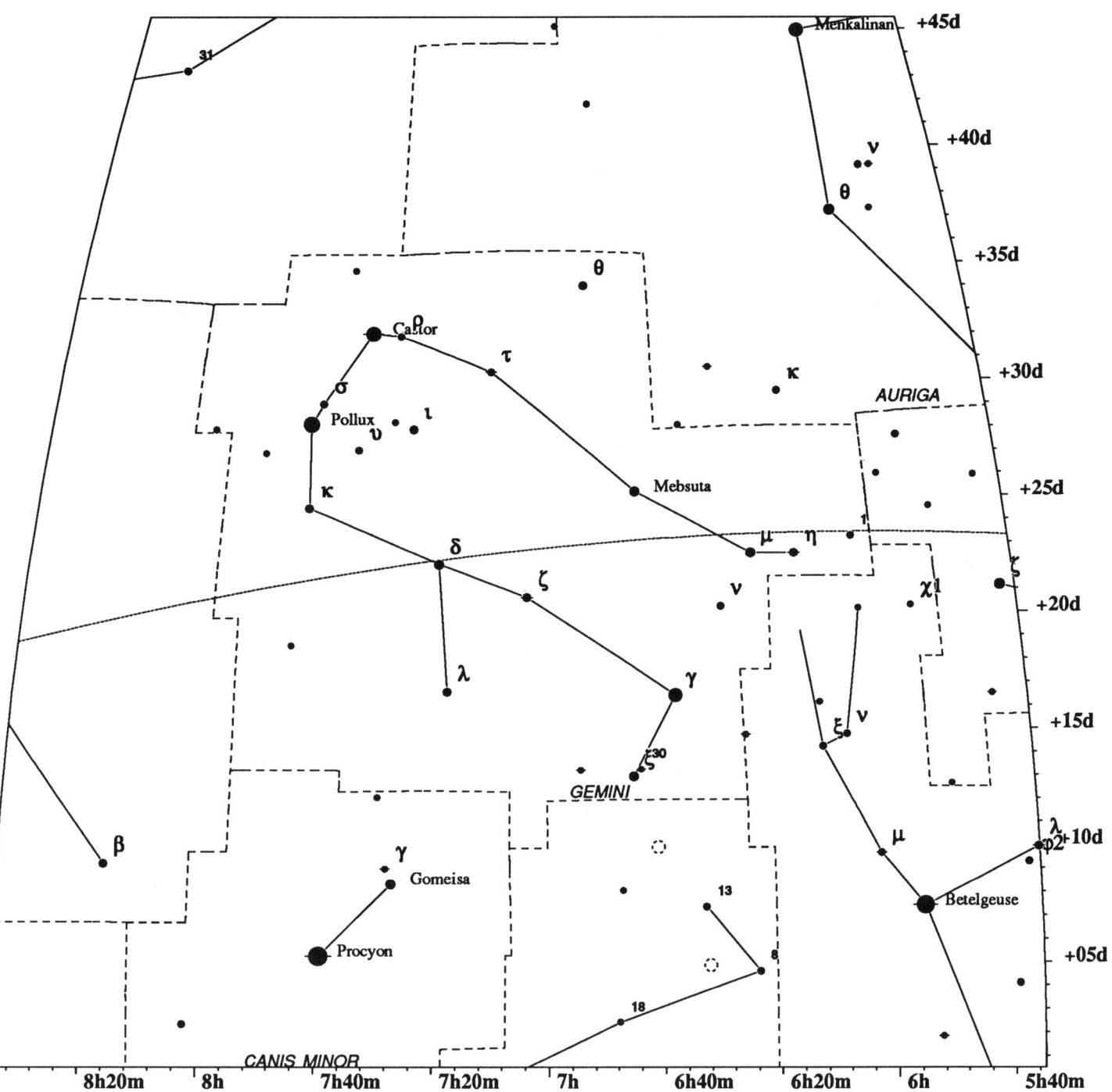

Observe the constellation and fill in the missing magnitudes and colors.

Star	Mag	Color		Star	Mag	Color
Castor	1.7	blue		μ Gem	2.9	red
Pollux	1.1			η Gem	3.3	red
σ Gem		red		κ Gem	3.6	yellow
τ Gem	4.4	red		δ Gem		blue
Mebsuta	3.0	yellow		γ Gem	1.9	

Leo

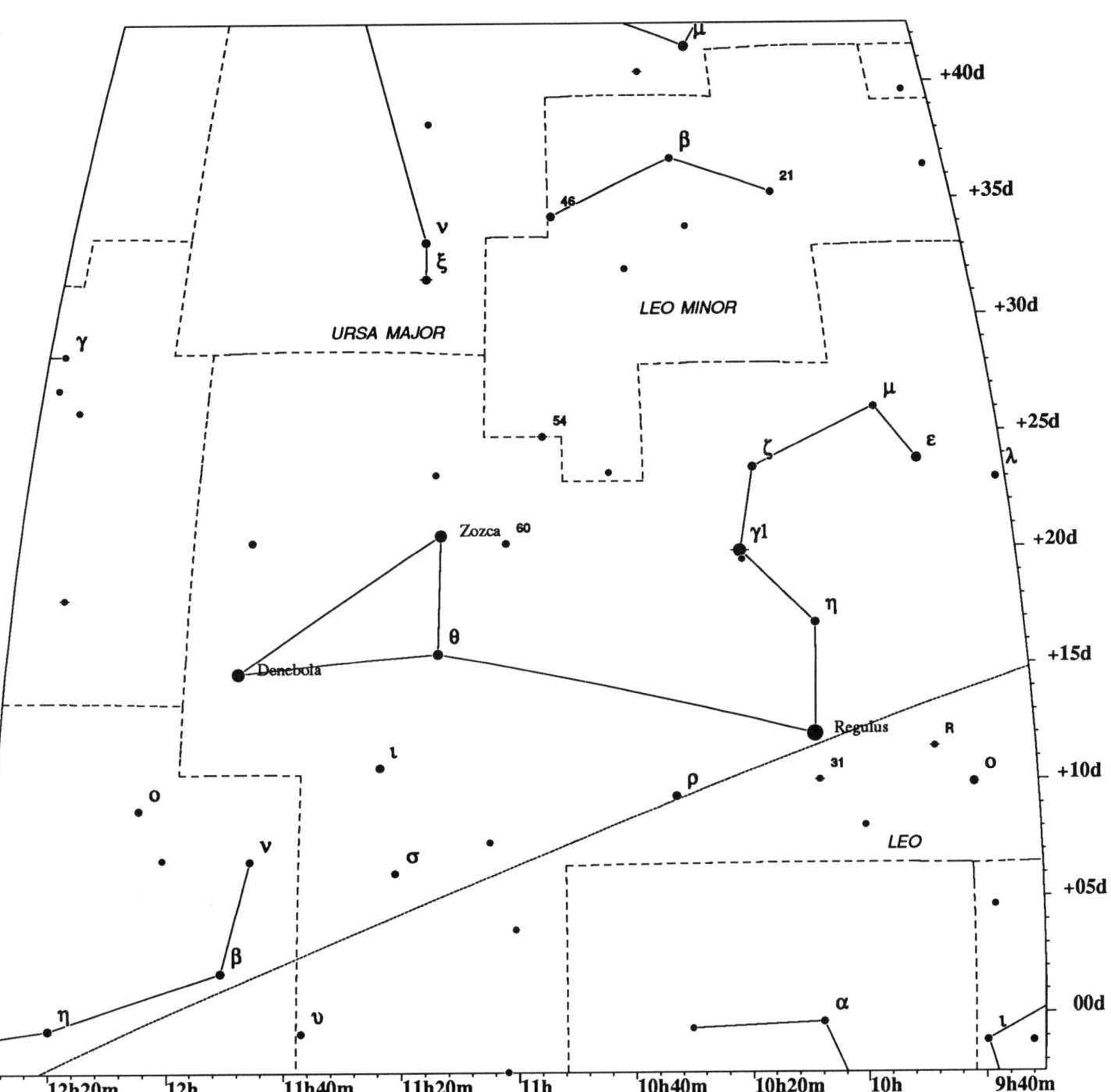

Observe the constellation and fill in the missing magnitudes and colors.

Star	Mag	Color
ε Leo	3.0	yellow
μ Leo	3.9	yellow
ζ Leo	3.4	blue
γ¹ Leo		yellow
η Leo	3.5	blue

Star	Mag	Color
Regulus	1.3	
θ Leo	3.3	blue
Zozca		blue
Denebola	2.1	blue

Corvus

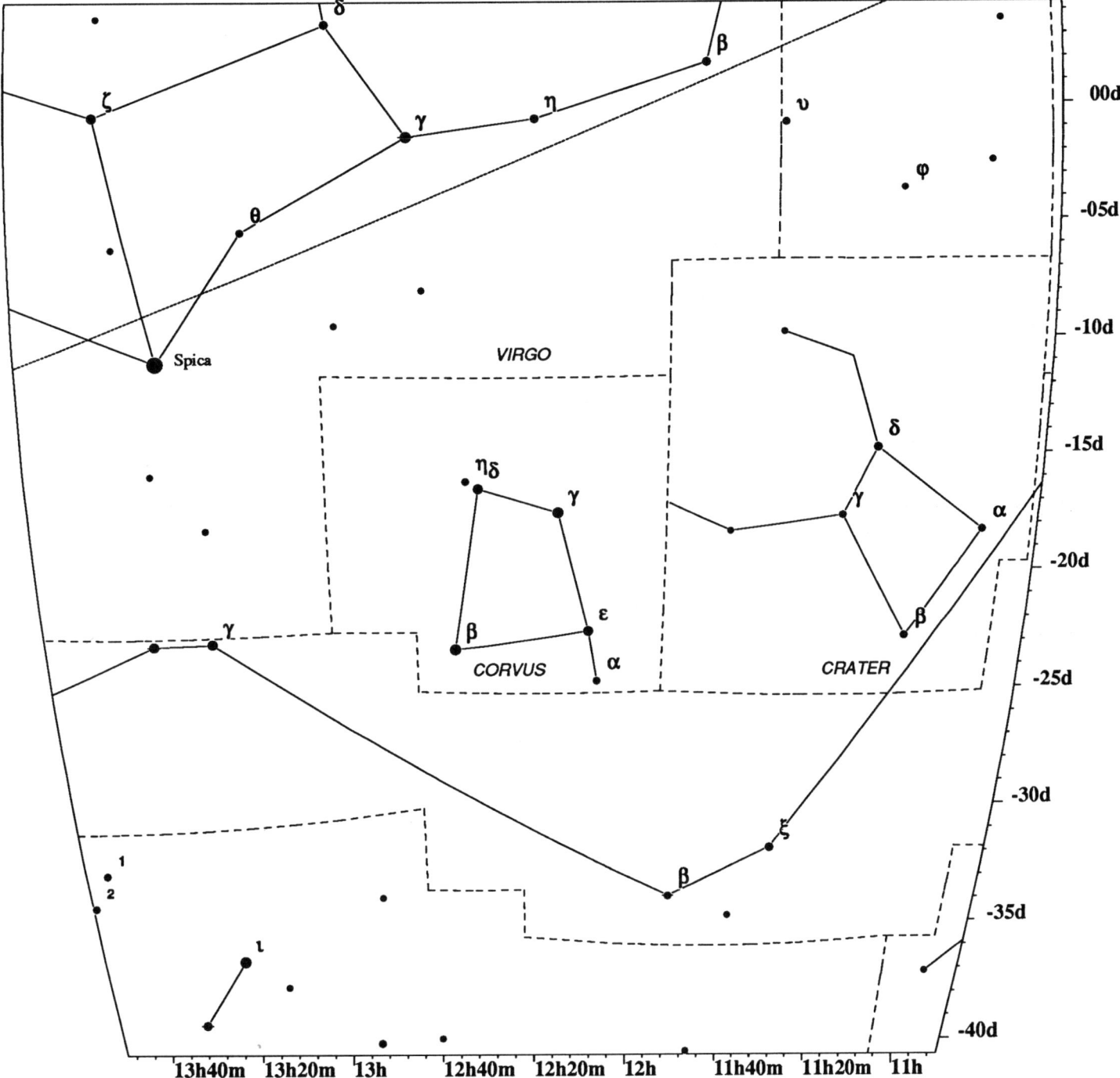

Observe the constellation and fill in the missing magnitudes and colors.

Star	Mag	Color
α Crv	2.6	
ε Crv	3.0	yellow
γ Crv		blue

Star	Mag	Color
δ Crv	2.9	blue
η Crv	4.3	blue
β Crv		yellow

Ursa Major

NAME: _____

SECTION: _____

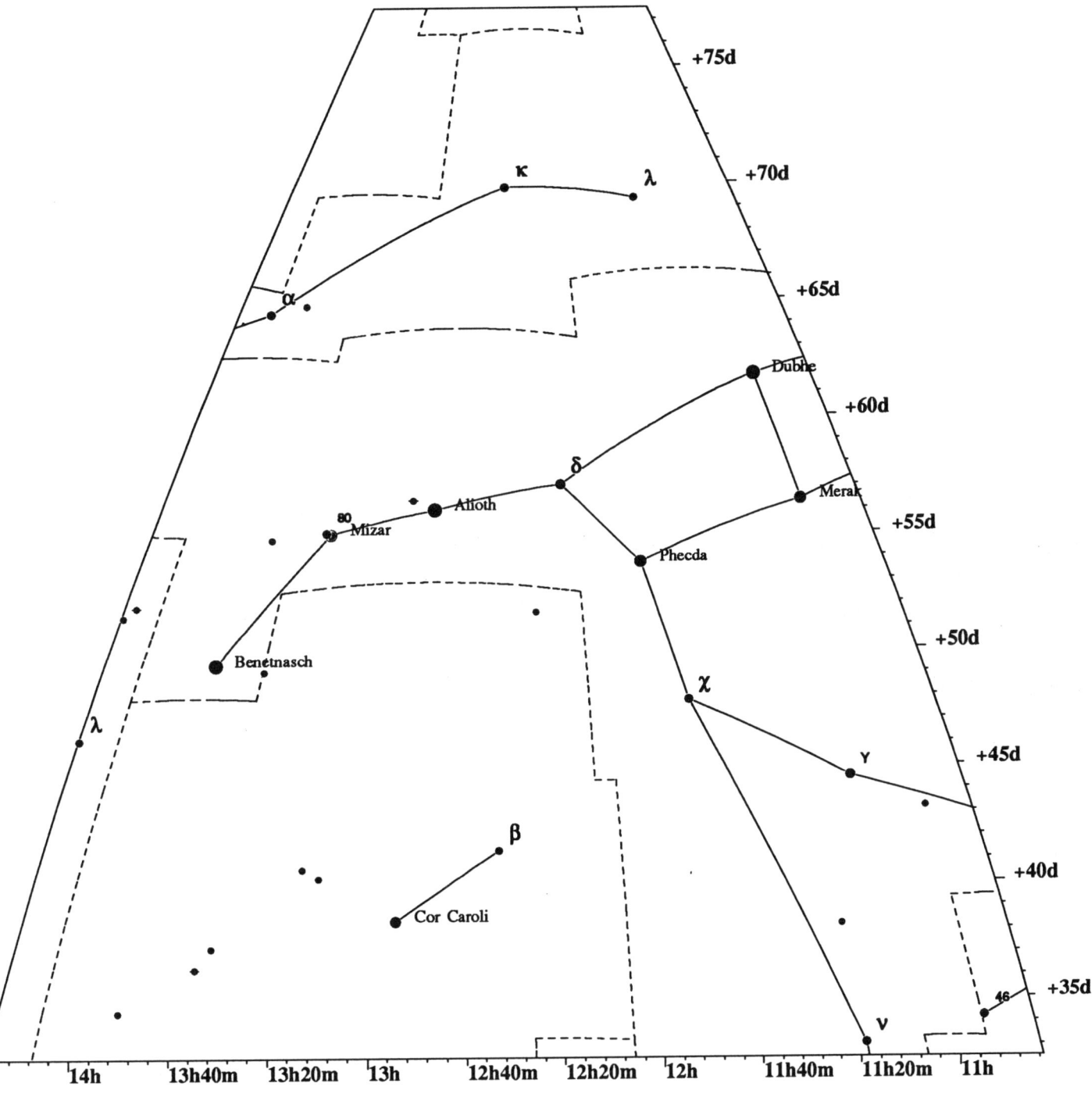

Observe the constellation and fill in the missing magnitudes and colors.

Star	Mag	Color
Merak		blue
Dubhe	1.8	yellow
Phecda	2.4	
χ UMa	3.7	yellow

Star	Mag	Color
δ UMa	3.3	blue
Alioth		blue
Mizar	2.3	blue
Benetnasch	1.9	blue

Bootes

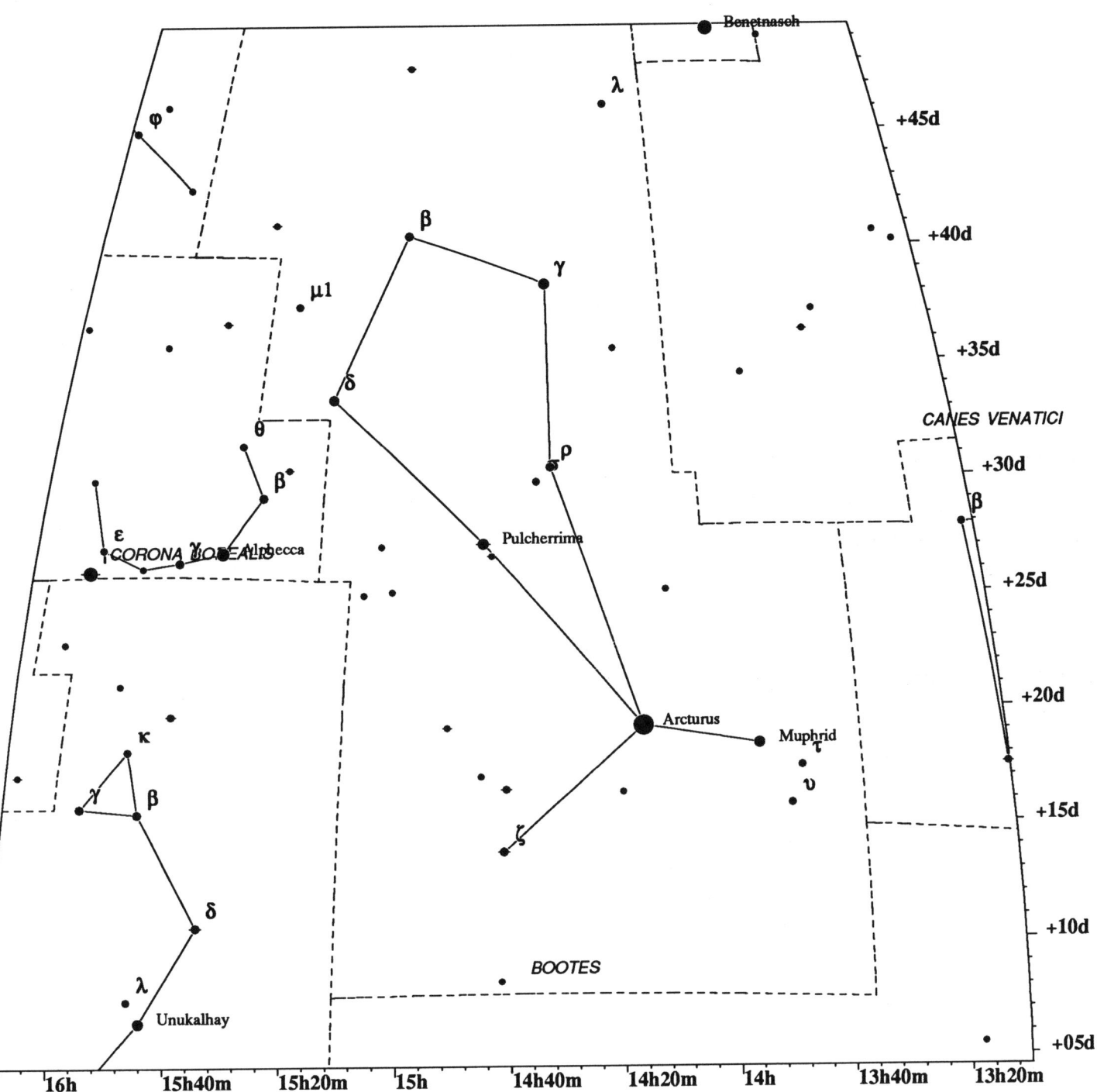

Observe the constellation and fill in the missing magnitudes and colors.

Star	Mag	Color		Star	Mag	Color
Muphrid	2.7	yellow		Pulcherrima	2.4	red
Arcturus	1.3			β Boo	3.5	yellow
ρ Boo	3.6	red		δ Boo		yellow
γ Boo		blue				

Scorpius

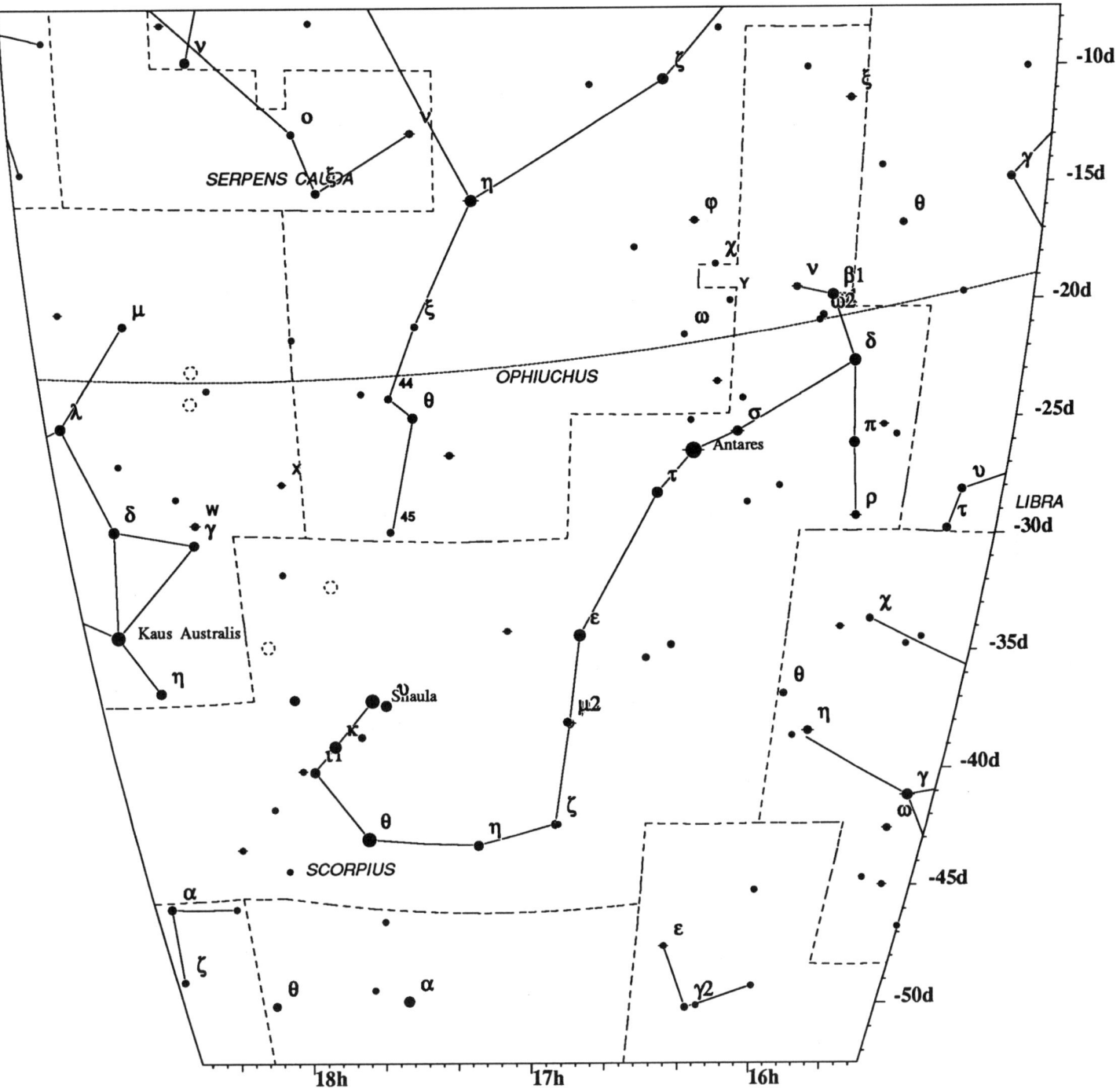

Observe the constellation and fill in the missing magnitudes and colors.

Star	Mag	Color		Star	Mag	Color
β¹ Sco		blue		τ Sco	2.8	blue
δ Sco	2.3	blue		ε Sco	2.3	yellow
π Sco	2.9	blue		θ Sco	1.9	blue
σ Sco		blue		Shaula		blue
Antares	0.9					

OBJECTIVES

After completing this observational project the student will be able to:

1. safely observe the Sun with a telescope using projection or solar filters.
2. identify by name solar features seen on white light photographs.
3. determine the Zurich/Wolf number from photographic observations.

STUDENT MATERIALS

one 12-exposure roll of 400 speed 35mm color print film (or 24-exposure film, if necessary)

OBSERVATORY EQUIPMENT

equatorially-aligned telescope with clock drive and solar filter
35mm camera with cable release
telescope-camera mounting hardware
masking tape

STUDENT REQUIREMENTS

These observations may be done individually or with a partner (two people, not groups). Observations are to be done during a solar photo session under the supervision of a lab instructor. After having the photos developed, do a sunspot count based on one of your solar images. Turn in your photo and sunspot count as **Fig. 3**, along with your **Photographic Data Table.**

INTRODUCTION

During this exercise you will observe the Sun with small telescopes. Solar observing can be dangerous. **NEVER LOOK DIRECTLY AT THE SUN WITH YOUR NAKED EYE OR OPTICAL AID WITHOUT PROPER SOLAR FILTERS.** Some commercial telescopes have a dark filter which attaches to the telescope's eyepiece. These filters are *never* to be used because they may crack due to the intense heat of the Sun. If this happens during observing a severe retinal burn will result leaving

Fig. 1: A Celestron C8 equipped with a solar filter and 35-mm camera.

you permanently blind in one eye. These filters are not safe and should be thrown away. The only safe solar filters are those which intercept the sunlight before it enters the telescope. These filters come as **off-axis** and **full-aperture** types as shown in **Fig. 1**. During this exercise you will use one or both of these two kinds of filters.

PROCEDURE

I. Observations

With the aid of your lab instructor, set up one or more telescopes equipped with white light solar filters (**off-axis** and/or **full-aperture**, as shown in **Fig. 1.**).

1. Check that the filters are taped in place to avoid an accident which could be caused by a gust of wind.

2. Mount a low-power eyepiece such as a 40-mm so that the entire Sun can be seen in the field of view.

3. With the aid of your instructor point the telescope at the Sun. **DO NOT LOOK THROUGH THE FINDER OR TELESCOPE.** It is best to use the technique of minimizing the shadow size of the telescope. Your instructor should demonstrate this method for you.

4. Observe the Sun and locate any visible sunspots. Note that the spots tend to be in groups. Also most spots have a dark central area called the umbra which is surrounded by a more lightly shaded area, named the penumbra.

5. Load the camera with film and fill out the information on the Photographic Data Table.

6. Mount the T-ring onto the camera body. (**Note:** each camera company has different lens mounts and your T-ring must be made for the camera model you are using).

7. Remove the eyepiece and visual back from the telescope and mount the camera in its place using a short extension tube as shown in **Fig. 1**.

8. Be sure the solar filter is in place and that the telescope is aimed at the Sun. Also check that the declination and right ascension axes are locked in place.

9. Using the declination and right ascension slow motion knobs, center the Sun in the camera.

10. Focus the telescope very carefully. If the Sun is not well focused you cannot get good photographs. This is not trivial and may take some practice.

11. Mount a cable release in the threaded hole on top of the shutter release button.

12. So that you can concentrate on what you are doing, let a partner record your exposure on the data table.

13. Set the camera shutter speed at $1/60$ of a second. Cock the camera and depress the cable release plunger. If all has gone well you just took your first photo of the Sun. Repeat this step again using the same shutter speed of $1/60$ of a second.

14. Repeat step 13 above for shutter speeds of $1/125$, $1/250$, $1/500$, and $1/1000$ of a second. You should now have two exposures at all of the shutter speeds. Be sure your partner has recorded each exposure, including mistakes, so that you will be able to figure out later which exposure was the best. (**Hint:** One of the shorter exposures is usually best on a clear day.)

15. Rewind the film and remove it from the camera.

16. Let your partner take their photographs while you record the exposures.

17. Have your film developed at a commercial photographic lab. You may want to tell them to print all the frames because they are astronomical photos of the Sun.

18. After your prints come back, sort them by frame number order. Pick out the best exposure and place it in the space provided in **Fig. 3**. Fill out the photo information requested in the figure.

19. Determine the Relative Spot Number as outlined in **Part II**.

II. Determination of Zurich/Wolf Number

Sunspot numbers are an important indicator of solar activity. Spots can be single or in groups. The Relative Spot Number (**RSN**) was introduced by Wolf using the Zurich 3-inch refractor. The RSN is not a simple sunspot count but instead is a number that represents the relative intensity of solar activity. Wolf proposed that the spot numbers (**n**) and groups (**g**) be combined so that groups represent ten times more activity than single spots. Mathematically, this can be represented as

$$RSN = (10)g + n \qquad (1)$$

Notice in the example of **Fig. 2** that (**n**) includes each individual umbra even if it is within a spot group. Also, individual spots are considered as a group.

1. Use your photo in **Fig. 3** and count the number of spot groups (**g**). Remember that a single spot counts as a group. If two nearby groups appear to be connected in any way by faculae or filaments, consider this as one group, not two. Record the value of (**g**) in the space provided in **Fig. 3**.

2. Again use **Fig. 3** and count the number of individual umbras (**n**). Record the total value (**n**) in the blank provided.

3. Use **eq. (1)** to calculate the **RSN** and record your answer in **Fig. 3**.

Turn in the data table and **Fig. 3** within two weeks after you take your photos or by the last day of your lab class, whichever comes first.

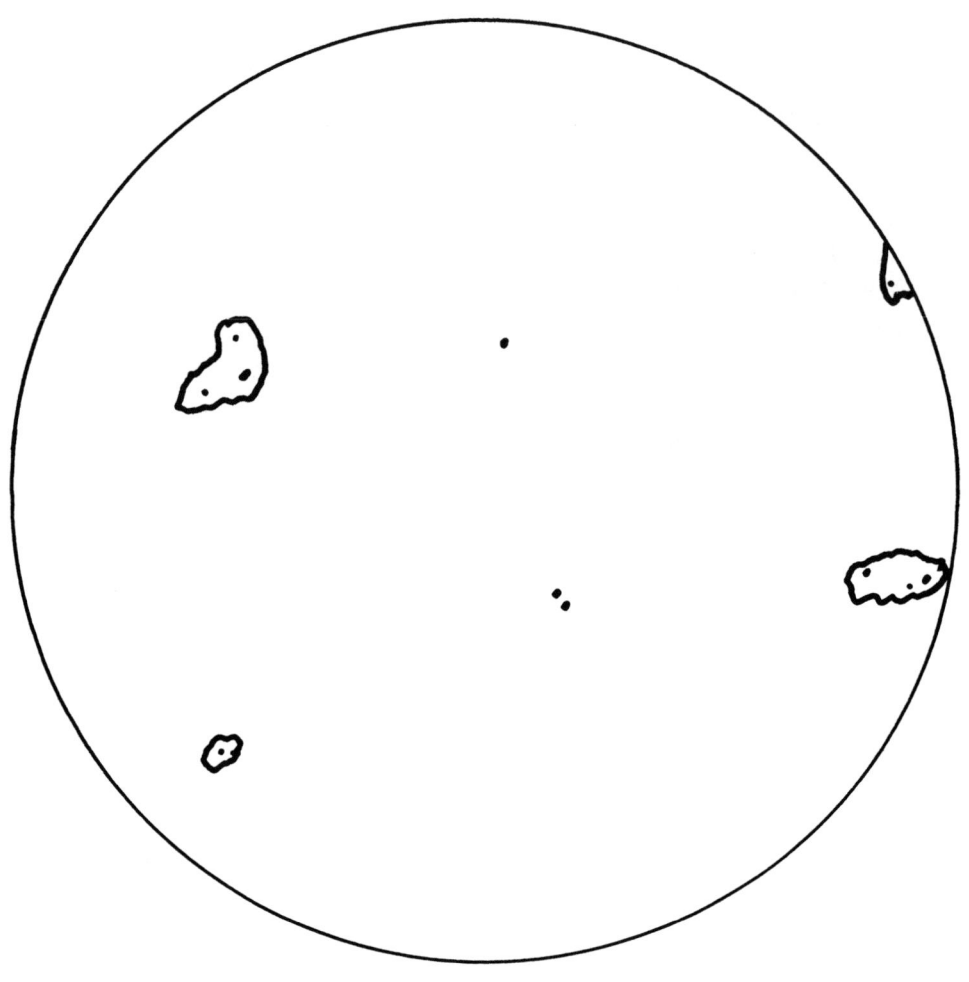

Date:	m/d/y	**g:**	6
UT:	h:m	**n:**	11
		RSN:	71

Fig. 2: An example of how to estimate the Relative Spot Number.

Photographic Data Table

FRAME	SUBJECT	EXPOSURE	EYEPIECE
1			
2			
3			
4			
5			
6			
7			
8			
9			
10			
11			
12			
13			
14			
15			
16			
17			
18			
19			
20			
21			
22			
23			
24			

NAME: ______________________________

SECTION: ______________________________

Place photo

in this space

Date: ______________________________

Exposure time: ______________________

Estimate of Relative Spot Number from photo above

g = ______________________________

n = ______________________________

RSN = ____________________________

Fig. 3: Student's photograph of the Sun and estimate of the RSN.

OBJECTIVES

After completing this exercise the student will be able to:

1. point a telescope at a selected star cluster, nebula, etc.
2. use a star chart to locate faint objects within a star field.
3. photograph the brighter star clusters, nebulae, etc.
4. describe the types of objects photographed.

STUDENT MATERIALS

penlight or flashlight
pencil

OBSERVING EQUIPMENT

equatorially aligned telescope with clock drive
illuminated reticle
camera with telephoto lens
400-speed film
cable release
piggyback mounting hardware
clock with second hand
star atlas

INTRODUCTION

Piggyback photography is one of the simplest ways to take photographs of the night sky. This technique uses the telescope only to guide the camera which is mounted on the telescope piggyback-style as shown in **Fig. 1**, below. This configuration makes locating the star field easier and it also makes guiding the telescope less critical.

Fig. 1: Piggyback camera arrangement with a typical Schmidt-Cassegrain telescope.

As you can see in **Fig. 1**, the camera is equipped with a lens of its own. Usually this is a small telephoto lens, but a wide-angle lens may also be used. The choice of lenses depends on the type of photo you want to make. For example, if you want to photograph the Milky Way, the wide-angle lens would be a good choice. However, if you are trying to photograph a smaller object, such as the Pleiades or the Orion Nebula, a 135-mm or 200-mm telephoto lens would be a good selection. In this observation session, you will take piggyback photographs of one or two of the objects listed in **Table I**, or some other object chosen by your instructor.

PROCEDURE

Before you arrive, the lab instructor should have the telescope set up and polar-aligned.

1. Load film into the camera.

2. Mount a telephoto lens (135 mm, 200 mm, C90, etc.) onto the camera.

3. Mount the camera to the piggyback bracket on the telescope's tube, as shown in **Fig. 1.**

4. Place an illuminated crosshair eyepiece into the eyepiece holder of the telescope.

5. Aim the telescope at a known bright "setup star" such as Vega, Capella, etc. Use the crosshair eyepiece to center the star within the telescope's field of view.

6. Look up coordinates for this "setup star" in a star atlas or a celestial almanac. Adjust the telescope's setting circles so they are reading the "setup star's" coordinates. Recheck that the star is still centered on the crosshair. If it is not, carefully repeat steps 5 and 6.

7. Adjust the camera's aim so that the "setup star" is seen near the center of the camera's viewfinder. This ensures that both telescope and camera are pointed at the same area of the sky.

8. Most star clusters and nebulae are too faint to be visible with the unaided eye. Therefore, you may need to look up the object's coordinates in order to point the telescope. Move the telescope in declination and right ascension until it is pointing at the object you want to photograph.

9. If all has gone well, you should be able to see a faint, fuzzy object in the finder scope. If not, check over the setup starting with step 5. If you see the object, center it within the telescope's field of viewing using the crosshair eyepiece. Depending on the object's brightness, you may or may not be able to see it within the viewfinder of the camera. If you have done step 7 properly, the object should be in the camera's field of view even if you cannot see it with your eye.

10. Mount the cable release into the small hole in the camera's shutter release button. Set the shutter speed to **B**, or **bulb**, for a time exposure. Focus the lens to infinity. Check that the lens f-stop is set to its lowest value.

11. Set the telescope drive-track rate to the **guide** position.

12. Look into the telescope eyepiece and find a "guide star." Use the handpaddle to move the telescope until the "guide star" is centered on the crosshair. Because of gear-train error in the clock drive, it may be necessary to guide the telescope during the exposure. To do this, use the buttons on the handpaddle box. If the guide star wanders off the crosshair, move it back by pressing the correct button. You may need to practice this technique before you take your first photograph. When you feel comfortable with guiding, go to step 13.

13. Start the exposure by pressing the cable release and locking the cable so the shutter stays open. Record the object's name, the lens f-stop, and the exposure's starting time in **Table II**. When you are ready to end the exposure, unlock the cable release to close the shutter. Record the exposure's ending time and duration in **Table II**.

14. Repeat steps 8 through 13 on as many objects as the instructor allows.

15. Rewind the film into the cassette.

16. Have the film developed at a commercial photo lab.

17. Turn in one of your photographs as part of **Fig. 2** and provide the requested information about the photo you turn in.

18. Answer the questions about your photograph.

Table I

SEASON	NAME	CONSTELLATION	OBJECT TYPE	SUGGESTED LENS
Fall	Milky Way	Cygnus, Aquila	our galaxy (Great Rift)	normal or wide-angle
	Double Cluster	Perseus	two open clusters	telephoto
	M31	Andromeda	spiral galaxy	telephoto
	North American Nebula	Cygnus	nebula	telephoto
Winter	Pleiades	Taurus	open star cluster	telephoto
	M42	Orion	nebula	telephoto
	M35	Gemini	open star cluster	telephoto
	M44 (Beehive)	Cancer	open star cluster	telephoto
Spring	M3	Coma Berenices	globular star cluster	telephoto
	M5	Serpens	globular star cluster	telephoto
	M51	Ursa Major	spiral galaxy	telephoto
Summer	M13	Hercules	globular star cluster	telephoto
	M92	Hercules	globular star cluster	telephoto
	Galactic Center	Sagittarius	our galaxy (numerous clusters and nebulae)	normal or wide-angle

Table II

Piggyback Photography Log

UT Date: _____   Lens Focal Length: _____

Film Type: _____   Film Speed: _____

FRAME NUMBER	SUBJECT	f-STOP	START TIME	END TIME	EXPOSURE LENGTH	COMMENT	STUDENT NAME
1							
2							
3							
4							
5							
6							
7							
8							
9							
10							
11							
12							
13							
14							
15							
16							
17							
18							
19							
20							

Questions

In order to answer these questions you will need to consult your astronomy textbook or some other astronomy reference book.

1. Is the object you photographed an open star cluster, globular star cluster, galaxy, or a nebula?

2. What is the distance to the object?

3. In what constellation is the object located?

4. What is the apparent magnitude of the object?

NAME: ______________________________

SECTION: ______________________________

Place photo of object

in this space

Star: ______________________________

Date: ______________________________

Time: ______________________________

Mag: ______________________________

Film type: ______________________________

Exposure length: ______________________________

Fig. 2: Student photograph of object.

OBSERVING EXERCISE — PHOTOGRAPHIC PHOTOMETRY OF VARIABLE STARS

25

OBJECTIVES

After completing this observational project the student will be able to:

1. photograph the sky using a camera piggyback on a small telescope with a clock drive.
2. locate a variable star on a photograph by comparing photographs to a star chart.
3. estimate stellar magnitudes on a photograph by comparison of these images to *The AAVSO Variable Star Atlas*.

STUDENT MATERIALS

penlight or flashlight
pencil

OBSERVATORY EQUIPMENT

equatorially aligned telescope with clock drive
illuminated reticle
camera with telephoto lens and cable release
piggyback mounting hardware
clock with second hand
finding charts for variable to be observed

INTRODUCTION

This observing exercise involves taking a time exposure of a variable star using the technique of piggyback photography. For this project, long-period Mira variable stars have been selected. These variables will be photographed with a telephoto lens which is guided for a few minutes using a telescope with a sidereal clock drive.

In piggyback photography, the telescope is used to guide the camera during the several-minute time exposure. The camera itself is equipped with a telephoto lens which is used to take the photographs. This configuration is shown in **Fig. 1** of **Lab 24**. We

are using this type of setup because it makes guiding the telescope less critical and locating the star field around the variable easier.

As a group the Mira-type variables are red giant stars which pulsate. This means their atmospheres expand to become more reddish and brighter, and then contract to become more bluish and fainter. Visually, this pulsation can be seen as a periodic brightening and dimming of the star. This brightness variation has a range of 4 to 10 magnitudes. The time between two successive maxima is the pulsation period. All Mira-type variables have periods from 100 days up to about 700 days, with each individual star having its own unique period within this range.

The long-period variables do not have a perfectly repeating cycle. Each cycle is somewhat different from the previous cycle. Mira itself, the prototype, has a maximum brightness of 2nd magnitude, but occasionally its maximum may only be 5th magnitude. Similarly, its minimum brightness ranges from 8th to 10th magnitude. Even the length of each cycle varies between 310 and 370 days with an average period of 332 days. Thus it is important for someone to monitor these variations.

PROCEDURE

A. Photography of the Variable Star

Your instructor should provide you with a "finding chart" for each star you will observe. These charts should give the magnitudes for comparison stars which are located near the variable. A commercial source for such charts is *The AAVSO Variable Star Atlas* published by Sky Publishing.

1. Load film into the camera.

2. Mount a small telephoto lens (200-500mm focal length) onto the camera.

3. Mount the camera to the piggyback bracket on the telescope's tube.

4. Put an illuminated crosshair eyepiece into the eyepiece holder of the telescope.

5. Aim the telescope at a known bright "setup star" such as Vega, Capella, etc. Use the crosshair to center the star in the telescope.

6. Look up the coordinates for your "setup star" in a star atlas. Adjust the telescope's setting circles so they are reading the "setup star's" coordinates.

7. Adjust the camera so that the "setup star" can be seen near the center of the camera viewfinder. This ensures that both telescope and camera are pointed at the same area of the sky.

8. The variable may not be bright enough to be seen visually or even in the camera's viewfinder. Thus, you need to look up the coordinates of the variable to be observed in **Table I**. Move the telescope in declination and right ascension so that it will be pointing at the variable.

9. If you are lucky, you may be able to see a few bright stars in the telescope's finder and in the camera's viewfinder. If so, compare them to the finding chart for the variable to see if they match the star field around the program star; if not, you must hunt for it. If that fails, start over at step 5 with a new "setup star."

10. After you have found the variable star field, it is time to start photographing the sky. Mount a cable release into the small hole in the camera's shutter release button. Set the shutter speed knob to **B** for **bulb**, or time exposure. Focus the lens to infinity and check that the f-stop is set to its lowest value (i.e., 3.5, 5.6, etc.).

11. Flip the track-rate switch from **set** to **guide**.

12. Look into the telescope eyepiece and find a guide star. Use the handpaddle to move the telescope until the guide star is centered on the crosshair. Because of gear-train error in the clock drive, it may be necessary to guide the telescope

during the exposure. To do this use the buttons on the handpaddle box. If the guide star wanders off the crosshair move it back by pressing the correct button. This may take some practice before you can start your photograph. When you feel comfortable with guiding, go to step 13.

13. Open the camera's shutter using the cable release and lock the shutter open. Record the variable star's name and the start time of the exposure on the observing log. After you have exposed the film several minutes, close the shutter by unlocking the cable release. Record the exposure length on the observing log.

14. Repeat steps 8 through 13 on another variable.

15. Rewind the film into the cassette.

16. Have the film developed at a commercial photo lab.

B. Obtaining a Photographic Magnitude

1. After you get the prints back from the photographic lab sort them by variable star name. Refer to the observing log made during the photography session to help with this sorting process.

2. Locate the variable star on the photograph by comparing the star pattern to the finding chart for the variable. This has the potential to drive you crazy, but it is the only way to identify your program star. After you are sure you have found it make tick marks on two sides of the star's image, like the markings on the finding chart.

3. Compare the image of the variable to the standard comparison stars which are labeled on the finding chart. The magnitudes of the comparison stars are labeled beside each star's image. Because there are already so many dots on the chart the decimal points have been omitted. Thus, a magnitude of 6.2 is shown as 62, and 8.9 is 89, etc.

Find some comparisons that are brighter (i.e., they have a large diameter and whiter images) and some which are fainter than the variable. Now you have the variable surrounded by comparisons of different magnitudes. Carefully estimate which of the comparisons the variable most closely resembles. It is likely that the variable will have a magnitude that is between the magnitudes of two "comps." Thus you will need to estimate visually the variable's magnitude. You should be able to do this to ±0.2 magnitudes for bright variables.

4. Attach your photograph of each variable star field on **Figs. 2** and **3**. Be sure to record the star's name, date and time of photograph, exposure time, film type, and magnitude estimate on each figure.

Turn in **Figs. 2** and **3** within three weeks of the observing date or by the last day of your lab class, whichever comes first.

Table I

STAR	RA		DEC		MAX.	MIN.	PERIOD
	hrs.	min.	deg.	min.	Mag.	Mag.	(days)
o Cet	02	16	−03	12	3	10	332
R Tri	02	34	+34	03	6	12	266
U Ori	05	53	+20	10	5	12	373
R Cnc	08	14	+11	53	6	11	362
R Leo	09	45	+11	40	6	11	313
R Vir	12	36	+07	16	7	12	146
χ Oph	18	36	+08	47	6	9	334
R Aql	19	04	+08	09	6	12	293
U Cyg	20	18	+47	44	7	11	465
T Cep	21	08	+68	17	6	11	390
R Cas	23	56	+51	07	5	12	431

NAME: ______________________________

SECTION: ______________________________

Place photo of variable star
in this space

Star: ______________________________

Date: ______________________________

Time: ______________________________

Mag: ______________________________

Film type: ______________________________

Exposure length: ______________________________

Fig. 2: Student photograph of a Mira variable star.

NAME: ______________________________

SECTION: ______________________________

Place photo of variable star

in this space

Star: ______________________________

Date: ______________________________

Time: ______________________________

Mag: ______________________________

Film type: ______________________________

Exposure length: ______________________________

Fig. 2: Student photograph of a Mira variable star.

OBSERVING EXERCISE — OUTDOOR LIGHTING AND THE ASTRONOMICAL ENVIRONMENT

26

OBJECTIVES

After completing this simulation, the student will be able to:

1. recognize by sight different types of outdoor lighting sources such as Mercury vapor, low pressure Sodium, etc.
2. describe the good and bad effects of each style of lighting fixture combined with its light source.
3. make suggestions for lighting improvements where needed.

STUDENT MATERIALS

camera loaded with high speed color print film (slide film is all right *but* you will have to convert the slides into prints)

pen or pencil to record where each photo was taken

STUDENT REQUIREMENTS

Each student is to take his or her own pictures and to do individual work on this lab. Double prints cannot be shared between two students. If this is done, neither student will get credit for completing this lab exercise. Turn in your Photography Log table, six photos of outdoor lighting, and the answers to the questions at the end of the lab.

INTRODUCTION

In general outdoor night lighting is increasing at a rapid rate because of a perception of improved nighttime safety. Much of this lighting is scattered into the night sky and makes astronomical observations difficult. More importantly, if the light is going into the sky it is not lighting the ground or entry ways to buildings. So, this light and the electrical energy (i.e., the power bills) used to produce it are being wasted by trying to light up the universe (sort of like leaving the door open when you go outside).

In this lab exercise, you will use various resources such as books, magazines, and the Internet to learn about good and bad lighting effects. You will then go out into your community and take pictures of both good and bad lighting and describe the positive and negative results of each lighting situation. Some of these lighting sources may be as close as your own yard or apartment parking lot. Finally, you will make suggestions how poor lighting situations can be improved.

PROCEDURE

Your first task is to learn what constitutes good and bad lighting from both economic and astronomical points of view. There are several excellent sources of information on this subject. A fantastic book on observing in light-polluted skies is *City Astronomy* by Robin Scagell. This book can be found in the astronomy section of many public libraries. The first part of this book describes many types of outdoor lighting and includes pictures. These photos and descriptions will be a great help to you for completing this lab. Many monthly astronomical magazines, such as *Sky and Telescope* and *Astronomy*, have regular articles on light pollution and how to improve it. These magazines are available in most libraries and book stores. Of course the Internet has lots and lots of information dealing with light pollution. A good starting point would be to look at the International Dark-Sky Association's web page at **www. darksky.org** and follow any links you want to in order to learn about outdoor lighting and how to improve it.

After you have read up on the subject, it is time to go outside and spot good and bad lighting. As you drive around town in the evening, start looking for good and poor types of lighting. Pay attention to private security lights in yards, street lights, parking lot lights, lights in community parks, industrial lighting, bill board lighting, etc. After you get a feel for the different types of lighting in your community, take photographs of both good and poor lighting. In the Photography Log table, record the frame number, date, and location for each picture taken. Do not feel obligated to take enough pictures to fill the entire table unless you want to, but you may actually take more photos than you will turn in. You will need to turn in at least six photographs which you have taken.

After your photos are processed, use the information entered into the Photographic Log to sort the photos. Select examples of both good and bad lighting and mount six of them on the pages provided at the back of this lab. Be sure to fill in the information at the bottom of each photo page.

PHOTOGRAPHY LOG

Frame Number	Date	Location
example: 1	*ex: mm/dd/yy*	*ex: Walmart parking lot, Rockbridge Road, Stone Mountain, GA*

Questions

1. Do you think that the lighting in your community is basically favorable or unfavorable for astronomical observing?

2. Do you think that the lighting in your community is wasteful of energy? Explain why you think so.

3. How might community leaders make lighting changes which will decrease the amount of light pollution and save the community and industry money?

4. Is there any evidence that bright lighting decreases the crime rate?

PLACE

PHOTO

HERE

Location:

Date:

Type of Lighting:

(incandescent, Mercury Vapor, low pressure Sodium, etc.)

Why is this type of lighting good or bad? Include in your discussion something about the spectrum of the light source and its shielding to direct light downward toward the ground.

PLACE

PHOTO

HERE

Location:

Date:

Type of Lighting:

(incandescent, Mercury Vapor, low pressure Sodium, etc.)

Why is this type of lighting good or bad? Include in your discussion something about the spectrum of the light source and its shielding to direct light downward toward the ground.

PLACE

PHOTO

HERE

Location:

Date:

Type of Lighting:

(incandescent, Mercury Vapor, low pressure Sodium, etc.)

Why is this type of lighting good or bad? Include in your discussion something about the spectrum of the light source and its shielding to direct light downward toward the ground.

PLACE

PHOTO

HERE

Location:

Date:

Type of Lighting:

(incandescent, Mercury Vapor, low pressure Sodium, etc.)

Why is this type of lighting good or bad? Include in your discussion something about the spectrum of the light source and its shielding to direct light downward toward the ground.

```
┌─────────────────────────────────────────┐
│                                         │
│                                         │
│                                         │
│                PLACE                    │
│                                         │
│                PHOTO                    │
│                                         │
│                 HERE                    │
│                                         │
│                                         │
│                                         │
└─────────────────────────────────────────┘
```

Location:

Date:

Type of Lighting:

(incandescent, Mercury Vapor, low pressure Sodium, etc.)

Why is this type of lighting good or bad? Include in your discussion something about the spectrum of the light source and its shielding to direct light downward toward the ground.

PLACE

PHOTO

HERE

Location:

Date:

Type of Lighting:

(incandescent, Mercury Vapor, low pressure Sodium, etc.)

Why is this type of lighting good or bad? Include in your discussion something about the spectrum of the light source and its shielding to direct light downward toward the ground.

INTERNET EXERCISE: EXPLORING THE SOLAR SYSTEM

27

OBJECTIVES

After completing this lab, the student will be able to:

1. make a list of current NASA missions involved in exploration of the Solar System.
2. discuss each mission's purpose and/or current results.
3. describe any new technological developments related to each mission.
4. discuss the relevance of each mission to society.

STUDENT MATERIALS

pencil
note pad

LAB MATERIALS

The instructor should provide the following item:
high speed computer with Internet connections

STUDENT REQUIREMENTS

Students may work alone or in teams of not more than three. However, each student is expected to write his own mission reports, not simply copy from other team members. Turn in all of your mission reports at the end of your lab period.

INTRODUCTION

At any given time, NASA may have missions related to exploring the Solar System. These may include direct flights to planets, asteroids, or comets. Sometimes these missions are carried out using high altitude balloons or as part of a Space Shuttle flight.

In order to be cost-effective, some missions may have multiple purposes. For example, the Voyager missions to the outer planets also made measurements of the interplanetary medium and observations of bright stars while in route to each planet. No sense wasting time just coasting when you could also take advantage of the space craft's other abilities.

In this lab you will attempt to find several current Solar System missions. These may include the most recent competed mission, a mission in progress, or a mission about to be launched. Do not use missions which have been superceded by a more current mission. However, you may need to refer to these previous missions in order to best interpret the most recent results of the current mission or to explain why another mission is needed.

PROCEDURE

1. Read over the report forms so that you will know what type of information to look for about each mission. Use a note pad to write down bits of this information as you find it.

2. The NASA site at **http://www.nasa.gov** is a great place to begin your search. You may also want to use a search engine such as Lycos, Yahoo, etc., to locate additional information or to locate any private missions. Try to identify at least three missions.

3. On separate Mission Report forms give the title and launch date of each mission found.

4. Answer the questions on the report forms about each mission. Use additional pages if necessary.

5. Staple your report forms together and turn them in by the end of lab class.

MISSION REPORT FORM 1

MISSION TITLE: _____ LAUNCH DATE: _____

1. Make a list of any URLs you located which contain information about this mission.

2. Describe the mission's purpose.

3. Describe any new technology (if any) developed for this mission.

4. State any results obtained by the mission or anticipated results from the mission.

5. Discuss the relevance of this mission to society (i.e., why would anyone other than a scientist care about such a mission?).

MISSION REPORT FORM 2

MISSION TITLE: _____ LAUNCH DATE: _____

1. Make a list of any URLs you located which contain information about this mission.

2. Describe the mission's purpose.

3. Describe any new technology (if any) developed for this mission.

4. State any results obtained by the mission or anticipated results from the mission.

5. Discuss the relevance of this mission to society (i.e., why would anyone other than a scientist care about such a mission?).

MISSION REPORT FORM 3

MISSION TITLE: _____ LAUNCH DATE: _____

1. Make a list of any URLs you located which contain information about this mission.

2. Describe the mission's purpose.

3. Describe any new technology (if any) developed for this mission.

4. State any results obtained by the mission or anticipated results from the mission.

5. Discuss the relevance of this mission to society (i.e., why would anyone other than a scientist care about such a mission?).

INTERNET EXERCISE: SPACED OUT TELESCOPES

OBJECTIVES

After completing this lab, the student will be able to:

1. make a list of some current, or planned, telescopes in space.
2. discuss the types of observations the telescope can make or will make.
3. discuss why these observations are important to our scientific knowledge of the universe.
4. describe any new technological developments related to each mission.
5. discuss the relevance of each mission to society.

STUDENT MATERIALS

pencil
note pad

LAB MATERIALS

The instructor should provide the following:

high speed computer with Internet connections

STUDENT REQUIREMENTS

Students may work alone or in teams of not more than three. However, each student is expected to write his own mission reports, not simply copy from other team members. Turn in all of your mission reports at the end of your lab period.

INTRODUCTION

Currently there are several astronomical telescopes orbiting the Earth. The most famous of these is the Hubble Space Telescope. It is the largest of the space telescopes and operates at wavelengths in the infrared, visible, and ultraviolet. The images it produces are extraordinary and highly publicized, which has made it famous. However, there are other space telescopes operating in the far-ultraviolet, x-ray, and gamma ray regimes of the spectrum. These telescopes are sponsored by NASA, NSF, ESA, foreign governments, universities, and private enterprise. Some of them are long-term missions which last several years and others are one-shot missions lasting only a few minutes. During this lab, you will attempt to identify several of these astronomical platforms. These may include recently completed programs, current missions, and possibly some planned missions in the future.

PROCEDURE

1. Read over the report forms so that you will know what type of information to look for about each. Use a note pad to write down each bit of information as you find it.

2. Some places to start your search include the following sites: **http://www.nasa.gov**, **http://www.ball.com/aerospace/cobe.html**, and **http://www.stsci.edu**. You may also want to use a search engine such as Lycos, Yahoo, etc., to locate additional information or to locate any other space telescopes. Try to find three different telescopes or missions.

3. On separate Space Telescope Report forms, list the title and launch date for each space telescope identified.

4. Answer the questions on the report forms about each mission. Use additional pages if necessary.

5. Staple your report forms together and turn them in by the end of lab class.

SPACE TELESCOPE REPORT FORM 1

MISSION TITLE: _____ LAUNCH DATE: _____

1. Make a list of any URLs you located which contain information about this mission.

2. List the wavelength band passes in which the telescpoe operates (i.e., x-ray, gamma ray, etac.).

3. Describe any new technology (if any) developed for this mission.

4. Describe some of the observations obtained by the telescope or describe anticipated observations to be made in the future.

5. Why are the observations listed above important to science?

6. What big questions do these observations help to answer which are important to human beings like you and me? (For example: COBE observations help confirm the Big Bang Theory and the origin the universe. These observations provide a link in the chain that helps us learn more about the origin of the Earth and humans on the earth.)

SPACE TELESCOPE REPORT FORM 2

MISSION TITLE: _____ LAUNCH DATE: _____

1. Make a list of any URLs you located which contain information about this mission.

2. List the wavelength band passes in which the telescope operates (i.e., x-ray, gamma ray, etc.).

3. Describe any new technology (if any) developed for this mission.

4. Describe some of the observations obtained by the telescope or describe anticipated observations to be made in the future.

5. Why are the observations listed above important to science?

6. What big questions do these observations help to answer which are important to human beings like you and me? (For example: COBE observations help confirm the Big Bang Theory and the origin the universe. These observations provide a link in the chain that helps us learn more about the origin of the Earth and humans on the earth.)

SPACE TELESCOPE REPORT FORM 3

MISSION TITLE: _____ LAUNCH DATE: _____

1. Make a list of any URLs you located which contain information about this mission.

2. List the wavelength band passes in which the telescpoe operates (i.e., x-ray, gamma ray, etc.).

3. Describe any new technology (if any) developed for this mission.

4. Describe some of the observations obtained by the telescope or describe anticipated observations to be made in the future.

5. Why are the observations listed above important to science?

6. What big questions do these observations help to answer which are important to human beings like you and me? (For example: COBE observations help confirm the Big Bang Theory and the origin the universe. These observations provide a link in the chain that helps us learn more about the origin of the Earth and humans on the earth.)

INTERNET EXERCISE: PLANETARY CONNECTIONS

OBJECTIVES

After completing this lab, the student will be able to:

1. describe the contributions to planetary science of three different scientists.
2. discuss the world events surrounding each of these four scientists.
3. draw any connections which may link these four scientists together in some way.

STUDENT MATERIALS

    pencil
    note pad

LAB MATERIALS

The instructor should provide the following item:

    high speed computer with Internet connections

STUDENT REQUIREMENTS

Students may work alone or in teams of not more than three. However, each student is expected to write his own reports, not simply copy from other team members. Turn in all three of your reports at the end of your lab period.

INTRODUCTION

Scientists do not work in a vacuum (at least not without a space suit). They are influenced by other scientists and world events which surround them. Many times scientists make discoveries because their work has been influenced by other scientists or individuals working on similar problems. Sometimes the wrong person may receive the credit for a discovery because he or she expanded and popularized someone else's work. Sometimes discoveries are made accidentally by a scientist working on a completely different problem. Regardless of how scientific knowledge is obtained, it does not become generally accepted until society agrees to accept it. Recall Galileo and the problems he had with the Roman Catholic Church. Think of the modern controversy between biologists and theologians over Darwin's Theory of Evolution. Currently cloning has taken center stage. Science is done from within a social frame work. What scientists work on is influenced by social events such as wars, plagues, politics, etc.

Learning about science does not always involve learning about scientific discoveries. Sometimes it means learning about scientists themselves. During this lab, you will try to find to the discoveries of three scientists who were, or are currently, working on problems of the Solar System. You will attempt to draw threads of similarity between them to see if they influenced each other in some manner. Finally, you will attempt to relate the work of each scientist to the backdrop of the society in which he or she worked and how that social connection may have affected their science. Some of these scientists will be rather easy to track down, while others may be difficult. I hope you will find this study of scientists and their lives interesting.

PROCEDURE

Pick at least three scientists from the list below. You are to use Internet search engines such as Yahoo, Lycos, etc., to find out what contribution(s) each of them has made to the study of the Solar System. The best way to do this is to click on **search** and then enter the astronomer's name in the search box. Another place to start is **http://www.yahoo.co.uk** and click on **science**, then **astronomy**, then **astronomers**. As you obtain information about each scientist, try to establish the social background that each of them was working under. Were there wars or other political events, illnesses, financial constraints, religious beliefs, etc., which in some way affected their scientific philosophy and discoveries? In addition, try to establish links between the three scientists you have chosen. Some of the links may be strong and others might be rather thin. Do the best you can to establish some relationship between your scientists no matter how thin the link. As you find information, jot it down on your notepad so you can use it later to write up your lab report about each scientist. As you study one person's work you may be led to study someone else on the list. Do not feel obligated to stick to your initial selections. If you find that it seems difficult to find information about one of the scientists you have selected, then simply pick someone else. Do not spend the entire lab period hunting down information that is hard to obtain. The purpose of this lab is to learn about science by studying scientists, not to make your search difficult. Answer the questions about each person on the forms provided on the next few pages. When you are finished, staple your reports together and turn them in.

Choose from this list

- Aristotle
- Claudius Ptolemy
- Nicholas Copernicus
- Johannes Kepler
- Galileo Galilei
- Tycho Brahe
- Isaac Newton
- Edmund Halley
- Giovanni Schiaparelli
- Percival Lowell
- Giovanni Cassini
- Christian Huygens
- William Herschel
- Caroline Herschel
- Urbain Leverri
- Carl Sagan
- Carolyn Shoemaker
- Clyde Tombaugh

SCIENTIST REPORT NUMBER 1

SCIENTIST'S NAME: _____ BORN / DIED: _____

1. Write a short discussion about the life and times of this scientist. Be sure to include world events, religious beliefs, etc., which may have influenced his or her scientific studies.

2. What was this person's major scientific contributions to the study of our Solar System?

3. What connections, if any, can you make between this person and any work done by some of the other scientists in the original list? This should include how one person's work may have affected the science of the person in this report.

SCIENTIST REPORT NUMBER 2

SCIENTIST'S NAME: _____   BORN / DIED: _____

1. Write a short discussion about the life and times of this scientist. Be sure to include world events, religious beliefs, etc., which may have influenced his or her scientific studies.

2. What was this person's major scientific contributions to the study of our Solar System?

3. What connections, if any, can you make between this person and any work done by some of the other scientists in the original list? This should include how one person's work may have affected the science of the person in this report.

SCIENTIST REPORT NUMBER 3

SCIENTIST'S NAME: _____   BORN / DIED: _____

1. Write a short discussion about the life and times of this scientist. Be sure to include world events, religious beliefs, etc., which may have influenced his or her scientific studies.

2. What was this person's major scientific contributions to the study of our Solar System?

3. What connections, if any, can you make between this person and any work done by some of the other scientists in the original list? This should include how one person's work may have affected the science of the person in this report.

INTERNET EXERCISE: COSMIC CONNECTIONS

OBJECTIVES

After completing this lab, the student will be able to:

1. describe the contributions of three different scientists to the science of Cosmology.
2. discuss the world events surrounding each of these scientists.
3. draw any connections which may link these scientists together in some way.

STUDENT MATERIALS

pencil
note pad

LAB MATERIALS

The instructor should provide the following:

high speed computers with Internet connections

STUDENT REQUIREMENTS

Students may work alone or in teams of not more than three. However, each student is expected to write his own reports, not simply copy from other team members. Turn in all of your reports at the end of your lab period.

INTRODUCTION

Scientists do not work in a vacuum (at least not without a space suit). They are influenced by other scientists and world events which surround them. Many times scientists make discoveries because their work has been influenced by other scientists or individuals working on similar problems. Sometimes the wrong person may receive the credit for a discovery because they expanded and/or popularized someone else's work. Sometimes discoveries are made accidentally by a scientist working on a completely different problem. Regardless of how scientific knowledge is obtained, it does not become generally accepted until society agrees to accept it. Recall Galileo and the problems he had with the Roman Catholic Church. Think of the modern controversy between biologists and theologians over Darwin's Theory of Evolution. Currently, cloning has taken center stage in the life sciences. The study of cosmology has deep scientific and religious significance and is one of the hottest topics in astronomy today. As cosmologists learn more about the creation of the universe, their scientific results will affect our religious and social structure.

Learning about science does not always involve learning about scientific discoveries. Sometimes it means learning about scientists themselves. During this lab you will try to find the discoveries of three scientists who were, or are currently, working on problems in the field of cosmology. You will attempt to draw threads between them to see if they influenced each other in some manner. Finally, you will attempt to relate the work of each scientist to the backdrop of the society in which they worked and how that social connection may have affected their science. Some of these scientists will be rather easy to track down, while others may be difficult. I hope you will find this study of scientists and their lives interesting. As you research each of your scientists look at the social and religious influences both on their practice of science and of their scientific results on society.

PROCEDURE

Pick at least three scientists from the list below. You are to use Internet search engines such as Yahoo, Lycos, etc., to find out what contribution(s) each of them has made to the study of cosmology. The best way to do this is to click on **search** and then enter the astronomer's name in the search box. Another place to start is **http://www.yahoo.co.uk**, and click on **science**, then **astronomy**, then **astronomers**. As you obtain information about each scientist, try to establish the social background each of them was working under. Were there wars or other political events, illnesses, financial constraints, religious beliefs, etc., which in some way affected their scientific philosophy and discoveries? In addition, try to establish some links between the three scientists you have chosen. These connections may be easy, difficult or impossible to establish. Do the best you can. As you find information, jot it down on your note pad so you can use it later to write up your lab report about each scientist. As you study one person's work you may be led to study someone else on the list. Do not feel obligated to stick to your initial selections. If you find that it is difficult to find information about one of the scientists you have selected, then simply pick someone else. Do not spend the entire lab period hunting down information that is hard to obtain. The purpose of this lab is to learn about cosmology by studying scientists working in the field, not to make your search difficult. Answer the questions about each one on the forms provided on the next few pages. When you are finished, staple your reports together and turn them in.

Choose from this list

- Henrietta Leavitt
- Vesto M. Slipher
- Harlow Shapley
- Kip Thome
- George Lemaitre
- Edwin Hubble
- Milton Humason
- Fred Hoyle
- Arno Penzias & Robert Wilson
- Steven Weinberg
- Stephen Hawking
- Alexander Friedmann
- Albert Einstein
- Jacobus Kapteyn
- William de Sitter

COSMOLOGIST REPORT NUMBER 1

SCIENTIST'S NAME: _____ BORN / DIED: _____

1. Write a short discussion about the life and times of this scientist. Be sure to include world events, religious beliefs, etc., which may have influenced their scientific studies.

2. What was (were) this person's major scientific contribution(s) to the study of Cosmology?

3. What connections, if any, can you make between this person and any work done by some of the other scientists in the original list? This should include how one person's work may have affected the science of the person in this report.

COSMOLOGIST REPORT NUMBER 2

SCIENTIST'S NAME: _____   BORN / DIED: _____

1. Write a short discussion about the life and times of this scientist. Be sure to include world events, religious beliefs, etc., which may have influenced their scientific studies.

2.   What was (were) this person's major scientific contribution(s) to the study of Cosmology?

3.   What connections, if any, can you make between this person and any work done by some of the other scientists in the original list? This should include how one person's work may have affected the science of the person in this report.

COSMOLOGIST REPORT NUMBER 3

SCIENTIST'S NAME: _____   BORN / DIED: _____

1. Write a short discussion about the life and times of this scientist. Be sure to include world events, religious beliefs, etc., which may have influenced their scientific studies.

2. What was (were) this person's major scientific contribution(s) to the study of Cosmology?

3. What connections, if any, can you make between this person and any work done by some of the other scientists in the original list? This should include how one person's work may have affected the science of the person in this report.

VISITING AN OBSERVATORY

OBJECTIVES

After completing this lab, the student will be able to:

1. describe the types of telescopes at the observatory visited.
2. list the scientific instruments at the observatory visited.
3. make a list of any astronomical objects viewed while at the observatory.

STUDENT MATERIALS

Students schould bring the following items with them to the observatory:

    pencil
    writing board or pad
    penlight or flashlight
    one of the report forms at the end of this lab

OBSERVATORY EQUIPMENT

The observatory should provide the student with the following:

1. access to telescopes through which the students can observe
2. a tour of the facilities and a description of any observing instruments used at the observatory
3. an astronomer to answer student questions and to give a simple tour of the night sky

STUDENT REQUIREMENTS

Students doing this lab should turn in the Observatory Report form. This form is to be completed individually by each student. The observatory visits should be fun and you will miss out on the best part of astronomy if you simply copy a friend's report. If you do this, it will not count as a completed lab.

INTRODUCTION

Attending an observatory open house or a special observing session provided for your class should be one of the most enjoyable experiences you will have in your astronomy course. There may be observatories in your area which hold regular open houses for the general public. These are usually operated by small colleges or universities. Your lab instructor can tell you when and where such open houses are being held. If there are no such facilities, then your lab or lecture instructor may be willing to hold observing sessions somewhere on campus using small portable telescopes. These telescopes will provide you with an excellent view of the moon, planets, binary stars, and the brighter nebulae in the sky. A little preparation on your part can make your observing experience more rewarding.

Several days before going to the observing facility, you should read up about telescopes in general and about what things are currently visible in the night sky. Your textbook has at least one chapter that covers telescopes. Skim through this to refresh your memory about different types of telescopes and mountings. This material will usually be heavily slanted towards professional telescopes and observatories. However, you may also want to be familiar with amateur telescopes which you are also likely to encounter on the lawn of the observatory or at a campus observing session for your class. Both *Sky and Telescope* and *Astronomy* magazines have articles and advertisements about amateur telescopes. They also have monthly sky charts which tell you what can be seen in the early evening sky. These magazines can be purchased at most bookstores and one or both are usually available in libraries. Their respective websites are **www.skypub.com** and **www.kalmback.com** (click on the Astronomy magazine icon). By making this preparation in advance, you will be better prepared for the terms and jargon used by any astronomers you may encounter and you will also be in a better position to ask intelligent questions of any astronomers you may meet.

TERMS YOU SHOULD KNOW

aperture

eyepiece

magnification

refracting telescope

Newtonian reflecting telescope

Cassegrain reflecting telescope

Schmidt Cassegrain telescope

equatorial mount

altitude-azimuth mount (alt-az mount)

Dobsonian mount

charge-coupled device (CCD)

north celestial pole

celestial equator

zenith

horizon

PROCEDURE

Preparation for Observing

1. Obtain a list of observatories and their public observing schedule. Your lab instructor will probably be able to help you with rounding up this list.

2. Watch the weather reports and look for a potentially clear night which also occurs on a night listed as a public night at one of the observing sites.

3. Before attending, round up any materials you may want to take with you such as flashlights, star charts, writing materials, insect repellent, etc.

4. You should dress appropriately. Wear pants and comfortable shoes. You may be climbing some stairs, or standing on deck planks; high heels and skirts are not recommended. Most observatories are open to the outside air. If it is cold outside, be sure to bring a jacket, coat, gloves, etc.

5. Before you attend, it may be a good idea to make one last check of the weather. If it has become overcast, you may want to reconsider and try a different night when you can see something. If it is clear, then go out and enjoy the beauty of the starry sky.

At the Observatory

6. If a tour is given, be sure to participate in it. As you tour the facility, look around and see what telescopes and instruments are available for astronomers to use. Ask observatory personnel questions you might have about the observatory.

7. If it is a clear night, look through every telescope available for student and public viewing. It will blow your mind! If any telescopes are set up for hands-on use, you should try pointing them at something in the sky. It's a real challenge, but fun.

8. Make a list of every astronomical object you view during the evening. This should include unaided eye observations of constellations and bright stars and binocular or telescopic views of astronomical objects like the moon, planets, binary stars, nebulae, etc.

9. Before leaving, have one of the astronomers at the observatory sign and date your observing report. This is proof that you actually attended. Turn in this report to your lab instructor. (**Note:** there are two report forms because GSU students are expected to go observing once per semester in a two-semester lab sequence. So, one is to be used by ASTR 1010 students and the second is to be used by ASTR 1020 students.)

OBSERVATORY REPORT for 1st Semester

NAME OF OBSERVATORY: _____ **LOCATION:** _____

WEATHER CONDITIONS: _____

In the space below describe any telescopes and instrumentation you saw or used while at the observatory. You may need to use some of the terms listed at the beginning of this lab.

List below any astronomical sights you may have viewed such as constellations and bright stars (give their names), the moon, planets, binary stars, nebulae, etc.

ASTRONOMER'S SIGNATURE: _____ DATE: _____

OBSERVATORY REPORT for 2nd Semester

NAME OF OBSERVATORY: _____ **LOCATION:** _____

WEATHER CONDITIONS: _____

In the space below describe any telescopes and instrumentation you saw or used while at the observatory. You may need to use some of the terms listed at the beginning of this lab.

List below any astronomical sights you may have viewed such as constellations and bright stars (give their names), the moon, planets, binary stars, nebulae, etc.

ASTRONOMER'S SIGNATURE: _____ **DATE:** _____